Abolition and Queer Justice

The publisher and the University of California Press Foundation gratefully acknowledge the generous support of The Dido Fund in making this book possible.

Abolition and Queer Justice

EDITED BY
Allyn Walker and Aimee Wodda

UNIVERSITY OF CALIFORNIA PRESS

University of California Press
Oakland, California

Library of Congress Cataloging-in-Publication Data

Names: Walker, Allyn, editor. | Wodda, Aimee, editor.
Title: Abolition and queer justice / edited by Allyn
    Walker and Aimee Wodda.
Description: Oakland, California : University of
    California Press, [2026] | Includes bibliographical
    references and index.
Identifiers: LCCN 2025012315 (print) | LCCN 2025012316
    (ebook) | ISBN 9780520399082 (cloth) |
    ISBN 9780520399099 (paperback) |
    ISBN 9780520399105 (ebook)
Subjects: LCSH: Police abolition movement—United
    States. | Prison-industrial complex—United States. |
    Sexual minority activists—United States. | Critical
    criminology—United States.
Classification: LCC HM883 .A26 2026 (print) |
    LCC HM883 (ebook) | DDC 363.20973—dc23/
    eng/20250615
LC record available at https://lccn.loc.gov/2025012315
LC ebook record available at https://lccn.loc.gov
    /2025012316

GPSR Authorized Representative: Easy Access System
Europe, Mustamäe tee 50, 10621 Tallinn, Estonia,
gpsr.requests@easproject.com

34 33 32 31 30 29 28 27 26 25
10 9 8 7 6 5 4 3 2 1

to everyone who dreams

Contents

Introduction

Envisioning Queer Justice

ALLYN WALKER, SAINT MARY'S UNIVERSITY
AIMEE WODDA, PACIFIC UNIVERSITY

What images come to mind when you see the word *justice*? Maybe they're of a blindfold, sword, and scale? Courtrooms and judges? Police and arrests? We're taught to associate the idea of justice with punishment, distributed fairly, by well-meaning people, against those who have caused harm. Over time, our societies have created entire *systems* using this concept of justice to separate good people from the bad, to keep the good safe and to keep dangerous people in line.

But for queer people, *justice* often conjures different images.[1] Police, judges, and prisons are part of a system that, time and again, criminalizes us and puts us at risk of harm. This is especially true for Black trans women and other queer people of color. During the time we conceived of and organized this book, queer people have found ourselves in the middle of a rising wave of lawmaking aimed at separating us from the rest of society. We have—not for the first time—been defined as the "dangerous people" that the system must keep in line.[2]

We know this is not just, so we can't rely on our systems to define justice for us. We therefore must envision our own ideas of justice. Queer justice does not have to be grounded in punishment. It doesn't have to involve police or courts. For us, justice may come in the form of chosen families, allies, or homes where we've felt belonging, schools where we feel safe to be ourselves, mutual aid projects where we offer each other legal, financial, or food assistance, jobs where we're shown we are valued, sports where we're welcomed as equal participants, health care providers who listen to us and consider our needs. Justice, for us, may be any and all these things, and more. Queer justice is ours to imagine and build.

Imagining a future built on queer justice is challenging, but we can start by identifying what we don't want that future to look like. This is where abolition comes in. On the one hand, abolition is about the literal defunding and dismantling of carceral systems: police, prisons, courts, and other structures that exist to surveil and punish. On the other, abolition can extend beyond these goals, allowing us to consider building societies free of false binaries of "good" and "bad" people, of "us" versus "them." Abolition can challenge us to see all people as deserving of resources and support.

Queer people have long been engaging in anticarceral resistance work.[3] But even with our histories of working toward these efforts, too often writing focused on abolitionist possibilities remains sidelined within criminology—even within more progressive queer, feminist, and other critical subfields. We, Allyn and Aimee, along with contributors to this volume Amanda Petersen and ash stephens, wrote an article addressing this issue, titled "Why Don't We Center Abolition in Queer Criminology?"[4] But there remains so much more to say. And so, we conceptualized a volume that would highlight abolitionist work within and around queer criminology to challenge our fields toward abolitionist goals and projects.

ABOLITION: A CRUCIAL STEP TOWARD QUEER JUSTICE

Those who study criminology from a critical point of view already share considerable common ground with abolitionists. We all understand that the systems our society has created to control and punish are harmful, contributing to violence against communities, families, and individual lives. We recognize that these systems are set up for those with wealth and power, and they continue to benefit those with wealth and power, while oppressed people are targeted. And we know that Black people, Indigenous people, other people of color, disabled people, queer people, people from low-income backgrounds—all these marginalized "others"—are harmed by the criminal legal system most of all, especially people at the intersections of those identities.[5]

These understandings are shared between abolitionists and queer, feminist, and critical criminologists, and all our work has the goal of ending systemic harms. But while many critical scholars aim to improve the criminal legal system out of a belief that through reform the system can deliver justice, abolitionists believe that we can never create justice through surveillance, arrests, or incarceration. And so, we need to get rid of our "deathmaking" system in order to push our world toward justice. Or, as Toniqua Mikell so evocatively describes it in "Dismembering the Powermonger: A BlaQueer Feminist Approach to Abolition," her chapter in this volume, we need to "vanquish" and "dismember" the violent creature that *is* the criminal legal system.

Defeating this creature requires bravery and creativity. It means rethinking what we've been taught about the criminal legal system as a source of protection and force for good, and thinking of new and more effective ways to protect one another. This might help explain why queer communities have been engaged in abolitionist efforts for so long. The main title of Max Osborn's chapter in this volume, "At Any Given Point in Your Life, You Can Be Wrong about Everything," hints at this: being queer often prompts us to question our identities, shifting our fundamental understandings about our lives and selves. This shift can prompt us to question the way we've collectively designed society, following our curiosity in a way that creates more opportunities for abolitionist thought. Queerness itself can open us up to creativity and trying new things.

Of course, it's not just our imaginations that make abolition a priority for queer people: we have also been targeted by the criminal legal system. In their chapter, "A Conversation on the Criminalization of Queer People, Abolition Feminism, and Resisting Carceral Harms around Child Sexual Abuse," jenani devi, Monica Ramsy, and Alison Reba talk about ongoing moral panic over queer and trans people as supposed threats to children and how this fear has been—and continues to be—weaponized to create laws that criminalize us. Amanda Petersen's chapter, "Queer against the Law," traces the roots of this moral panic. They remind us that because of our marginalization across time, queer politics have their roots in intersectionality and coalition building across marginalized groups, and that we need to resist the binaries of "good" queer people versus the criminal "other" to work toward a collective, liberatory future. Only in such a future can queer justice be realized.

FROM ABOLITION TO OTHER ONGOING SOCIAL MOVEMENTS

These conceptual divisions between "good" and "other" hold influence over us, pushing us to believe we need the protection only powerful systems can provide. Queer people in the United States and Canada are frequently told that we should support our criminal legal systems because we are given protection from violence via police, prisons, and anti-LGBTQ+ hate crime laws. In our personal and research experience, we have not been made safer by the criminal legal system.[6] Yet this line of reasoning continues and is found elsewhere: Allyn has been told that as a Jewish person who speaks out against anti-Jewish hatred, they should support the Israeli military; that a Jewish state, backed by a strong military, keeps Jewish people safe from the threat of a future Holocaust. And both of us have been addressed with messaging that all queer people should support Israel's military efforts against Gaza because Palestinians are—so the argument goes—inherently homophobic and transphobic.[7] Conversely, these arguments paint Israel as inherently pro-queer. Contrary to this binary logic, however, queer and trans people exist, form communities, and face disproportionate violence in both Israel[8] and Palestine,[9] just as they do in the United States and across the world. And the genocidal tactics of the Israeli military are a far greater threat to queer Palestinians than homophobia.

Liberatory protesting and organizing among, with, and on behalf of Palestinians has been going on from the early days of the Zionist movement.[10] Many abolitionists and queer activists have been working on this issue, caring about what happens to people in Gaza and supporting Palestinians and their right to autonomy, for decades—such as Angela Y. Davis,[11] Dean Spade,[12] and other queer organizers advocating for the Boycott, Divestment, and Sanctions movement.[13]

Most of the chapters in this volume had already been drafted by the start of the invasion of Gaza that began on October 7, 2023, and none of these chapters focus entirely on Palestine. Yet they are connected through the central goals of abolition. Abolitionists and queer activists teach us that what we need is not "protection" through violent systems that villainize and oppress targeted groups of people: what we need is solidarity. We have found particular inspiration in the "Everyone for Everyone" movement. Comparative ethnic studies scholar Dan Berger explains the logic of this movement through an abolitionist lens. On one level, the movement advocates for the exchange of hostages and prisoners: everyone for everyone. But on another level, as his article states, "From within a colonial system that insists that life is disposable, the proposal set forth by the families of the hostages contains the seed of a radically transformed society—one which grants, in the words of prison abolitionist Ruth Wilson Gilmore, that 'where life is precious, life is precious.'"[14]

These are messages of hope and peace. Yet abolitionists, queer organizers, and those protesting genocide in Gaza are often characterized as threats—even from within universities. In 2024, university administrations discouraged students and faculty alike from engaging in protests. They canceled their graduation ceremonies rather than allowing students critical of Israel to speak.[15] They suspended and expelled student protesters and even used the criminal legal system against students and faculty.[16] The Associated Press reported that around thirty-two hundred people were arrested on campuses across the United States over pro-Palestine demonstrations.[17] Faculty who could be seen with their hands in the air, being pushed to the ground by police, were later accused of battering the police officers who arrested them.[18] And as of early 2025, the Trump administration has begun targeting student protestors for deportation, including permanent residents who are not suspected of breaking any laws.[19] In some cases, these students' universities have aided efforts to deport them.

These patterns of criminalization—whether targeting queer people, Palestinians, or protesters—reveal how systems of oppression work together to maintain power through creating "others" who must be controlled. The work of abolition, then, requires us to work with one another to reject these divisions entirely, to refuse the logic that says some people must be surveilled, arrested, or imprisoned to keep others safe. Instead, we must work toward forms of justice that recognize everyone's inherent value and right to thrive. This brings us back to queer justice.

ORGANIZING THIS BOOK

The editors of this book are queer criminologists who have written about abolition, queer communities, and other subjects that challenge the status quo. Having experience with writing books and receiving pushback from those who want queer people to be deplatformed, we felt we had developed the right skill set to tackle the subjects of queer justice and carceral abolition within a project such as this.[20] But as two white academics, we hesitated before committing to this project, wondering if it was appropriate for us to take the lead on this. We decided instead to create a volume centering voices we don't often hear in our discipline. We envisioned our role in this project as gatherers of a collective, prioritizing contributions from Black and Latinx scholars, and other scholars of color, who have been discussing and writing about abolition for years. We also wanted to highlight the voices of other groups who are frequently marginalized in academic writing, including students, untenured professors and those who are not on the tenure track, and folks who have, or whose family members have, been targeted by the criminal legal system.

We reached out to queer criminologists whose work we were familiar with, telling them our goals for the book—to encourage engagement with abolitionist perspectives among people whose research, teaching, learning, and/or personal lives speak to queer criminology. We were looking for chapters related in some way to intersectional queer issues and abolition. We received several submissions and then issued a broader call for papers within queer criminology and surrounding fields. Scholars and activists in our communities responded to our call, and we crafted a book proposal that was enthusiastically accepted by the publisher. We are humbled by the work that appears in this book, and we have learned a great deal from the authors featured in this volume. Once we had interest from several authors, we grouped the submissions we received based on common themes and ended up with the following sections for this book.

Part One. Seeds of Change: Nurturing Our Abolitionist Growth

We received multiple submissions from queer criminologists presenting narratives of their own pathways toward abolitionist work. Many of those who wrote chapters for this section had gotten their start in criminology working toward what Critical Resistance refers to as "reformist reforms"—in other words, toward steps that, whether intentionally or not, would ultimately preserve and even strengthen the criminal legal system.[21] Abolitionists are often mischaracterized in the media and dismissed for supposedly impractical ideas, so we wanted to give those who pick up this book an opportunity to read directly from abolitionists, in their own words, about how they decided to work toward carceral abolition.

In "From the Hood to Queer Scholar: How I Became a Police Abolitionist," Susana Avalos reflects on their experiences growing up in a Salvadorian immigrant family in Bakersfield, California, where they faced overlapping threats from gang violence, United States Immigration and Customs Enforcement (ICE), and police. Motivated by these early experiences to understand and address injustice, they pursued academic studies in criminal justice. Within their chapter, they detail how their subsequent research on LGBTQ people's experiences with law enforcement, combined with their own identity as a queer, nonbinary person of color, shifted their perspectives, ultimately leading them to become a police abolitionist. While Rosa Squillacote writes that she was taught from a young age to understand the criminal legal system as oppressive, in her chapter, "Growing Up an Abolitionist," she too describes a journey of changing perceptions. Within its pages, she describes the process of visiting each of her parents in prison, starting at age twelve. She advises us to think how we are all affected by the carceral system and uses this commonality to urge us toward empathy—not just for incarcerated people, but for their families, as well as those who work in prisons.

In "So, You Like the Police, Huh?," Alessandra Early documents her evolving relationship with abolition as a Black queer woman criminologist. Incorporating personal history and professional experiences, she interrogates the meaning of work in criminology—a field inherently intertwined with a system that criminalizes and exploits those who share her multiple marginalized identities. "Queer Criminologists' Pathways to Abolition: A Québécois Autoethnography," written by Alexis Marcoux Rouleau, Karl Beaulieu, and Catherine Therrien, weaves together narratives to discuss how abolitionist thought and queerness are inherently entangled. In this chapter, the authors write about their experiences with victimization and describe how both the criminal legal system and the discipline of criminology itself deepened their sense of marginalization.

We end this section with a chapter blending personal experience and in-depth synthesis of criminological research. In "A Radical Vision for Prison Abolition," Jennifer Ortiz begins by describing her personal journey from reformer to abolitionist. Having worked in multiple areas of the criminal legal system out of an interest in creating positive change, she carefully walks readers through how she came to understand that the system cannot be fixed, as she proposes an evidence-based framework for a prisonless United States.

Part Two. Roots of Oppression: Unearthing Queer Criminalization

This section discusses a key factor for queer interest in abolition: the criminalization of queer communities, including the treatment of queer lives as disposable by legislators, police, and officials in courts, prisons, jails, detention centers, probation, parole, and elsewhere within the criminal legal system. The chapters in this section make linkages between past and present harm against queer communities by the criminal legal system, arguing for an abolitionist path forward.

Toniqua Mikell's "Dismembering the Powermonger: A BlaQueer Feminist Approach to Abolition" recommends and describes the "complete dismemberment of the criminal legal body." Mikell asks us to confront the tyrannical, deathmaking power of the violent criminal legal system and to recognize that its roots in misogyny, racism, and heterocentrism mean that it can never be reformed. In order to ensure the safety, freedom, and life chances of all people, she argues that the criminal legal system must be dismembered in order to make room for the more fertile ground of transformation and wild-seed justice.

Drawing on interviews he conducted with forty-two queer people in New York City, in his chapter, "'At Any Given Point in Your Life, You Can Be Wrong about Everything': Queer and Trans Perspectives, Community Care, and the Abolitionist Imagination," Max Osborn examines participant experiences with police violence and discrimination and their involvement in abolitionist advocacy. Many interviewees made connections between being queer and becoming involved in abolitionist organizing, transformative justice, and mutual aid. Osborn explores the idea of questioning gender norms as a pathway toward questioning other normative structures and building community with other marginalized communities. Relatedly, Amanda Petersen's chapter, "Queer against the Law," examines how queer responses to being labeled as criminal can either challenge or reinforce carceral logic. Borrowing from Cathy Cohen's critique of dominant queer politics, Petersen advocates for an abolitionist approach that—instead of denying the criminalization of queer communities specifically—rejects the practice of criminalization as a whole and argues for coalition building as a liberatory practice.

In the chapter "(Un)DocuQueer: Trapped within Bodies, Borders, and Systems," Karen Armenta Rojas calls for abolishing ICE, bringing in discussion about how ICE affects queer migrants specifically and how it reinforces Western, colonial ideas about gender binaries. She combines that discussion with her personal experiences, tying in commonalities between coming out as queer and coming out as undocumented, which highlights shared experiences as being the "other" and the systemic harm that leaves undocumented queer people vulnerable when their status becomes known.

The concluding chapter in this section, jenani devi, Monica Ramsy, and Alison Reba's "A Conversation on the Criminalization of Queer

People, Abolition Feminism, and Resisting Carceral Harms around Child Sexual Abuse," traces how adultism has shaped the "parents' rights" movement, how this movement has framed queer existence as enabling child sexual abuse, and how this creates barriers to preventing child sexual abuse. The authors argue for an abolitionist theory of change that acknowledges the underlying individual, social, economic, and political conditions that contribute to child sexual abuse. They recommend centering prevention and healing, not disposability and punishment, as the path forward.

Part Three. Branches of Progress: Reaching for Queer Justice in Criminology

The final section of this book encourages the field of criminology to work toward abolitionist goals, challenging queer, feminist, and other critical criminologists to consider how their work can move away from preserving the criminal legal system. In this section, authors urge our fields to work toward liberatory justice in the way that Black women, queer, and trans abolitionists have been advocating for over decades. Candice Crutchfield writes about these leaders and their work in her chapter, "Critiquing Criminology: Toward an Abolitionist-Centered Pedagogy and Discipline." Throughout the chapter, she examines how the discipline of criminology has often contributed to the expansion of the very systems it claims to challenge and advocates for transforming the academy—beginning in the classroom.

Many of our colleagues work together with the police in an attempt to improve conditions for queer and trans people. What other options do we have? Emma Russell writes about this in her chapter, "From Prison to Police Abolition: Challenging Queer Criminology's Investments in the Police," which struggles with the historical and contemporary ties to the police and the prison industrial complex within the discipline of criminology and details how mainstream queer organizations are materially and symbolically connected to policing and punishment. It can be intimidating for many criminological researchers to imagine what separating our work from the criminal legal system might look like. And yet, we *can* imagine it—as ash stephens and Jane Hereth do in their chapter, "'Queer' Means Centering Criminalized Survivors: Lessons from Abolition Feminism." In order to center survivors of interpersonal violence, they encourage queer criminologists to "apply an abolition feminist lens to resist the overreliance on policing and punishment to address violence," and they demonstrate how to do so throughout their piece.

We close out the volume with Ihsan Al-Zouabi's chapter, "Toward a Pedagogy of Possibility: On Abolitionist Teaching." Al-Zouabi explores abolitionist teaching as a transformative educational approach that challenges settler colonial and white supremacist systems in education, recommending not only teaching about abolishing the criminal legal system in the classroom, but applying a liberatory framework throughout our teaching practices to treat students in a just and healing way. She shares her own experiences as a Muslim, Arab student, bringing them back to the larger picture of global oppression, of Gaza, and collectively working toward a better world.

FURTHER RESOURCES

While there is a great deal of labor involved in editing a collectively written volume, we agreed from the start that it would not be in the spirit of what we're creating to financially benefit from the work produced by the book's contributors. Accordingly, we asked our contributors to provide suggestions for and vote on an organization working toward our shared vision of queer justice to be supported by the volume's royalties. The organization chosen by our contributors was alQaws for Sexual & Gender Diversity in Palestinian Society, a grassroots organization working at the intersection of gender, sexuality, and the broader struggle for Palestinian liberation. Founded by and for queer Palestinians, alQaws leads community-based initiatives, public advocacy campaigns, and educational programming to challenge social norms, combat gender-based and sexual oppression, and build safe, affirming spaces across historic Palestine. Their work includes leadership development, cultural and media interventions, support structures—like a national support hotline for LGBTQ people, connecting queer and trans Palestinians to friendly therapists—and other organizing efforts rooted in decolonial, feminist, and intersectional frameworks.[22]

It's common for abolitionists to be asked what alternatives we envision for police, prisons, and other components that comprise the carceral system. This is an impossible question to answer, because abolition is just as much about creating a world that has no use for police and prisons as it is about the actual dismantling of these institutions.[23] While we therefore do not have suggestions for "alternatives," we did want to highlight other projects suggested by our contributors. Each of these projects addresses root causes of violence and other forms of harm by providing resources to those who need them, or they respond to violence, or both.

In addition to alQaws, contributors suggested other mental health support resources: Call BlackLine and Trans LifeLine. Call BlackLine runs a confidential hotline for people in crisis or who wish to report negative, physical, and inappropriate contact with police and vigilantes. They prioritize Black, Black LGBTQI, Brown, Native, and Muslim community members and do not share caller information with law enforcement or state agencies.[24] Trans LifeLine runs a hotline for trans people in or out of crisis, staffed by trans and nonbinary peers. Trans LifeLine does not engage in nonconsensual active rescue, such as calling 911, emergency services, or law enforcement.[25]

Multiple suggestions included organizations that provide resources for incarcerated people, formerly incarcerated people, or others who may need legal help, and advocate for abolitionist causes. These included Critical Resistance, Black & Pink, the Sylvia Rivera Law Project, and the Tranzmission Prison Project. Founded by a group of activists, including Angela Y. Davis[26] and Ruth Wilson Gilmore,[27] Critical Resistance runs campaigns to close prisons and detention centers and to defund and demilitarize the police, hosts community events, runs prisoner mail programs and a prisoner solidarity phone line, and develops resources for abolitionist educators and working groups.[28] Black & Pink runs an active solidarity pen pal program and newsletter for incarcerated LGBTQIA2S+ people and people living with HIV/AIDS, and provides housing and financial resources to people returning to their communities after incarceration.[29] Founded by Dean Spade,[30] the Sylvia Rivera Law Project provides legal services for trans people, including immigration assistance, name change/gender marker change help, and assistance for incarcerated people.[31] The Tranzmission Prison Project is an LGBTQ+-focused prison abolition/advocacy group providing free books, zines, prisoner resources, and other means of support to incarcerated folks nationwide.[32]

Another category of organization was restorative justice services. Hidden Water was suggested by a contributor; they run restorative justice-based healing circles, connecting people affected by child sexual abuse based on shared personal experiences. They hold groups specifically for men, for LGBTQIA+ people, for neurodivergent people, and for Spanish speakers. Hidden Water also runs family circles for family members who have all participated in separate circle work, and they run an active child sexual abuse prevention program.[33]

A couple of our contributors suggested other community-powered initiatives that address gaps in conventional institutions. For example, Bluestockings Cooperative, a queer, trans, sex worker–owned and run bookstore in New York City, runs a "free store" within its walls. Through the free store, their nonprofit organization, Bluestockings Cares, offers food, drinks, clothing, hygiene products, safer sex kits, Plan B, naloxone, fentanyl test strips, and more—all 100 percent free to anyone who stops in and asks.[34] Finally, the Just Practice Collaborative was suggested; this organization, cofounded by Mariame Kaba,[35] holds a monthly virtual peer learning space for groups and organizations working to collectively intervene in and respond to crises without police.[36] All these organizations, and so many more projects that exist and have yet to be developed, can help us reimagine what justice means, who and what keeps us safe, and how we can build thriving communities without relying on systems of punishment and control.

There is so much more to say about this book: on queer justice, on abolition, on resisting systemic violence, on what's at stake. Fortunately, our contributors say most of it for us (and far better than we could). We invite you to read their words on the pages ahead.

NOTES

1. Throughout this book, the authors of each chapter have chosen language that feels right to them to refer to people in two-spirit, lesbian, gay, bisexual, transgender, queer, questioning, intersex, asexual, and other communities related to nonnormative gender, sex, and sexuality (2SLGBTQIA+ communities). Similarly to its use in "queer criminology," when we use the term *queer* in this introduction, we use this as an umbrella term for people whose gender, sex, and/or sexuality fall outside of societal norms.

2. For example, Mogul, Ritchie, and Whitlock, *Queer (In)Justice: The Criminalization of LGBT People in the United States*; Movement Advancement Project, "HIV Criminalization Laws"; Trans Legislation Tracker, "Learn: U.S. Anti-trans Legislation History," 2024, https://translegislation.com/learn.

3. See, for example, Feinberg, "Street Transvestite Action Revolutionaries"; Stanley and Smith, *Captive Genders: Trans Embodiment and the Prison Industrial Complex*.

4. Walker et al., "Why Don't We Center Abolition in Queer Criminology?"

5. Within this volume, chapter authors use varied terms for the complex web of agencies and institutions that criminalize, surveil, and punish on behalf of the state. We use *criminal legal system* in this chapter in direct opposition to the more commonly used *criminal justice system*. Although some writers prefer not to use the term *criminal* because of its stigmatizing use when applied to individual people, we use *criminal* here not to describe people but to describe

the legal system we are referring to (i.e., as opposed to the civil legal system). Other common terms include the *prison-industrial complex*, the *criminal punishment system*, and the *carceral system*.

6. For example, Walker, "Police Do Not Protect Us, and Other Lessons I Learned as a Queer Victim"; Wodda and Panfil, *Sex-Positive Criminology.*

7. Schrader, "Palestinians: LGBTQ+ Not Welcome Here—Opinion."

8. Bagno/Maariv, "Israel Sees Record Number of Anti-LGBTQ+ Incidents in 2022—Report."

9. O'Neal, "Gaza's Queer Palestinians Fight to Be Remembered."

10. Tamarkin, "Why Queer Solidarity with Palestine Is Not 'Chickens for KFC.'"

11. Davis, *Freedom Is a Constant Struggle: Ferguson, Palestine, and the Foundations of a Movement.*

12. Spade, "Under the Cover of Gay Rights."

13. Prager, "Queer People Organizing in Solidarity with Palestine Continues to Grow."

14. Berger, "The Abolitionist Logic of 'Everyone for Everyone.'"

15. For example, Mzezewa, "USC Has Canceled Its Main Graduation."

16. "Noelle McAfee, Emory University's Philosophy Department Chair, Detained in Pro-Palestine Protest"; "'I Barely Did Anything': Video Shows Emory Professor Thrown to the Ground, Arrested during Protest."

17. Sampath et al., "For College Students Arrested Protesting the War in Gaza, the Fallout Was Only Beginning."

18. O'Connor, "Prosecutors Have Levied Serious Charges against Pro-Palestine College Protesters."

19. Fadel et al., "'Citizenship Won't Save You': Free Speech Advocates Say Student Arrests Should Worry All."

20. Walker, "Transphobic Discourse and Moral Panic Convergence: A Content Analysis of My Hate Mail"; Walker, "Preventing Child Abuse Should Not Be Controversial. My Own Hate Mail Reveals That It Is."

21. Critical Resistance, "Reformist Reforms vs Abolitionist Steps in Policing"; Critical Resistance, *Reformist Reforms vs. Abolitionist Steps to End Imprisonment*; Gilmore, *Golden Gulag: Prisons, Surplus, Crisis, and Opposition in Globalizing California*, 242.

22. alQaws for Sexual & Gender Diversity in Palestinian Society, "alQaws for Sexual & Gender Diversity in Palestinian Society," 2024, https://alqaws.org/siteEn/index.

23. Kaba and Hayes, "A Jailbreak of the Imagination: Seeing Prisons for What They Are and Demanding Transformation."

24. Call Blackline, "Call Blackline," n.d., https://www.callblackline.com/.

25. Trans LifeLine, "Trans LifeLine," 2025, https://translifeline.org/.

26. Davis, *Are Prisons Obsolete?*; Davis, *Freedom Is a Constant Struggle: Ferguson, Palestine, and the Foundations of a Movement*; Davis et al., *Abolition. Feminism. Now.*

27. Gilmore, *Abolition Geography: Essays towards Liberation*; Gilmore, *Golden Gulag: Prisons, Surplus, Crisis, and Opposition in Globalizing California*; Gilmore, *Change Everything: Racial Capitalism and the Case for Abolition.*

28. Critical Resistance, "Critical Resistance: Beyond the Prison Industrial Complex 1998 Conference"; Critical Resistance, "Critical Resistance," 2025, https://criticalresistance.org/.

29. Black & Pink, "Black & Pink," 2025, https://www.blackandpink.org/.

30. Spade, *Normal Life: Administrative Violence, Critical Trans Politics, and the Limits of Law*; Spade, *Love in a F*cked-up World: How to Build Relationships, Hook Up, and Raise Hell Together*.

31. Sylvia Rivera Law Project, "Sylvia Rivera Law Project," 2025, https://srlp.org/.

32. Tranzmission Prison Project, "Tranzmission Prison Project," n.d., http://www.tranzmissionprisonproject.org/about-us/.

33. Hidden Water, "Hidden Water," 2025, https://www.hiddenwatercircle.org/.

34. Bluestockings Cooperative, "Free Store," n.d., https://bluestockings.com/about-us/free-store.

35. Kaba, *We Do This 'til We Free Us: Abolitionist Organizing and Transforming Justice*; Kaba and Ritchie, *No More Police: A Case for Abolition*.

36. Just Practice Collaborative, "Just Practice," n.d., https://just-practice.org/just-practice-collaborative.

PART ONE

Seeds of Change

Nurturing Our Abolitionist Growth

CHAPTER 1

From the Hood to Queer Scholar

How I Became a Police Abolitionist

SUSANA AVALOS, UNIVERSITY OF MISSOURI–KANSAS CITY

The year was 2004. The place: Bakersfield, California. I was eleven years old and had recently moved into a new neighborhood where shortly thereafter my immigrant parents separated. This new neighborhood differed from the previous one; there were mixed demographics (i.e., Black, Hispanic, and White people), whereas my previous neighborhood consisted of White, middle-class people. Unlike my previous block, which was often quiet unless children were playing outside, this one was loud. People were constantly walking up and down the street, and my next-door neighbors openly did drugs and drank alcohol in their front yard. On this block, most of the yards were unkempt, there was trash in the gutters, and everyone kept to themselves. The kids were nowhere to be seen, hidden away in their homes to protect them from the violence that soon became our shared nightmare.

When people learn that I was born and raised in California, I often hear statements like, "You are so lucky. It must be amazing living in that sunny state!" To some extent, for some people, it may be. But for my family and neighbors, our experiences did not fit the narrative of the "California dream." Before moving to Deborah Avenue in Bakersfield, California, we did not live in the best places, but we would soon experience the worst. Between 2004 and 2010, it felt like every day there was a drive-by shooting or a physical altercation that resulted in the police being called.

It would be years before I recognized my block as the "hood," an area where gang-related violence and crime rates were high. Within this context, the hood inhabits precise coordinates: California Avenue to the north, Brundage Lane to the south, Washington Street to the east, and Chester Avenue to the west. Deborah Avenue did not inhabit those coordinates per se, but it was just on the outskirts of Chester Avenue within its own centralized pocket of violence when the Bloods decided to settle here. As a child, I often heard mentions of the hood by my older brother, neighbors, or school friends, but I did not make the connection that I lived there until I was about thirteen years old. I knew the violence we experienced there was abnormal, but I did not know we lived in one of the worst neighborhoods in the area. Maybe I should have paid more attention to the red flags, such as sleeping on the ground because our mattresses were covering the windows just in case there were stray bullets. Or being taught to drop on the floor like "soldiers" to avoid being struck by a stray bullet. Yet, as a child, I did not make the link, or maybe I did not want to.

The first deaths I witnessed were of a rival gang member of the Bloods and his girlfriend after gunfire was exchanged between them and my neighbors. I was thirteen years old. By this time (2006), the gun violence had gotten progressively worse. While I may have been naive to the violence in the neighborhood years prior, at thirteen I knew it was a matter of time before something like this would happen, given the increased rate of drive-bys. By this time, seeing the police in our neighborhood was commonplace, but my family never dared to call them, for two specific reasons. First, my mother, a Salvadorian immigrant, was afraid of Immigration and Customs Enforcement (ICE) due to a fear of deportation and family separation, so any person who looked like a law enforcement official made her feel uneasy. That uneasiness is something we all became familiar with, despite me and my siblings being US citizens. Today, our mother is a California resident, but even now, that fear lingers for us. Second was the fear of potential retribution by our neighbors. We did not want to become just another evening news story. "Family of five, murdered in their home" replayed in my mind whenever I thought about calling the police.

Generally, the police are tasked with maintaining public safety and order. Except for my family and neighbors: we came to be fearful of the police, not because we did not trust them or were afraid they were going to harm us (at least during this time), but because our lives were on the line should we be labeled as "snitches" by our neighbors. In neighborhoods like the one I lived in, being labeled as a snitch could have severe and sometimes lethal consequences. To us, the police represented an additional danger that was not worth the potential "safety" we'd get out of interacting with them. As such, despite police officers threatening us with criminal obstruction, we stayed quiet. My mother, who fled El Salvador due to gun violence, told the officers she did not speak English. This put her at risk of having ICE called on her, but she would rather have been deported than potentially murdered in her home with her children.

In 2010, the gun violence ended abruptly when one of our neighbors was murdered (one of the main members of the gang) and the others incarcerated. At seventeen, I had gone through experiences others could not fathom and had grown so accustomed to the violence that even after they were gone I still slept on the floor and felt uneasy when outdoors. Over time, I started to let my guard down, but even now, I struggle with post-traumatic stress from these experiences. While writing this chapter and reflecting on my experience, I find it difficult to comprehend that we spent seven years in that situation and made it out physically unharmed. Others were not so lucky.

As my siblings and I got older, we were taught how to interact with the police by my older brother outside of the neighborhood context. My brother was a Salvadorian migrant who was brought to the United States when he was eleven. As soon as he arrived here, he learned to speak English, and given the climate in El Salvador at the time (heavy military/police presence, gang violence), he was very observant of his surroundings and the police in the United States. As a teenager, when we lived on Deborah Avenue, he noticed that people of color were more likely to be profiled and thus interact with police officers more often than White people. Based on his experiences and the experiences of his friends with the police here in the United States, he taught us the importance of being safe around the police once we were old enough to drive. I remember vividly how those conversations varied depending on whether he was talking to me (a person who identified as female at the time) or my younger brother. While we were both told to keep our driver's license and car insurance handy, I was told to be aware of my surroundings and to be respectful when interacting with the police. Conversely, my younger brother was told to quickly turn his car off, sit up straight, maintain eye contact with the officer, keep his hands on the steering wheel, and be quiet. At the time I was confused as to why I was told different information, but after learning during my master's program that men and boys of color were more likely to be profiled and mistreated by the police, I understood that while there was a risk of being profiled and mistreated as a female-presenting person of color, the risk was not as high for me as it was for my three male siblings.

FROM THE HOOD TO QUEER SCHOLAR

Although there was no sociocultural expectation for me, as a first-generation student, to attend college, the prospect of it was intriguing. Much to the opposition of my mother, who believed I was wasting my time and should be "working a real job," I applied to college. My mother could not comprehend why I made this decision, given that we were a lower-class, low-income family that occasionally struggled with food and money insecurities. To her, my going to college meant one less person working to keep the house afloat. At the time, my older brother had married, had a child, and moved out of the home. This left my mother, a single parent, with me and my two younger siblings to care for (they were sixteen and eleven years old at the time). Since she was a single parent and largely looked to me to help her keep track of my younger brothers, it was up to me to raise my siblings while she worked two jobs. Girls and women in Hispanic households are often looked to as "second mothers" or caregivers, or at least this was the case for me and my Hispanic girlfriends. Thus, it was my responsibility to be a caretaker while she was away, despite one of my brothers being a year younger and being fully capable of helping with home duties, such as caring for our eleven-year-old brother and doing other chores around the home. So, to ease her worries, I worked full-time while also attending college full-time at age seventeen and helped raise my brothers. This was very difficult, but I managed. After all, since the age of eleven when my father left our home, I had already been caring for them while she was away.

Based on my exposure to gang violence, I became interested in studying criminal justice, with a focus on crime and deviance. I wanted to know why people committed violent acts, what happened to these people once they were incarcerated, and what role the criminal legal system played in addressing violent crime, largely because I saw my neighbors commit very violent acts and not be held accountable for them. I made the decision to attend community college and earned an associate's in administration of justice. Upon graduation, I felt as though I did not learn enough, so I transferred to a four-year university. I subsequently earned my bachelor's in criminal justice with a minor in psychology. However, similarly to when I earned my associate's, I felt like there was more to learn, especially regarding the police, as the courses I took for my bachelor's largely lacked context on the historical roots of policing and its treatment of marginalized people. So I applied to graduate school.

During my master's, I learned more about policing, its colonial ties (i.e., how the police were developed as slave patrols), and how police treatment of marginalized and minoritized communities significantly differed from police treatment of White people. This fascinated me, given my background, and challenged my preconceived ideas of what it meant to be a "criminal." To me, criminals were people of color, since that is what I was exposed to, but learning about police profiling, harassment, and abuse made me realize things were not so black and white. Then, midway through my master's program, George Floyd, a Black man, was killed by police officer Derek Chauvin. Chauvin pinned George Floyd to the ground with his knee for nine minutes, while George pleaded for his life, calling out to his mother before he passed away. A video of this interaction went viral and gained global attention. Protests erupted and calls for justice, accountability, reform, defunding, and abolition came shortly after. It was this moment that truly shifted my perspective of what justice really was and what role police officers play, if any, in the protection and safety of their communities.

At the same time, I was learning about the subfield of queer criminology while also coming to terms with my own identity. When the global COVID-19 pandemic began, I came out as queer and nonbinary. Who I was and what these identities meant terrified me, based on what I saw in the media regarding the treatment of LGBTQ people, the personal experiences shared by my LGBTQ friends, and what I read about in queer criminological research. In that research, I learned that LGBTQ people were harassed, discriminated against, abused, and criminalized at higher rates than cisgender and heterosexual people by criminal legal actors and the general public, largely due to homophobic and transphobic beliefs.[1] To make matters worse, I learned that LGBTQ people of color had worse experiences than their White counterparts, especially if they were trans women of color.[2] That information was largely unsurprising, given the country's history with racism and the stories of racism shared by my brothers and their friends, and what I saw happen on my block. However, this made me realize how having multiple marginalized identities could subject people to worse treatment.

Because I was a queer, nonbinary person of color, reading these accounts exacerbated my existing fear of the police, but mostly it made me driven to right these wrongs. For the duration of my master's program, I became interested in police interactions with LGBTQ people. I conducted a meta-analysis for my master's thesis that exposed me to all existing literature on LGBTQ people's experiences with the police (it was not much). The findings were as expected, given what I had learned about their interactions with marginalized and minoritized people beforehand. I found that the police profiled LGBTQ people based on queer criminal archetypes and stereotypes of these communities as "deceptive" or "predatory";[3] that police physically, emotionally, and sexually abused people in these communities;[4] and when LGBTQ people interacted with or entered the criminal legal system, court and correctional staff treated them with the same contempt.[5] Most shockingly, I found that police were the third-largest category of perpetrators of violence against LGBTQ people and that LGBTQ youth were subject to treatment similar to that of LGBTQ adults.[6] The more time I spent immersed in the literature, the more I came to understand why police should not be interacting with the public, especially LGBTQ people. During this time, abolitionist perspectives were briefly mentioned in the literature and came to make sense to me because interactions between LGBTQ people and the police were abysmal, thus demonstrating that these two groups should not be interacting with one another. But I had my doubts. Who would respond to calls of violence, like the violence my family experienced? While the police did not improve our sense of safety, they always came and were seemingly ready to take action. If police abolition were to occur, who would take their place?

HOW I BECAME A POLICE ABOLITIONIST

It was not until I entered my PhD program that I came to fully understand police abolition. I realized at that point that my knowledge about it was limited. I had ideas about abolition as a movement that sought to eliminate police without putting too much thought into what this would do to communities like the one I was raised in. I admit I fed into the narratives put forth in the media regarding police abolition, namely, that it was a pointless cause and that crime would be rampant if police were abolished. But over time, I came to realize that the police were not creating safety for my family and community members—crime continued to be an issue despite their presence.

I thought back to the neighborhood I was raised in on Deborah Avenue. Sure, police arrived when they were called, often hours or days later, but when they arrived, the people on my block were viewed as being guilty of wrongdoing despite often being crime victims. We were threatened with incarceration, and the fear of family separation loomed over us and other immigrant families in the neighborhood. Despite the police coming when they were called, our neighborhood still struggled. No efforts were made to improve our quality of life or reduce gang violence. The police came and went, and nothing changed. People continued to die, drive-bys did not end, and every day for seven years we cowered in fear. Likewise, people of color and other marginalized communities continue to be mistreated, profiled, and criminalized at disproportionate rates, despite multiple efforts to reform the police. To me, it is clear that reform does not and cannot improve the circumstances and conditions of neighborhoods like the one I was raised in. Police reform does not stop people of color from low-income neighborhoods from being profiled, mistreated, and criminalized, nor does it improve the circumstances of people who are in constant contact with the criminal legal system and its actors.

As I have reflected on my lived experiences and knowledge of police treatment toward marginalized and minoritized communities, it has become evident that for our society police reform is not enough. Events such as the police murders of George Floyd, Eric Garner, Tony McDade, and Breonna Taylor, among many others, and the literature consistently point at the failure of police to improve the safety of society.[7] Instead, reforms provide police agencies with more resources (e.g., money, equipment) that militarize them and give them more power to inflict damage on those who are most disadvantaged, especially people of color and LGBTQ people.[8] Indeed, it is argued, and I agree, that police reform gives police more power, legitimacy, and money while business continues as usual.[9] Rather than implement robust structural reform, most reforms have been programmatic, where police agencies are offered large funding packages to improve their "presentation of self" by undergoing additional job training, with the idea that police treatment of these communities will improve.[10] And yet, low-income people, people of color, LGBTQ people, and other marginalized communities continue to be subject to ill-treatment by the police, often choosing to endure their victimization because they do not trust the police to believe or help them.

What we as a society should instead be doing is investing in education, health care, housing, employment opportunities, mental health services, and other community resources. For example, we should be investing in youth engagement, mentorship, and education programs (e.g., after-school programs, job training, mentorship initiatives) that target at-risk youths that live in neighborhoods like the one I was raised in. I suggest this specifically because the education we received in my community was subpar, and this could have provided constructive outlets and educational opportunities to reduce the likelihood of becoming involved with the legal system. Investment in restorative justice programs, housing and homelessness services, and community-based safety initiatives could help build strong, interconnected communities where residents could collectively address issues of safety and conflict resolution and work toward prioritizing healing, accountability, and repairing harm without relying on the police.

For centuries, police reform has largely failed to produce any positive or lasting effects, as evidenced by the current mass incarceration problem in the United States, despite police reforms after the war on poverty, the war on crime, and the war on drugs.[11] As such, people have taken matters into their own hands. Across the country, grassroots organizations mostly led by people of color (e.g., INCITE!, Critical Resistance, Black Lives Matter, One Million Experiments) have been working to eliminate the use of police and instead rely on one another to overcome issues that arise in their neighborhoods.[12] While envisioning a world without the need for police or a criminal legal system is difficult, it is not unimaginable.

Abolition is multifaceted. An abolition framework seeks to address the real problems people have, it seeks to reduce and avoid perpetuating different forms of oppression, and it advocates for divesting from police agencies and prisons and instead investing in their communities. An abolition framework is a way to brainstorm various solutions to prevent, stop, and respond to harm and to eradicate the conditions that create harm.[13] Rather than focusing on reforming the way police respond to certain situations or interact with certain people, abolitionists are interested in addressing the root causes of these problems, such as toxic masculinity, the heteropatriarchy, capitalism, racism, homophobia, transphobia, and so on, without relying on the legal system and instead relying on themselves.

Based on my lived experiences and knowledge acquired as a queer criminologist, it has become clear to me that police abolition is necessary because the alternative has not been working and does not show signs of sustainability. This newfound knowledge of abolition has undoubtedly changed the way I do research and teach, especially when it involves discussions about the police. I used to believe that it was possible to reform the police, that implementing more training and holding police accountable could change the way police treat the people they are tasked with protecting. Indeed, when I came to Old Dominion University, I hoped to research the police and seek ways to improve their interactions with LGBTQ people. This is no longer the case. Now, my research explores how people create safety, what safety means to them, and how it can differ between people. I focus on what we as a society can collectively do at a personal and structural level to make our lives better without involving or relying on the legal system. In my classroom, I discuss alternatives to policing and incarceration and have critical conversations regarding our need for agents of social control. Much like when I was younger, my students often struggle to imagine a society without police. Having these conversations can be difficult, especially from the perspective of a criminologist, but they are not impossible or improbable. The work by INCITE!, Critical Resistance, Black Lives Matter, and One Million Experiments demonstrates that we have more power than we think we do to effect meaningful change. We need to get comfortable with getting uncomfortable to confront these realities and actually do something about them.

NOTES

1. Casey et al., "Discrimination in the United States: Experiences of Lesbian, Gay, Bisexual, Transgender, and Queer Americans"; James et al., *The Report of the 2015 U.S. Transgender Survey*; Panfil, "Young and Unafraid: Queer Criminology's Unbounded Potential."

2. Carpenter and Marshall, "Walking While Trans: Profiling of Transgender Women by Law Enforcement, and the Problem of Proof."

3. Carpenter and Marshall, "Walking While Trans: Profiling of Transgender Women by Law Enforcement, and the Problem of Proof"; Mogul, Ritchie, and Whitlock, *Queer (In)Justice: The Criminalization of LGBT People in the United States*; Woods, "Queer Contestations and the Future of a Critical 'Queer' Criminology."

4. Grant et al., *Transgender Discrimination Survey*; James et al., *The Report of the 2015 U.S. Transgender Survey*.

5. Buist and Stone, "Transgender Victims and Offenders: Failures of the United States Criminal Justice System and the Necessity of Queer Criminology"; Malkin and DeJong, "Protections for Transgender Inmates under PREA: A Comparative Study of Correctional Policies in the United States."

6. Garnette et al., "Lesbian, Gay, Bisexual, and Transgender (LGBT) Youth and the Juvenile Justice System"; Hunt and Moodie-Mills, "The Unfair Criminalization of Gay and Transgender Youth: An Overview of the Experiences of LGBT Youth in the Juvenile Justice System"; Snapp et al., "Messy, Butch, and Queer: LGBTQ Youth and the School-to-Prison Pipeline"; Braunstein, "The Five Stages of LGBTQ Discrimination and Its Effects on Mass Incarceration."

7. Alexander, *The New Jim Crow: Mass Incarceration in the Age of Color-blindness*; Balko, *Rise of the Warrior Cop: The Militarization of America's Police Forces*; Hinton, *From the War on Poverty to the War on Crime: The Making of Mass Incarceration in America*; Simon, *Mass Incarceration on Trial: A Remarkable Court Decision and the Future of Prisons in America*.

8. Balko, *Rise of the Warrior Cop: The Militarization of America's Police Forces*; Purnell, *Becoming Abolitionists: Police, Protests, and the Pursuit of Freedom*; Walker et al., "Why Don't We Center Abolition in Queer Criminology?"

9. Purnell, *Becoming Abolitionists: Police, Protests, and the Pursuit of Freedom*.

10. Hinton, *From the War on Poverty to the War on Crime: The Making of Mass Incarceration in America*.

11. Alexander, *The New Jim Crow: Mass Incarceration in the Age of Color-blindness*; Hinton, *From the War on Poverty to the War on Crime: The Making of Mass Incarceration in America*.

12. Purnell, *Becoming Abolitionists: Police, Protests, and the Pursuit of Freedom*; Walker et al., "Why Don't We Center Abolition in Queer Criminology?"

13. Purnell, *Becoming Abolitionists: Police, Protests, and the Pursuit of Freedom*.

CHAPTER 2

Growing Up an Abolitionist

ROSA SQUILLACOTE, JOHN JAY COLLEGE, CITY
UNIVERSITY OF NEW YORK

I grew up in Washington, DC, in the 1990s, with socialist parents—and I do not remember ever understanding the criminal legal system except as a tool of oppression. In that era, in the middle of exponential growth of the carceral state, the concept of carceral abolition was inarticulable.[1] My childhood and adolescence were saturated by the discourse of the War on Crime that evolved into the War on Terror. These "wars" defined my generation. The fact that they were obvious failures was immaterial. (Social science had long established that prisons were expensive and ineffective in reducing crime; George W. Bush's lies about weapons of mass destruction were notorious.) Ideology will trump material reality almost every time. And the ideology of punishment lies deep within our American culture. It is perhaps easy to question how so many people believed these lies so easily. But that is how ideology functions. We are told to (and agree to) believe certain things, and rejecting those beliefs is hard work. It is hard partly because there is little language to talk about it. The critical thing to understand about prisons and carceral institutions is the silence that defines them. Abolition's first goal is to rip the carceral state open, to understand it and make it visible.

FAMILY HISTORY: GRANDPARENTS

I grew up with a different ideology. My parents were committed leftists who came from activist families. My mother's parents were involved in civil rights work in the 1950s in Chicago; my grandfather helped found the Chicago chapter of the HOMES project during the early 1950s. HOMES helped integrate Chicago residential neighborhoods. He worked for the National Labor Relations Board in Milwaukee for most of his career, eventually becoming regional director.

My father's parents were German refugees who fled the Nazis. My Oma's family was Communist; my Opa's was Jewish and socialist.[2] My Oma's parents left Germany in the 1920s to avoid arrest or execution by the Nazis. While my Oma was living with her own grandparents as a child, the SS came to her home and arrested her grandfather and her uncles. Her favorite uncle pretended to be his brother (the brother was most active in the KPD, the German Communist Party) and was beaten so badly his jaw was broken. One of the arrested uncles was tortured and died within days after his release. The uncle they were looking for eventually fled to France, then Spain, where he was killed in battle during the Spanish Civil War. Her grandfather was rearrested during the war and was killed in the Buchenwald concentration camp just before it was liberated. Her favorite cousin was drafted into the Nazi military and bravely faced death by willfully defying an order on his navy ship; he was accused of mutiny, shot, and tossed overboard. My Opa's family fled Germany via Poland, where they stayed with relatives who were all later killed in concentration camps. My Opa and his brother were sent to what were essentially labor camps on farms to work off the debt the family owed getting their papers allowing them to escape. They then fled to Czechoslovakia, where they spent several years and my Opa, as a teenager, joined a Communist youth group.

The last story my Opa told me before he died was of a time when he and two other members of the youth group were wheatpasting anti-Nazi posters and got caught. He and the other young man drew attention toward themselves so that the young woman with them would be able to run away and avoid being raped. They were almost beaten to death before she was able to get other members of the Communist group to rescue them. My Opa's mother got the family tickets on the last boat to leave for America. When he said he didn't want to leave, she said that she would inform on all his Communist friends if he didn't go. So, he left. All his friends from that group were killed in camps, and his girlfriend was killed in one of the camps known for doing medical experiments on women. In the United States, Opa enlisted as soon as he could and was a medical paratrooper in WWII, seeing firsthand some of the worst brutality of the war, including the Battle of the Bulge. After the war, he went to look for whatever family was left in Displaced Person camps. He had PTSD for the rest of his life. My Oma also never recovered from her childhood trauma and from the upheaval she experienced both as an immigrant and from political repression as a Communist in the United States. When I was growing up, the family pictures on their walls were all stories of who had been killed by the Nazis or who had been traumatized by political repression in the United States. I grew up on stories of racial violence in the United States and Nazi atrocities in Europe. I was never naive about the repressive role of the state.

But then when I turned twelve I was confronted by this reality very harshly. I woke up one day and there were FBI agents knocking on the door of my childhood home, telling me that my parents had been arrested. They would serve fifteen and seventeen years in federal prisons, and our family became defined by this new reality.

HISTORY: THE SILENT CARCERAL GENERATION

It was hard. Prison is a world unto itself—by design—and people on the outside with loved ones inside exist in a liminal state, neither here nor there, but always somewhere in between. That existence is also by design—the suffering of family members. When I was growing up, one in thirty children had a parent in prison. But it wasn't something people ever talked about. I told a girlfriend in high school by just showing her a letter from my mom postmarked Tallahassee Federal Correctional Institution (FCI). She recognized the stamp, saying her stepfather was locked up. We never talked about it outside of that. Millennials are a generation defined by the presence and the silence of prison, police—the growth of the carceral state is rooted in our childhoods. It is important to understand ourselves this way, to understand ourselves as experiencing the presence of the carceral state and the silence of it, even if you did not (or think you did not) experience it directly. More likely you had a friend with a cousin the family didn't talk about or shared a bus ride with people going to visit someone inside. As my stepmother, and longtime activist, Lisa Stand has said, "Do you think you don't know anyone with a loved one locked up? Think again. We are everywhere."[3]

The first thing I want to say about abolition is that it is not just a political necessity for "people directly impacted by the carceral state"—because *we are all* directly impacted by the carceral state. Some people's "safety" comes at the expense of others'. Some people's stability comes at the expense of others'. Everyone—from guards to inmates, victims to criminals, and people who have only had friendly police officers giving them directions—all require the abolition of the current carceral institutions and the abolition of the carceral framework that has grown alongside the American state. The silence of this state has left a generation in profound ignorance of itself. But it is closer than you think (and something that has become more clear, perhaps, since the police repression of Occupy, Black Lives Matter, Cop City, and the current college solidarity encampments for Gaza).

Abolitionism should be able to articulate the reality and the silence of the carceral state, in order to be able to effectively challenge it.

FAMILY HISTORY: PRISON VISITS

My parents were arrested in 1997 and sent to federal prison. From the time I was twelve until I was twenty-nine, I had a parent in prison. It is still difficult for me to think about that time—and it is hard for me to write this now.

This was my life for those years: holidays on the road driving to prison, the sound of bolted doors buzzing open, Ziploc bags of quarters for vending machine food, fifteen-minute recorded phone calls, not ever being able to have a private conversation, crying in front of other visitors, prison staff watching to make sure you didn't hug too much. That was the bulk of my life. And it is still with me, every day. When I hold my kids, when I hear a loud door buzz, when I celebrate holidays at home, when I am driving—I am thinking about prison, and freedom. The two are inextricably linked. Every phone call, every contact had a beginning and an end defined by walls.

I said previously that prisons create a liminal space for visitors, for loved ones. We live outside the walls, but part of us is always inside. The barrier of the wall, the surveillance, the barbed wire—it keeps us out or in, but we are always crossing that barrier, even if only in spirit.

What is there to say about prison visits? My worst visit was the first time I saw my father after my parents were convicted. The first year after their arrest (1997–1998), they were held at a federal detention center. That facility was like what you see in movies—talking on a phone while looking through plexiglass windows, sitting in a row with other visitors. My mom got special visits during that year, so a couple of times we were able to go in and hug her. My father didn't, so I couldn't hug him until the first time my Oma took me to see him in prison after the trial, after they were convicted. We were new and didn't know the rules of visitation yet, so we arrived late. I got to touch my dad for the first time in a year, and an hour later we had to leave. I was thirteen, and I cried and I screamed, and the guards took me and my Oma away while my dad looked on and had to go back inside. The guards let me and my Oma cry in the bathroom for a few minutes but then told us it was time to leave. They just kept saying visiting had ended and we should have come earlier. I was thirteen and the state tore me, sobbing, away from my father. I hadn't been able to touch him in a year.

This is important to remember: most stories I will tell, that people tell, about prison visits are brutal and heartrending. But people are people and find a way to laugh and create good memories. During one of the first visits to my father at the detention center, I was waiting at the window for him to get called out. One of the other inmates saw my face and immediately went back in to get my father. My father and I were new at that place, but I had his face. This stranger saw me and recognized my father. It was a moment that made me feel close and connected, despite the window. My mother was first sentenced to Tallahassee FCI, and she worked in the kitchen and created elaborate ice cream recipes. She amused us at every visit with the new flavors and names she came up with: Purple Passion, the Pear-fect Vanilla, Mandarin Orange Chocolate. Here's a later story: One of the inmates in my father's prison had found a stray cat and managed to keep him hidden as a pet. It was a bit of an open secret, but the cat was out of the bag when he was caught by a surprise inspection by guards they didn't know. Still, for a time there was a furry companion that brought people joy.

People visiting prisons are usually women. I remember seeing them dressed to the nines, high heels and beautiful dresses and elaborate hairstyles. It's a chance to see a loved one, and we all liked to look our best if we could manage it. Of course, often we couldn't manage it. There were long lists of rules about what we were allowed to wear. No khakis, no flip flops, nothing tight fitting. The rules were so convoluted it was hard to keep track. Once I asked a guard (when I first arrived, while waiting to be processed) if my clothes met the visiting standards. He said they were fine, and I waited in processing for an hour only to be told when I got to the door that no, in fact, my clothes were not appropriate. I had to go find a store to buy sweatpants and missed precious hours with my family.

Bureaucracy can be used to punish people for nothing, for existing. Rule changes come out of nowhere and hit you hard. One of the constant questions of prison visits was whether there was a rule change for visitation you hadn't heard about in time—a particular color of clothing or style of shoe that might no longer be allowed. Once, they changed their policy so that underwire bras were not permitted. Several women were turned away before others got the idea to just cut the wire out of their bras in the bathroom. These random changes were ostensibly for safety, but visitors always understood their real purpose: to make our lives harder, to punish us.

The awkwardness of going through puberty is painful enough for most people. I remember when I was no longer allowed to sit on my father's lap or to wear certain clothes—prison guards looked at my body and told me I was too old. Prison visits put your family intimacies on display. There are no secret vulnerabilities—every blush, discomfort, anger, sadness is on display for whoever is watching.

Prison visiting rooms are a very specific space—not free, not unfree. We are together but reminded at every moment it is only temporary. The inmates have more freedom than when inside; we have less than when outside. (Whatever the guards say, goes. Don't ever forget that.) At 10 a.m. at Petersburg, every visit was interrupted by "the count." Every inmate stands up and goes to the back of the room while they are counted to make sure no one has slipped through the gates, the bars, the locks, the guards. Once my brother and I—while in high school—took the Metro north to Danbury FCI to visit our mother. At Danbury, you had to arrive before the count or after; the count could take an hour, so if you were late you were going to be very late. My brother and I took the train to Danbury, then walked the fifteen or so minutes from the train to the prison, mostly on the shoulder of a state highway. We ended up missing count and weren't allowed to wait inside. So, we went outside to wait at the front entrance. It started to hail. Someone came out to tell us we weren't allowed to wait there, either. So, we walked fifteen minutes along the side of the highway back to the train station. Somehow the prison rules reached outside the prison to punish us while we trudged through the town.

Different facilities had different rules. In Petersburg (Virginia), visitors had to wait in an outside structure with plastic paneling and heat lamps that (usually) worked in the winter. There was a phone and you'd have to call up to let the guards know who you wanted to see. Veteran visitors would arrive early and keep track of who arrived in what order—new people had to have the informal rules explained to them. Visitors tended to look after each other: in conversation, assuring that everyone knew the rules, exchanging tips and advice and experiences; or in silence, sitting and waiting together.

Visiting people in prison is subject to that peculiar bureaucratic combination of rules and discretion, institutions and people. The rules and the institution were always punishing. Some guards made prison visits bearable. Others made them more painful. Sometimes the same guard would do either, depending on the day. I remember visiting and knowing, "Oh, this guard is here, I won't have to take my bra off today." Or I would hear people advise each other about what to say to a particular guard. We navigated the moods and the rules of the prison world—always knowing that, as bad as this is, it's so much better than being inside. We, the loved ones outside, were the lucky ones. Prison visiting is a state of constant tension, resentment, gratitude. Most of all, though, it is a state of determined optimism fueled by love and connection with those inside. It is punishment and traumatizing, and it is your only option for that moment of looking into someone's eyes and hugging them.

More than all of that, prison visits were (are) inarticulable. I'm trying my best to describe them accurately, and this is one small drop in one large bucket. Prisons are invisible to those who don't have people inside. When you do have someone inside, you become a little invisible, too. The New York City subway maps show the outline of Rikers Island but don't label it. The first fight of abolition is to make the carceral state visible—really visible—to people outside. There was a brief campaign called "See Rikers," where activists put stickers with "RIKERS ISLAND" printed on them over the island outline on the subway maps. That is an act of abolition—to make the invisible visible, to make it articulable and thus able to be challenged.

THE POLITICAL LIMITS OF REFORMIST REFORMS

I was able to attend Berkeley School of Law, and I thought I would go on to criminal justice reform policy work. I found much of law school to be a major disappointment, with no real opportunity to understand the full scope of the carceral state. In my first semester, I worked in a student clinic—supposedly a "street law" program that teaches children incarcerated in juvenile prisons a "know your rights" course. Many of the boys had been incarcerated for several years, and the clinic was considered a friendly joke. They knew, and we knew, that whatever rights they had in theory meant nothing to their lives. What was the purpose of our clinic? It was mere performance. The biggest impact we had in that clinic was to organize a book drive. We collected books to donate to the prison library because during one session when we came to the prison, the boys complained that they had been denied recreation time for a week—meaning they were kept in their cells for the one hour a day when they got to enjoy "free recreation." I cannot describe to you looking at the cells lining the "free time space" we held the clinic in and trying to understand how keeping teenage boys locked up and unable to move achieved any purpose at all. One of the kids complained that they didn't even have books to read. This was the beginning of my understanding of the pointlessness of legal reform, of the limits of law. They did not need law students' legal advice. They needed to not be locked up.

My second year in law school I took a class taught by a Berkeley professor and two legal scholars from Mexico. The class focused on criminal due process rights; their question revolved around how to incorporate American due process protections into Mexican constitutional law. They talked about the success of American criminal policy in reducing crime and showed documentaries on how Giuliani-trained officers were sent to Mexico City to advise local police departments. This was years before the Black Lives Matter movement, when Guiliani was still seen by liberal society as the savior of NYC. The depth of the faculty's and students' faith in American criminal due process protections stunned me.

Other classes and clinic work I did led me to understand that many elements of the "criminal justice reform" of that era were politically ineffective. I remember being deeply disillusioned. The political world of legal reform movements seemed to me doomed to irrelevance. (This is not to diminish the important work that many good people have done! It is just to say that the opportunities to participate in effective political change were not readily available to law students at that elite institution.)

After law school, I came back to New York and helped create the Police Reform Organizing Project (PROP) in the fall of 2011, at the beginning of Occupy Wall Street. When we were putting together the idea for PROP, common wisdom was that any project that targeted the NYPD was doomed to fail. People who lived with police harassment certainly wanted change, but the media and popular culture still thought of the NYPD as the heroes of 9/11 and the force that took down NYC's crime wave. It was fortuitous, then, that PROP began so close to Occupy, as we were able to participate in the swift shift of public opinion. The NYPD's oppressive tactics against Occupy protestors—and in particular, a widely shared photograph of an officer pepper spraying a couple of penned-in young white women—changed the tenor of public conversations about the NYPD in totally unforeseen ways.

Occupy gave way to the Stop Stop-and-Frisk movement in New York, including the 2012 Floyd trial that held the NYPD's stop-and-frisk tactic to be unconstitutional. This also led to the rise of the Black Lives Matter movement and uprisings protesting violent/racist policing. Popular media, such as the book *The New Jim Crow* and the documentary *13th*, provided a framework that gave voice to a much broader and fundamental criticism of carceral institutions and the carceral state as inherently racist.[4]

However, that shift in framework did not result in strategically successful demands or in meaningful changes to NYPD policy or practice. After Mayor de Blasio's election in 2013, stop-and-frisk numbers declined, but ticketing/arrest practices increased for petty acts such as dancing on the subway.[5] De Blasio's meager attempts to limit the power of the NYPD resulted in a dramatic public conflict. Officers stood and silently turned their backs on de Blasio and issued vague threats to his family.[6] At the same time, de Blasio failed to make any significant policy changes.

The political goals of the police reform movement at that time focused on litigation and legislation. *Floyd v. NY* was a federal court decision that overturned the NYPD's racist stop-and-frisk policy.[7] One of their primary policy goals was the Community Safety Act— legislation that expanded the definition of discrimination and created a new administrative official (inspector general) who would have oversight powers over the NYPD (although this office actually only has the power to make recommendations and request information). This law passed and provided legitimacy to the political claim that the NYPD was too powerful and needed to be reined in. But this law also failed to result in any changes to NYPD policy and practice.

While in the last year of de Blasio's tenure as mayor there was some reduction in the NYPD budget, most of that reduction came from merely shuffling school safety officers to the Department of Education instead of the NYPD.[8] But still, the NYPD's budget was decreased for the first time in decades. And at the same time, the summer of uprisings after George Floyd's death led to flagrant abuses by the NYPD, which de Blasio failed to address in any meaningful way. In fact, during the 2020 summer of uprisings, it seemed like the NYPD ran the city and de Blasio was unable to stop them.[9] One NYPD planned response to a protest in the South Bronx included flooding in officers from all over the city, kettling protesters until the 8 p.m. curfew, then violently assaulting and arresting everyone.[10] The NYPD faced serious criticisms for its abusive response to protesters. And yet, in the next Democratic primary for the mayoral election, New Yorkers elected an avowedly "tough on crime" former cop as mayor. Eric Adams was elected with broad support from the outer boroughs.[11] His tenure as mayor has been better for the NYPD than for New Yorkers. The Close Rikers movement that had some promise has effectively died. Bail reform efforts have been rolled back, and the promise of progressive district attorneys has not yet been felt.

I went to graduate school in part to understand the limits of criminal justice reform, in particular, to understand why police departments seemed so resistant to change. Two notable elements of my research in grad school have stood out to me. The first is that the carceral state is almost entirely bureaucratic. Bureaucracies are only indirectly influenced by litigation or legislation, and they are often characterized as largely undemocratic; at the same time, bureaucracies are marked by a high level of discretion on the part of frontline workers. That is to say, individual workers—like police, prison guards, teachers, DMV personnel, people working in food stamps offices, and so on—have a fairly significant amount of discretion in how they apply or enforce the rules they are bound to. For prison visits, guards frequently used their discretion to make visits either better or worse. That choice was usually informed by how much they saw themselves in the visitors—how much they could or couldn't empathize. This discretion should be critical to the abolition movement, since it tells us that workers in carceral institutions have some choice in how they carry out their work. How can we influence that choice?

The second element I found in grad school research is that the growth of mass incarceration is rooted in a series of reform movements. Prisons themselves are reforms away from public punishment, such as stocks. The expansion of carceral institutions (probation and parole, in particular) were introduced to reduce prison populations.[12] The carceral state has a way of turning reforms into expanding institutional power; today, this is manifested by the creep of carceral logic into other administrative/bureaucratic institutions.[13] One of the reasons for this is that reforms are always externally imposed but internally carried through. That is, it is the workers who are being regulated who enact the new rule. In such conditions, isolated from dynamic democratic accountability, the carceral state uses reforms to expand itself.

These experiences tell me something critical about the politics of abolition: (1) the carceral state is a bureaucratic one, which requires moving outside of traditional political strategies of litigation/legislation; and (2) workers within the carceral state hold a unique position of power and must be incorporated into any politics of abolition.

In 2010, Adrien Schoolcraft secretly recorded conversations in his precinct and released those tapes. He was subsequently abducted by the department and involuntarily held in a psychiatric ward. He was released after three days due primarily to public scrutiny. The costs of speaking out against NYPD practice are high. And yet officers continue to do so, some more or less publicly. Despite the costs, some officers object to the work they are required to do. They object to the racial discrimination, they object to the constant surveillance of communities, and they believe there are better ways to ensure public safety. The fact that there are both objections and retribution suggests the very thing that abolitionists risk ignoring: different police officers feel differently about their job, and that feeling causes some police officers to act differently. In a recent lawsuit, minority officers are directly challenging the NYPD's quota policy as an explicitly racist policy. In August of 2017, one hundred law enforcement officers marched in support of Colin Kaepernick. In one prisoner strike in Alabama, prison guards engaged in a sick-out and "had communicated their plans to F.A.M. [Free Alabama Movement] members, and expressed their support for non-violent and peaceful demonstrations against the human rights conditions existent at Holman."[14] The actions come from the workers; abolition politics can only benefit by seeing these actions and these workers, by incorporating them into our understanding of the carceral state.

In law school, some of the clinic work I was able to do included working with a broad coalition of partners, including radical prison abolitionist groups like All of Us or None. I remember some of those meetings included parole and probation officers; I don't think corrections officers were ever present. But parole and probation workers—two strong arms of the carceral state—were voluntarily working with a reform coalition to make it easier for people to get decent work when they got outside. Why? I didn't think to ask that question then, but in retrospect it is clear that on some level they understood the limits of and were critical about their work. In the mid 2010s, I attended a conference of women unionists—the UALE Women's School. Being surrounded by women from all parts of the labor world was a profound experience. It really was people from all over the labor world, too—white collar and blue collar. One of the group discussions we held addressed the Black Lives Matter movement. Two of the women at my table were offended by the framing of the conversation; they both had worked as corrections officers and talked about the danger and difficulty of that job. They talked about violence from inmates, the brutal work conditions. Conditions of employment and conditions of confinement are often the same conditions, after all. I remember feeling that there was a bit of a missed opportunity. What would a more open conversation have looked like? Labor is uniquely situated to provide a platform for difficult conversations about carceral work.[15]

These conversations will not be easy, they will not always be productive, and they will not be sufficient. Abolition must rely on much more than carceral workers. But it must also take into account these workers, if only because they are a critical part of the material reality of the carceral state. They help shape that reality. As I said previously, there were some moments in visiting prison when correction officers' discretion could be kind—but it usually wasn't. I would not have wanted to sit down with a corrections officer to talk about the harmful effect their job had on me. I don't think I would have been able to. At the same time, they actually saw the same world I did. They were also stuck in the invisible carceral world.

SEEING THE CARCERAL WORLD

It is one thing to not see something. It is something else to not be seen. People inside are rendered invisible; mass incarceration has effectively disappeared millions of people. The effects of that ripple outward, in political ways (census counts, unemployment statistics) and in psychological ones. When you have a loved one inside, you are also always a little bit invisible. When you visit inside, you also disappear. But, of course, you don't really disappear. You just move into another world— the carceral world. The carceral world is a material one, it is not abstract. When you are in that world, it is all-consuming. It informs how you act, how you feel, how you think. The reality is too all-consuming to imagine yourself outside of it. Questioning that world— getting angry at the guards or the rules or the waiting—feels like it has no purpose. So, you teach yourself, convince yourself, to accept that world. You could say "I want to abolish prison" with the same sense as "I want a million dollars." Prisons have done their job very well—the reality they impose is very convincing. I have been trained to be quiet in response to certain noises; it's part of my nervous system now.

But it is not only people who are locked up and their families who are rendered invisible by the carceral state. People who work in these institutions are usually from economically depressed areas without meaningful alternative job options.[16] In NYC, working as a police officer is one of the few avenues toward respectable work with a decent salary and a strong union (and job protections) without the need for a college degree. This holds true across carceral institutions. Carceral workers are often from the same economically dispossessed conditions as victims of the carceral state.[17]

To believe in the abolition of the carceral state, you have to accept certain seeming contradictions. These contradictions have to do with the distinction between criminal and victim, or between good and bad. People who harm others are themselves harmed by the carceral state. People who work in prisons and who abuse prisoners are—often— themselves victimized by the economic brutality of our current political order. Prisons, police—the carceral state writ large is an institution full of people who have few other options.

Of course, these are only contradictory on the outside. They find their resolution in human reality. We are all of us good people and bad people and hurting people who have hurt other people. To the extent one can ascribe any genuine attempt by the institutions and workers within the carceral state a desire to help the world be a better place, the failure of that goal comes from those institutions' (and workers') failure to understand the subjects of the carceral state as people. The corrections officer or police officer or probation officer must recognize themself in the prisoner/suspect/returning citizen. Those people who sit outside the carceral system must do this also—that is, see themselves in the people who are locked up. Those of us who work to dismantle this system have perhaps a harder task—to see ourselves in the very people whose jobs we want to abolish.[18]

In furtherance of our goal of abolition, we must understand the objective conditions of carceral institutions as they exist today: the structural reality of the institution of correction officers/police, the social and work conditions of their lives, and the kind of control that these bureaucrats have over their actual labor power. We know that not all police officers go into this work for the same reasons, and not all police officers feel the same way about their work. That is reality as much as the fact that police killed over six hundred civilians in 2023.[19] We cannot afford to ignore either truth if we take our goal of abolition seriously.

CONCLUSION

This is a critical challenge for contemporary abolitionist work. The righteous anger of people who see the cruelty of these institutions does not easily make room for nuance. We want prisons to close, now. We want the police to disband, now. We cannot afford to wait—the people inside cannot afford to wait. And yet wait we must, and while we wait we must attack the institutions directly as much as possible. But "attack" has many meanings, and in order to use the most effective one, we have to understand these institutions as accurately as possible.

Many police officers are avowed white supremacists. Many others are just trying to do their often tedious and unpleasant job.[20] The key is to focus on the *person*—the person who has been locked up and the person doing the locking. If my experiences have taught me anything, it is that we have to begin with that first step of recognition. People who work in the carceral state—even the "bad" ones—are people who are often themselves stuck in a situation in which they have little control over their own lives.

People who work in carceral states must be acknowledged by the abolition movement. These people *are* the most tangible articulation of the institutions they work in. They must be part of any changes. I know that sounds . . . well, naive is perhaps the kindest word. But it is not without precedent. There have been demonstrations of solidarity between guards and inmates, between Black police officers and Black Lives Matter activists.[21] One of the only public records of the NYPD's illegal quota system comes from arbitration pursued by the police union (the Police Benevolent Association), which continues to collect stories about officers being forced to use quotas to pursue broken windows arrests. This is important, because the quota system is one of the main drivers of abusive police practice in the city. Quotas behind broken windows are almost certainly responsible for Eric Garner's death. And police officers—like other workers—do not like quotas, which make their work more onerous. Quotas are a prime example of the relationship between the conditions of police work and the consequences of police work. Abolitionists must highlight this connection, a connection that reflects the reality of the social conditions of carceral institutions and thus is strategically useful.

The landmark Public Renewables legislation in New York State includes a section to retrain people currently working in fossil fuel industries for green energy jobs. Imagine if NYC retrained police to work in any other department of the city agency—to invest in utilities, sanitation, transportation, education, and so on. Imagine if NYC took one-eighth of the NYPD budget for the City University of New York. Abolitionism must understand itself as pursuing these goals not *just* for those harmed by the carceral state (we are all harmed by the carceral state), but as a path forward that provides *every* person the opportunity to be a more whole version of themselves.

NOTES

1. Herring, "Was a Prison Built Every 10 Days to House a Fast-Growing Inmate Population?"

2. *Oma* and *Opa* are German for "Grandma" and "Grandpa."

3. Stand, "Every Family Has One."

4. *13th*; Alexander, *The New Jim Crow: Mass Incarceration in the Age of Colorblindness*.

5. Lennard, "New York City's Cops Are Waging War on Subway Performers."

6. Rayman, Jorgensen, and McShane, "Hundreds of NYPD Cops Turn Backs to de Blasio in Protest as He Speaks at Funeral for Slain Officer Miosotis Familia"; Rubinstein and Mays, "Police Union Discloses Arrest of de Blasio's Daughter in Privacy Breach."

7. Floyd v. City of New York, No. 13–3088 (2d Cir. 2012).

8. New York City Independent Budget Office, "Fiscal History: NYPD."

9. Mystal, "Bill de Blasio Has Failed the Test of This Moment"; Rubinstein and Mays, "Police Union Discloses Arrest of de Blasio's Daughter in Privacy Breach"; Speri, "Bill de Blasio Promised to Change the NYPD. His Courage Failed Him, and Us."

10. Human Rights Watch, "US: New York Police Planned Assault on Bronx Protesters."

11. Editorial Staff, "New York Mayoral Primary Election: Live Vote Results."

12. Rothman, *Conscience and Convenience: The Asylum and Its Alternatives in Progressive America*; Walker, *A Critical History of Police Reform: The Emergence of Professionalism*.

13. Beckett and Murakawa, "Mapping the Shadow Carceral State: Toward an Institutionally Capacious Approach to Punishment."

14. Lewis, "Guards Join Striking Prisoners in Alabama."

15. Squillacote, "To the Editors."

16. "You know, a lot of people think the prison system isn't working. People think the prisons are just a place to put people who haven't learned to function in society, people who could be taught to be productive, if only society would give them a chance. It's really a shame, we just throw people away in prisons. But enough about the staff" (Lisa Stand, personal communication).

17. Beck, "Op-ed: New York Should Make Milk, Not Prisons"; Huling, "Building a Prison Economy in Rural America"; Kim, "Prison-Based Economic Development: What the Evidence Tells Us."

18. Conover, *Newjack: Guarding Sing Sing*; Stand, "What Kind of Job: A Series on Unions and Prisons."

19. Mapping Police Violence, "Mapping Police Violence," n.d., https://mappingpoliceviolence.org/.

20. Democracy Now!, "'Horrendous': Black Men Tortured by White Mississippi Police 'Goon Squad' React to Guilty Pleas"; Forman, *Locking Up Our Own: Crime and Punishment in Black America*.

21. Conlin, "Off-Duty Black Cops in New York Feel Threat from Fellow Police"; Lewis, "Guards Join Striking Prisoners in Alabama."

CHAPTER 3

"So, You Like the Police, Huh?"

ALESSANDRA MILAGROS EARLY, JOHN JAY COLLEGE, CITY
UNIVERSITY OF NEW YORK

Leaving campus during my second year as a PhD student, I drove a familiar route back home. Although this particular street is known as a speed trap, I thought nothing of it as I talked to my girlfriend on the phone and began driving downhill, my car gradually picking up speed. My conversation was abruptly cut short when I was jolted by the sound of police sirens and the increasingly bright lights flashing in my rearview mirror. As my heart dropped into the pit of my stomach, I told my girlfriend to call my mother and that I was going to record the interaction— I thought that day could be my last. After I pulled over, my hands trembled as I quickly deleted several apps on my phone to make space for a potentially long video. I rolled down my windows, placed my hands at "ten and two" on the steering wheel, locked my eyes on my review mirror, and tried to slow down my panicked breathing. Honestly, I do not think there are enough words to describe the insurmountable wave of relief I felt when I saw an older Black man get out of the police car. While I am well aware that not all "skinfolk are kinfolk," I felt a small comfort in seeing him instead of a white male cop.[1]

Growing up as a Black woman, I constantly received "The Talk" from both of my parents. Although commonly associated with conversations about sex, for many Black people, "The Talk" is a conversation on "race and race relations" and, in the context of the carceral system, it centers on how to survive or avoid interactions with the police.[2] Whitaker and Snell describe this ritual as a dialogue about "racial profiling and diffusing negative perceptions and stereotypes to avoid being hurt or killed by police during routine activities, such as driving or walking down the street."[3] For me, that manifested in exchanges where my parents shared their own experiences of being profiled, their avoidance or coping strategies, and familial stories, and even encouraged practicing how I would handle a potential situation. As an example, my father instructed me that if I got pulled over, always "roll down your windows, keep your hands on the steering wheel, and ask permission before you move or reach for anything." My mother told me about the time a family member, as a teenager, was profiled by a police officer who was looking for a suspect in his neighborhood. Although he had been playing in his front yard while his mother watched, the officer attempted to arrest him simply because "he fit the profile." Hearing this, his mother insisted on accompanying her son to the station. In response, the officer promptly changed his mind and walked away. These stories were in the back of my mind that day I got pulled over in St. Louis, mere miles from where Mike Brown was killed—a name that sparked the widespread protests in 2014 against police brutality.

"Do you know how fast you were going?" the officer asked me as his eyes scanned my car. I replied that I was unsure and apologized for being unsure. "License and registration," he said. As I looked at the passenger seat, a moment of panic swept over me as I realized that my purse was not by my side. I had placed it in my backpack, which was in the trunk of my car. I heard my mother's voice echoing in my head, reminding me that I should always keep my purse and documents close by at all times. I told the officer that I needed to access my trunk and he told me it was okay to exit my vehicle. As we walked around my car, the officer asked me how old I was and what I did for a living. Opening my trunk, I told him I was a PhD student in criminology and criminal justice at the University of Missouri—St. Louis. The officer smiled and shook his head in approval, then said, "Criminal justice? So, you like the police, huh? Is that what you study? Do you work a lot with the police?" Although anyone who knows me or is familiar with my work could guess my answers, I felt scared to tell him how his questions were complicated and charged. Instead, I pointed to other threads of connection: "I've had family members who work with police or who have been officers themselves. Also, as a criminology and criminal justice student, I've spent quite a lot of time studying the police. My department has worked closely with police departments and we even have a faculty member who is a retired officer." After I handed over my documents, the officer went back to his car to presumably look me up. Within a few seconds, the officer returned and we chatted some more. He then explained why he was going to let me off with a warning: "I'm going to let you off with a warning because you remind me of my daughter and because you're a criminal justice student. We need more people like you who are researching and working with police. We get a bad rap, but if more people look into this stuff, the better off we'll be. But don't speed again."

The cop walked back to his car, laughing. Once I returned to the driver's seat, I immediately called my mother and my girlfriend to debrief about the exchange as I drove back home. Although on the surface the interaction could be read as pleasant, pulling back the layers of police violence, white supremacy, systemic racism, and perceived Black solidarity provides some insight into my personal and ongoing struggle with abolition. Namely, I examine the overlap of my positionality as a Black queer person and a Black queer criminologist while unpacking the challenges of working within a field that was founded on the criminalization and brutalization of my predecessors. Drawing from personal experiences and supplemented by diverse bodies of literature, this chapter considers how my personal definitions of abolition have changed throughout different educational, professional, and social contexts. In doing so, I ask this question: "What does it mean to be within a discipline that is inextricably intertwined with, and benefits from, the carceral system?"

LEARNING AND UNLEARNING

Although abolition has certainly "[re]surfaced into popular discourse," it is historically associated with the "abolishment" of slavery.[4] For example, throughout my educational career, particularly within early educational contexts, abolition was commonly presented as the Thirteenth Amendment that passed due to President Lincoln's efforts. Generally, the narrative was that "Lincoln freed the slaves because he knew it was the right thing to do" or that the racialized encoding of law and society ended with his actions. However, as a young Black woman navigating majority white educational contexts, I have learned, as legal scholar Michelle Alexander describes, how these processes have shifted and remain embedded within "the basic structure of society."[5] I have distinct memories of sitting in classrooms as either the only, or one of a handful of, Black student(s) and feeling the unnerving gaze or reactions from my white peers whenever slavery came up. In one unforgettable moment from third grade, I had to talk about my family's history for a class presentation. Every student was required to stand on a stage in front of our families, friends, and teachers. We were encouraged to dress up in our cultural clothing and deliver a short speech in front. Although I am unsure of what I wore, I remember my speech was one of the shortest of the class and was something along these lines: "My name is Alessandra Milagros Early and I'm African American. I don't know our family's history. I only know that we came over on a boat." At the time, I could not isolate why my "speech" felt so embarrassing or why knots appeared in my stomach after several chuckles emerged from the crowd. Slavery's cruel and enduring legacy, from erasing a family tree to perpetuating racialized violence through the contemporary prison system, has been omnipresent in my life—but so has the power to resist, fight, and pursue alternatives such as abolition.[6]

In college and graduate school, abolition was a rare topic in class, so I pursued my own self-educational journey. Although scholars note that "abolition work and [criminology and criminal justice] education cannot be separated," most of my classes or coursework never explicitly discussed abolition.[7] However, deeply related topics, such as the explicit and implicit forms of racism underlying American society, piqued my interest, and I became drawn to research and conversations concerning the intersection of identity and the carceral system.

As an adult, my understanding of my queer identity deepened in tandem with my criminology and criminal justice–related research, and I read everything I could about the historical and contemporary criminalization of queer communities. The work exposed my discipline's historical, and contemporary, role in defining queerness as abnormal and justifying violence toward queer people through social and carceral system–related processes.[8] As Foucault wrote, criminalization and criminalizing narratives are mobilized to regulate the identities and behaviors of people and transform them into controllable "docile bodies."[9] I questioned why institutions such as prisons, which are supposed to deter crime, still existed when they "exacerbate the very conditions that they are supposed to address."[10] Again, I was forced to grapple with the painful and frustrating truth that the very foundations of the carceral system—the study of which I have dedicated the majority of my life and career to—were built on the efforts to eradicate my own people.[11] Does that foundational history entirely negate the modern-day carceral system? In other words, if the core (criminology's origins) of the apple (criminology) is rotten, can you still eat the fruit? While some may cheekily suggest cutting around the rot and eating the "fresh" parts of the apple, is that still an appropriate approach when we exit this metaphor and recognize that we're talking about people's lives? If no, then abolition, in whatever form it may take, feels like an imperative, not solely to correct long-standing wrongs but to prevent the state from enacting these harms today and in the future.

My discomfort and curiosity pushed me to seek literature by scholar-activists and critical academics who traced the history of punishment to consider how various institutions, like the carceral system and its apparatuses, can be interwoven with power and privilege that enacts violence toward those most vulnerable in society.[12] I became fascinated by the tension between those who push for "reformist reforms" that would patch up or alter the carceral system versus others who propose the "eventual dismantling of that system" described as "non-reformist reforms."[13] Although these two schools of thought were a useful framework for my initial foray into abolitionist circles, the notion of either keeping or immediately dismantling the carceral system and its apparatuses seemed too cut-and-dried, an oversimplification of potential solutions. Eventually, I read the works of abolitionists like Mathiesen, Davis, Moten and Harney, and Davis and Rodriguez, all of which expanded the notion of abolition.[14] For them, abolition was a process rather than something that abruptly occurred. For example, Mathiesen describes abolition as leaning into "the 'unfinished' . . . the sketch, in what is not yet fully existing."[15] In other words, abolition is a shift from relying upon the familiar system and embracing the possibility of creating new structures. Similarly, Moten and Harney suggest that abolition should not be centered on one particular structure, such as the prison; rather, it is "the abolition of a society that could have prisons . . . [and is] the founding of a new society."[16] Abolition can mean any number of pathways, all aiming to end centuries of violence, and that expansive approach feels like it could open doors to many different viable solutions to prevent further harm. Using that definition, the pursuit of abolition seemed not just realistic but an investment "in a long game," and that gave me hope.[17]

"WHAT'S THE ANSWER?": ABOLITION CONVERSATIONS IN SOCIAL SPACES

Although my research considers social spaces, gender and sexuality, identity formation, and substance use, I'm often met with a barrage of questions related to topics outside of my specialization within criminology spaces and beyond. Recently, a few acquaintances asked me about Port-land law enforcement's difficulty locating a serial killer. In other situa-tions, I am asked questions that are framed as professional but are really directed toward me because I am a Black queer woman. For example, over the years several people have asked me, "Why do you think there is so much Black on Black crime?" or "Is it hard being queer within crimi-nology?" However, the most interesting discussions that I have had are often centered on my personal and professional thoughts on the state of the carceral system or its apparatuses. In these exchanges, abolition is like a lightning rod. Conversations can immediately turn sour or lead to defensiveness and skepticism.

"Well, what will replace the carceral system? What will we do with people who commit crimes?" are questions I am asked. Criminologists and others demand simple answers on the spot whenever I simply float the idea of abolition. Scholars have described this phenomenon, mean-ing the hostility toward the concept of abolition, as manifesting from the organization of American society, language, and public sentiments related to conceiving possible alternatives.[18] For example, Burton and colleagues found that American public opinion toward punitiveness was dependent on whether those who committed an offense could be "redeemed."[19] Other studies have found that the majority of Americans are in favor of rehabilitation and reform rather than maintaining the current system.[20] However, abolitionist frameworks suggest that want-ing and mobilizing carceral system reforms would require an entire rethreading of society's fabric.[21] As an example, the gradual abolition of the carceral system and its apparatuses would require people to balance a desire for "the system to be less cruel and rehabilitative" with a desire for justice when they encounter victimization.[22] This monopolized dependency of the carceral system as a distributor of justice or compen-sation may be why carceral system–related institutions such as prisons and the police have become fixed aspects of American society.[23]

Even my language has sparked tension with legal practitioners and others within criminology, who continue to use denigrating terms to refer to people in the carceral system. My use of person-centered terms—for example, my preference to say "individuals who were formerly incar-cerated" over the commonly used "ex-con"—has signaled my abolition-ist orientation to some. On one occasion, while conducting research within a correctional setting, I had a rather confrontational conversation with a correctional officer who became irritated by my use of "people who are incarcerated" in lieu of "inmate." Although I had used the term in reference to some of my research interests, he bristled and sharply interrupted: "People who are incarcerated? That's a new one. We call them inmates here because that's what they are." Interactions like this have caused some abolitionists to advocate for the development of new and humanizing language to replace problematic and stigmatizing ways of referring to those entangled with the carceral system.[24] For example, Davis and Rodriguez expanded upon this notion by emphasizing that contemporary carceral system–related language "articulates crime and punishment in such a way that we cannot think about a society without crime except as a society in which all the criminals are imprisoned."[25] Furthermore, the rethinking of current language and the development of new language to describe the carceral system can also, as the authors note, facilitate further conversations on the ways in which "punishment is linked to poverty, racism, sexism, homophobia, and other modes of dominance."[26] For example, initial drafts of this chapter used the phrase "criminal justice system" until my editors highlighted the opportunity to further engage with abolitionist frameworks. I realized that my use of "criminal justice system" was a heuristic shorthand rather than a reflection of my faith in the system. I thought about my collegiate use of the term *prison industrial complex*, which always felt too abstract to me. Subsequently, I weighed the implications of terms like *criminal legal system*, *criminal punishment system*, and Roberts's use of the term *carceral punishment system*, all of which draw primary focus to specific aspects of the system (i.e., legal versus punishment) and are unable to capture the multifaceted and insidious ways in which the carceral system harms people.[27] Similarly, the use of the word *criminal* made me feel uncomfortable because it is a stigmatizing label. Ultimately, I decided to adopt Roberts's use of the word *carceral* and omit *punishment* to simply refer to the system as a *carceral system*, an adequate but far from perfect solution. In this regard, abolitionist frameworks and language, as I have grown to understand, can help address "the roots of harm and violence" by reframing how we consider and discuss punishment.[28]

CONCLUSION

While I call myself "a baby criminologist," a term borrowed from the queer phrase "baby gay," I have spent enough time in this field to know that the *a* in abolition is considered by many to be as scandalously controversial as *The Scarlet Letter*'s "A" for adultery. This chapter alone may likely be a source of contention for me in the future simply because it will contribute to the relatively small body of work that examines abolition within criminology. Some readers may feel defensive, skeptical, or even hostile. For instance, during a graduate school presentation in 2019, my copresenter and I discussed the ways in which gender and sexuality structure how people are sent to prison and their treatment once confined, per Acker and Britton.[29] After we finished, we were asked if there were ways to "fix" the gendering and sexualization of prisons so that they could function better. Although my copresenter and I explained that prisons reflect broader societal violence toward identities that have been marginalized, we were met with animosity and labeled "radicals" when we suggested that prisons could not be fixed.[30] That is, while prison abolitionists support reforms "to safeguard the lives" of those who are incarcerated, reforms have "resulted in bigger, and what are considered 'better,' prisons," which may resolve some immediate issues in the short term but only inflate the carceral system and its apparatuses and does little to address the root of these systemic problems.[31]

Generally, because abolition "has found a marginal home in the academy," it remains most prominent in activist and noncriminological spheres.[32] Within criminology and criminal justice professional spaces, the topic remains taboo. For example, while a search for *abolition* on the American Society of Criminology's website produces only fifteen results since 1999, a Google Scholar search produces a small but quickly growing body of abolitionist criminology and criminal justice literature. Largely, this disconnect may reflect what Bagaric describes as the positioning of abolitionists as "pragmatically naïve" idealists who want to "bulldoze prisons and jails tomorrow."[33] Yet abolitionist criminological work in reality does not produce a dedication to some otherworldly or utopian solution. Rather, these works can "pave a way for social change."[34]

Most notably, the emergence of what Walker and colleagues term "subfield[s] of criminological research," such as queer criminology, may be an opportunity for further inclusion of abolitionist perspectives within the discipline.[35] For example, although the Division of Queer Criminology has only formally existed since 2019, most queer criminological work has pushed for "reformist reforms" rather than complete abolitionism, which is more common in other subfields such as "queer and trans abolition."[36] Although subfields like queer criminology may exist on "the margins of criminology," there is, as Ball notes, power that can be drawn from this position.[37] In "mapping the margins" of criminology, to borrow from Crenshaw,[38] abolitionist and abolitionist-oriented subfields can remain vigilant and "retain a sharp-toothed quality."[39] This vision aligns most closely with my perspective as a young Black queer criminologist who remains critical of the carceral system while seeking abolitionist perspectives and solutions.

Truthfully, this chapter was one of the most difficult pieces of work to write and felt more complicated than my dissertation. Overall, I have come to the realization that it is the personal nature of abolitionism coupled with the sanitization of academia, rather than the inclusion of my own experiences, that have produced this sentiment. Because I am a scholar who holds identities that have been marginalized, sometimes my work may be read as advancing an agenda instead of scholarship grounded in research and experience. Put more simply, it is often the knowledge of those who are marginalized that is delegitimized or marked as inherently biased.[40] However, the growing acceptance that all research "cannot be value-free" and the importance of considering one's positionality and reflexivity has opened new avenues for transparency.[41]

My identity as a Black queer woman criminologist, personally and professionally, navigating and thriving in a world and discipline inextricably intertwined with, and benefiting from, a system dependent on the exploitation of my communities means abolition is almost inevitably part of my understanding of the future of the carceral system. As such, while my journey into abolitionism and abolitionist circles has only just begun, I have unlearned the notion of abolition existing only in the past as a reference to the enslavement of my ancestors. As I continue to interrogate and research the urgent need for abolition today, I embrace a "Black radical imagination," one that is a living and breathing move to change.[42]

NOTES

1. Guishard et al., "What We Not Finna Do: Respectfully Collaborating with Skinfolk and Kinfolk in Black Feminist Participatory Action Research," 6.

2. Anderson, Caughy, and Owen, "'The Talk' and Parenting While Black in America: Centering Race, Resistance, and Refuge," 477.

3. Whitaker and Snell, "Parenting While Powerless: Consequences of 'the Talk,'" 304.

4. Ben-Moshe, *The Tension between Abolition and Reform*; Sabati et al., "Dismantle, Change, Build: Lessons for Growing Abolition in Teacher Education."

5. Alexander, "The New Jim Crow," 179.

6. Davis, "Masked Racism: Reflections on the Prison Industrial Complex."

7. Martensen, "Teaching Abolition to Future Police Officers: A Reflective Essay on Pedagogies of Response and Care," 141.

8. Mogul, Ritchie, and Whitlock, *Queer (In)Justice: The Criminalization of LGBT People in the United States*; Woods, "Queer Contestations and the Future of a Critical 'Queer' Criminology."

9. Foucault, *Discipline and Punish: The Birth of the Prison*, 136.

10. Bell, "Abolition: A New Paradigm for Reform," 32.

11. Woods, "Queer Contestations and the Future of a Critical 'Queer' Criminology."

12. Alexander, "The New Jim Crow"; Foucault, *Discipline and Punish: The Birth of the Prison*.

13. Bell, "Abolition: A New Paradigm for Reform," 45.

14. Davis and Rodriguez, "The Challenge of Prison Abolition: A Conversation"; Mathiesen, "The Prison Movement in Scandinavia"; Davis, *Are Prisons Obsolete?*; Moten and Harney, "The University and the Undercommons: Seven Theses."

15. Mathiesen, "The Prison Movement in Scandinavia," 1.

16. Moten and Harney, "The University and the Undercommons: Seven Theses," 114.

17. Bagaric, Hunter, and Svilar, "Prison Abolition: From Naïve Idealism to Technological Pragmatism," 394.

18. Burton et al., "Belief in Redeemability and Punitive Public Opinion: 'Once a Criminal, Always a Criminal' Revisited"; Clarke, "Polls Show People Favor Rehabilitation over Incarceration"; Hart, *Changing Public Attitudes toward the Criminal Justice System*.

19. Burton et al., "Belief in Redeemability and Punitive Public Opinion: 'Once a Criminal, Always a Criminal' Revisited."

20. Clarke, "Polls Show People Favor Rehabilitation over Incarceration"; Hart, *Changing Public Attitudes toward the Criminal Justice System*.

21. Bell, "Abolition: A New Paradigm for Reform"; Davis, *Are Prisons Obsolete?*; Dilts, "Crisis, Critique, and Abolition."

22. Bagaric, Hunter, and Svilar, "Prison Abolition: From Naïve Idealism to Technological Pragmatism"; Keller, "Is 'Abolish Prisons' the Next Frontier in Criminal Justice?"

23. Dilts, "Crisis, Critique, and Abolition."

24. Bell, "Abolition: A New Paradigm for Reform"; Davis, "Masked Racism: Reflections on the Prison Industrial Complex."

25. Davis and Rodriguez, "The Challenge of Prison Abolition: A Conversation," 217.

26. Davis and Rodriguez, 217.

27. Levin, "After the Criminal Justice System"; Roberts, "Abolition Constitutionalism," 930–31.

28. Bell, "Abolition: A New Paradigm for Reform," 47.

29. Britton, "The Epistemology of the Gendered Organization"; Acker, "Gendering Organizational Theory."

30. Ball, "Queering Penal Abolition"; Mogul, Ritchie, and Whitlock, *Queer (In)Justice: The Criminalization of LGBT People in the United States*; Stanley and Smith, *Captive Genders: Trans Embodiment and the Prison Industrial Complex*.

31. Davis and Rodriguez, "The Challenge of Prison Abolition: A Conversation," 216.

32. Walker et al., "Why Don't We Center Abolition in Queer Criminology?"; Dilts, "Crisis, Critique, and Abolition."

33. Bagaric, Hunter, and Svilar, "Prison Abolition: From Naïve Idealism to Technological Pragmatism," 394.

34. Ruggiero, "How Public Is Public Criminology?," 158.

35. Walker et al., "Why Don't We Center Abolition in Queer Criminology?," 1443.

36. Walker et al., 1444.

37. Walker et al., "Why Don't We Center Abolition in Queer Criminology?"; Ball, "What's Queer about Queer Criminology?"

38. Crenshaw, "Mapping the Margins: Intersectionality, Identity Politics, and Violence against Women of Color," 1241.

39. Ball, "What's Queer about Queer Criminology?," 552; as cited in Walker et al., "Why Don't We Center Abolition in Queer Criminology?," 1454.

40. Bernal, "Using a Chicana Feminist Epistemology in Educational Research."

41. Greenbank, "The Role of Values in Educational Research: The Case for Reflexivity," 798.

42. Kelley, *Freedom Dreams: The Black Radical Imagination*, 138.

CHAPTER 4

Queer Criminologists' Pathways to Abolition

A Québécois Autoethnography

ALEXIS MARCOUX ROULEAU, UNIVERSITÉ DE MONTRÉAL
KARL BEAULIEU, UNIVERSITÉ DE MONTRÉAL
CATHERINE THERRIEN, UNIVERSITÉ DE MONTRÉAL

The Montréal School of Criminology in Québec, Canada, is notoriously steeped in the conventional, or mainstream.[1] Indeed, within graduate student production in our department, only 2 out of 408 theses or dissertations (0.5%) have explicitly researched lesbian or gay participants, while other members of the queer umbrella were left invisible.[2] Yet as graduate students within this department, our queerness has been fundamental to our relationship to criminology.

In this chapter, we untangle our dual perspectives as "outsiders within" criminology and our department, both as queer and as abolitionist students.[3] We discuss our pathways from queerness to abolitionism and highlight how our lived experiences challenge the field's and the department's status quo intellectually, politically, and emotionally. We show how abolitionism is the culmination of our queer standpoints and is rooted in our relationships to our marginalized communities. In closing, we discuss the future of the discipline from an abolitionist standpoint.

Like Walker and colleagues, we rely on autoethnography, meaning we unpack our experiences as queer and trans criminologists in academia and analyze these to achieve broader insights.[4] There are two main types of autoethnography: the evocative emotional type, which is turned toward oneself, and the analytical type, which aims to understand the social world through oneself.[5] We lean toward analytical autoethnography, yet we did attempt to highlight our emotional journeys throughout this chapter. In practice, each author answered the following writing prompts individually: Which turning points brought you to abolition-ism? How is your queer identity linked to abolitionism? How did your experience as a queer, critical criminologist within a conventional department influence your trajectory toward abolitionism? We then provided feedback to each other and iteratively teased out similarities and differences in our experiences in an attempt to reach a deeper understanding.

As a content warning, this chapter discusses many experiences of violence, including sexual violence, familial abuse, police brutality, street and cyberharassment, queerphobic and transphobic violence, and secondary victimization through contact with the criminal legal system. We also mention death threats, racist violence, and murder. We encour-age readers to take care of themselves before, during, and after engaging with this chapter.

ALEXIS

I am a survivor of many forms of interpersonal and institutional vio-lence. I grew up confined in an abusive home against my will, have survived sexual assaults and other forms of gender-based violence as a child and as an adult, and have experienced psychiatric institutionaliza-tion. This standpoint informs my research, my relationship to criminol-ogy as a discipline, and my relationship to police, prison, and psychiat-ric abolition.[6]

I've had horrible experiences with police as a student activist. In 2012, I participated in the Maple Spring, a Québec-wide student strike lasting over six months. I've stared into the eyes of riot police who, behind helmets and clear protective shields, grinned as they prepared to beat minors with batons. While engaging in peaceful protest, I have been charged by police riding gigantic horses. Apparently, this crowd control tactic evolved from wartime cavalry maneuvers—in any case, it is petrifying. Over those six grueling months, friends and acquaintances were added to police watchlists and brutally assaulted. I know of at least three activists who were disabled by so-called nonlethal weapons used by riot police.

Although growing up white and middle class shielded me from police violence until young adulthood, in 2012 I was brutally awakened to the fact that the criminal legal system does *not* exist to protect people whose positionality and values challenge the status quo. I have fervently hated the police since, having seen and felt in my bones how this institution exists only to protect dominant groups' interests. As a nonbinary, trans, queer, and multiply disabled person, this conviction has only been cemented since. If there is one thing queer history demonstrates without the shadow of a doubt, it's that police are not on our side.[7] Canadian research also shows that one in four to one in five trans people have experienced police violence and harassment.[8] Perhaps for this reason, there is a long tradition of abolitionist activism within trans communities.[9]

After the student strike, I went on to study sociology. Then my mental health plummeted—thank you, complex PTSD—and I stayed in a psychiatric wing. In the chronically depressed brain fog that ensued, I signed up for a criminology certificate. I had this vague notion of working with people found not criminally responsible for crimes due to mental illness, or as a criminal profiler, which I did not know was a police-adjacent job.

The first time I felt out of place in criminology was during my first week in the discipline, in 2014. I was flabbergasted when the Monday night lecturer made sexist, homophobic, and racist "jokes" over the first three hours. I do not remember what he said specifically, only that I felt ill. I wanted to drop the class, but it was mandatory. I stayed. In this and other introductory classes, I felt *so much* cognitive dissonance. Hearing my criminology professors and peers uncritically discuss police and incarceration was shocking and destabilizing. Having grown up held against my will in an abusive home from which I could not escape, I felt deeply empathetic toward incarcerated people. Thus, learning all about so-called "crazies" who commit crimes and "deserve" incarceration did not sit right with me.

The following semester, as I learned the words for all the ways I'd been victimized—crying on my way home every night—I also read a mandatory textbook filled with snarky and bigoted comments about justice-involved youth. It did not get better once I transferred to the bachelor's degree in 2015. A criminology professor ridiculed the concept of rape culture and joked that if young women in the program were kidnapped, no one would be the wiser, given how many women were enrolled. Fellow students heartily laughed as I stonily stared ahead.

It was also disheartening to steep in such a cis-heteronormative environment as an out and proud trans, nonbinary, and queer person. Only two classes mentioned queer and trans people in passing. In one, this was part of a discussion on abnormal sexual desires. In the other, we were taught outdated, cis-heteronormative concepts pertaining to gender expression, sexuality, and desire in prison. The concept of "pseudo-families" attempts to explain social dynamics in women's prisons, why some incarcerated women date each other, and why some have a butch gender expression.[10] The author claims that women create partnerships and pseudo-families as a way to compensate for lack of men and lack of heterosexual family dynamics in prison. In attempting to explain sapphic relationships and transgressive gender expression, she manages to reinforce heteronormativity. God forbid there be actual lesbians in prison! Another cis-heteronormative concept I learned about is the "deprivation of heterosexual relationships." This is framed as a specific pain caused by incarceration.[11] The author manages to both negate queer sexuality and equate it with sexual assault. I vividly remember pointing out how harmful this concept is, at the time; to her credit, the professor did take this feedback to heart. However, the concept of specific "pains of imprisonment," and by extension the pains caused by the deprivation of heterosexual relationships, is foundational to prison studies.[12] So although this professor may have reviewed how she discusses these concepts, they continue to proliferate within the discipline itself.

Beyond these barely camouflaged queerphobic theories, I regularly experienced transphobic and queerphobic micro-aggressions in university classes, bathrooms, and hallways. Once, a student followed me from the bathroom, down the hall, to my seat at the front of the auditorium to question my bathroom choice. It made me feel monitored and unsafe, to say the least. Although I joined a trans activist student organization, I remained extremely uneasy in the university setting.

During undergrad, further experiences of primary, secondary, and tertiary victimization fed my distrust of the criminal legal system and of other official recourses, which also affected my relationship to criminology. I'd always experienced street harassment, but as my gender expression shifted away from cisnormative standards these experiences grew (and remain overall) scarier. But what could I do about it? Street harassment is not a crime in and of itself, and related crimes like stalking and criminal harassment are extremely difficult to prosecute, should a victim wish to go that route. And now, as a full-fledged abolitionist, I would not opt for reporting street harassment either, as I do not believe in the solutions the criminal legal system has to offer.

Then in 2016, forty-nine trans and queer people were shot and killed at Pulse nightclub in Orlando, Florida. During a local solidarity vigil, the Québec premier addressed the crowd, stating that Montréal is an inclusive city. Frustrated by this inaccurate statement, a trans friend shouted "*¡Viva la revolución!*" and threw a paper ball at the premier.

He was arrested and—as preposterous as it sounds—found guilty of armed assault.[13] In the sensationalistic media coverage that followed, an interview I'd given to discuss nonbinary genders was finally published, one year after I'd sat down with the journalist. This led to me getting cyberharassed and to customers recognizing me at work. I felt unsafe and was afraid I'd get assaulted. Again, there was no legal recourse to protect me—not that the law is particularly effective or useful at protecting people. Hearing of my friend's treatment while in custody also reinforced my distrust of the criminal legal system, especially how it treats trans people.

Shortly after, I witnessed death threats against my trans partner and was involved in the ensuing criminal legal procedures. The case was dropped. The same year, I filed a complaint for sexual harassment at work; human resources concluded no harassment had occurred. Over those two or three years, I experienced multiple forms of victimization that were minimized, discarded, or simply left invisible to official systems. I felt like justice couldn't be served through conventional avenues.

In short, the criminology of the Other that I was taught in class contrasted strongly with my experiences as a marginalized person who'd been in contact with the criminal legal system and whose queer and trans chosen family had similar experiences. This "us" (intervention professionals and researchers) versus "them" (those in contact with the criminal legal system), which was consistently enforced, made no sense, given my experiences. To me, criminology was all about my kin, marginalized people.

Researching prisons since 2017 has formalized my commitment to abolitionism. As a graduate student I learned about prisons' failures toward incarcerated people and about injustices faced by multiply marginalized populations, such as racialized, poor, queer, and disabled people. This knowledge radicalized me, especially once it became tangible during fieldwork. Most of this fieldwork involved going to provincial prisons for women and interviewing people held therein. Although there were no prompts to this effect, many participants disclosed victimizations and other injustices they'd experienced in horrific detail. These interviews reaffirmed to me that the people whose experiences I study are my kin and that my scholarship needs to contribute to their liberation.

Mere months after my fieldwork, the pandemic started and the global uprising around anti-Black police violence resonated locally. With other marginalized grad students, we demanded accountability and changes within our criminology department, yet our demands were met with disdain.[14] In reaction to this, I launched an independent community education project around abolitionism for French speakers. Through this I decided to stop separating my abolitionist values from my research; I submitted my first abolitionist article shortly thereafter. Since then, I have gone on to spend a year as director of research at a trans-for-trans nonprofit that promotes access to justice for 2Spirit, trans, nonbinary, and gender nonconforming folks in so-called Canada. This nonprofit is explicitly abolitionist, as this aligns with community knowledges regarding the intersectional harms caused by the criminal legal and immigration systems: colonialism, racism, transphobia and transmisogyny, queerphobia, whorephobia, ableism, and more. As I circle back to my dissertation, I am as committed as ever to abolitionist theory and praxis.

Overall, my lived experiences as a trans, queer, and disabled person who has been on the receiving end of multiple institutions of control brought me to abolitionist thought, despite the conservative formal education I received. The intimate relationship between queerness and abolitionism is so inherent in my eyes that I got "ACAB" (all cops are bastards) and "trans riot câlisse"[15] tattooed onto my arm, on the same day. I did not do this on purpose, but it is fitting, I think.

KARL

Born in St-Jérôme, Québec, I saw the penal system and its imagery unfold in my social interactions from a very young age. St-Jérôme is a suburban city located near the urban center of Montréal (Tiohtià:ke) and is home to one of the provincial prisons. Residents of St-Jérôme and its surrounding areas must pass by the prison on a daily basis, as Route 117 leads directly to the prison's yard. This layout provides a panoramic view of the prisoners' lives and daily activities. Throughout my youth, this prison sparked conversations within my family, eventually serving to crystallize the binary categories that formed the basis of our education, such as good/evil and just/unjust. Those who had committed unjust actions and were deemed "bad" deserved punishment. I came from a "good family," so the prison was only relevant for the "Other." From a Foucauldian perspective, these were not just family conversations, but rather the power of the State succeeding in disciplining and autonomizing me, thus constructing my belief system around morality and justice.

My belonging in the LGBTQ+ community led me to question the moral and intersecting race, gender, class, and sexuality binaries at the foundation of our social system that allow for the "othering" of different social groups.[16] Growing up while being pushed and oppressed by norms and values helps one understand how social forces have a strong impact on individual pathways. It helps to understand how some choices tend to be nonchoices for many of us, complicating the notion of the good, the moral, and the just. Indeed, in 2012, Québec's youth were globally politicizing their living conditions as the longest student strike was shaking up austerity policies in place. White youth like me were experiencing police violence for the first time and critically reflecting upon its defense of bourgeois interests.

This social climate played a role in my desire to undertake undergraduate studies. I enrolled in a degree in criminology. Binaries practiced in Québec today are largely endorsed by criminology, reaffirming the good, the just, and the good life, notably in terms of sexual morality. I was surprised by the deeply normative theories and discussions that took place in our classes: several professors and students openly value the good life model as a means of combating crime. The heterosexist couple-family-work triad was easily recognizable. Furthermore, in a psycho-criminology course, homosexuality was even addressed as a risk factor. I was shocked, but when discussing it with other students, I learned it was deemed acceptable since we were in a Boy's Club Department.

At the same time, I sought out a job with a community organization that intervenes with queer sex workers. On the streets, I learned to distrust police officers present during outreach work. Slowly, I was led to confront the binary thinking that was ingrained in my education, which was also reinforced by my encounters with the prison and the conversations that followed. I gradually understood that social work practice, in its state today, contributes to the criminalization of certain bodies.

When I entered the master's program in criminology, it was spring 2020. At that time, I had to choose between a professional master's degree with a clinical internship or a research thesis. Our societies were facing the ongoing COVID-19 crisis, which exacerbated social and racial inequalities. A few days later, George Floyd was killed by police officers. In Montréal, the second wave of Black Lives Matter protests was at its peak, with activists calling for racial justice and to defund the police. In outreach work, the relationship with the police was even more of an issue than ever before. I decided to do my MA thesis on policing the homelessness crisis, while working as a practitioner in this field. As practitioners, we were desperate as we had nothing to help our clients, while the police gained power. We witnessed many human rights violations, especially toward queer bodies and sex workers, which was hurtful to me as a gay man. This echoed the HIV/AIDS crisis, where authorities fell back on control and fear instead of relying on local knowledges promoting sensitization, care, and love.

In the meantime, various professions in the United States and Canada took a stand on the magnitude of the racial inequalities being (re) exposed by this crisis. However, criminology and criminologists in Québec remained silent. Even worse, a professor in the department ridiculed the demands made by the Defund the Police movement. He advocated for stop and frisk (mass youth stops in "hot" neighborhoods). Being in such a privileged position as "to study" those issues, while people from my discipline called for more cops, I couldn't stay silent. We, queer and racialized communities, were finally in a fertile moment to rewrite the story about care and injustice. I had seen so much evidence from outreach workers, I couldn't stay silent. I published op-eds against the ideas conveyed by the professor.

At that moment, I felt so powerless. On the one hand, I was told that my concern for social justice could represent a threat to criminology organizations that do not wish to host students only to be criticized. On the other hand, regarding research, one professor assured me that the goal of academics is not really to "change anything." Another professor advised my cohort to smartly negotiate our critiques against policing as we need police forces' collaboration in order to access data. I felt that my ideas, my identity, and my experiences represented barriers both for practice and research in the field of criminology.

In short, I discovered a field that has few aspirations and tools to dismantle structural oppressions. While some areas of criminology acknowledge the discipline's reliance on punitiveness, specifically against marginalized communities, even our universities are plagued by carceral logics. Eventually, all these experiences, both in the field of social intervention and academia, led me to lose confidence in the power of institutions to seek social and racial justice.

CATHERINE

I have always felt marginal. Growing up, big secrets inhabited me and followed me everywhere I went. I couldn't put them down to breathe a little—they were MY secrets—and I couldn't risk anyone having access to them.

One day, my friend and I went for a walk and I thought I would ask if what my cousins were doing to me was normal. Just like that, it slipped right out of my mouth; I had dropped almost a decade of sexual trauma. My friend couldn't keep that information to herself like I asked her to. She called my mom. The latter was waiting for me with her arms crossed and let a long sigh escape as I entered the room. It felt like it was all my fault. She convinced me to go to the police station, so I followed her, not knowing that I had other options.

I don't remember much of what and how everything happened at the police station and how much time had passed before the police interview, but I do remember that part as it was a very traumatic experience. I had to recall every memory of almost a decade of incest while answering the detective sergeant's questions, like "Did it hurt?," "Was there blood?," "Why didn't you tell anyone?," "Was it consensual?," and so on. I was still a minor and that interrogatory felt like I was reliving everything. The wait after the police interview felt like forever. I still have emails of me telling the detective sergeant that I felt like I was not kept sufficiently informed and that I didn't understand half of his gibberish. I had to remind him that I was a teenager who wasn't familiar with the justice system. He replied that I could write a letter to the judge as a form of repair if I wanted to. I refused. I was seeing a psychologist and was diagnosed with PTSD.

Years after reporting those crimes, I received the judge's decision by mail. My abusers were sentenced to a few months of probation, with a curfew and a restraining order. It was not the closure I was hoping for. It felt so unfair. It really felt like I was getting punished over and over again just for existing. On top of the emotional neglect and the sexual abuse, I was excluded from my extended family. I'm not sure I wanted my abusers to be punished, but I was sure the justice system was all but just. I felt so alone.

My other secret was my queerness. I've never felt like a woman nor like a straight person, but it took me years to understand that it was even possible to not identify as a cis straight woman and that it was okay to be myself. Not being able to present myself, at first as a young queer person and later on as an abolitionist student, made me feel alone. Growing up, I didn't have queer models around me. I was, in fact, the only queer person I knew. For instance, there were only straight white couples on TV, or when there were lesbians, they were represented as sexual objects for men. Without realistic representations of queerness, it was very difficult to understand that I was queer, and I was ashamed to tell my friends and family, as homophobic slurs were often thrown around as jokes. This was happening at the same time as the emotional and sexual abuse in my family. I began questioning the justice system and the status quo quite early because I felt like I didn't belong anywhere.

Flash forward to the two years that I studied criminology at the undergraduate level. I felt uneasy. Something wasn't right. Indeed, the criminology department at the Université de Montréal is very conventional and the authors we learned about in the courses were all white Western men. Moreover, the courses overemphasized the repression of "delinquents," underemphasized victims, and often failed to address the social inequalities leading to the criminalization of marginalized people. My pondering continued in feminist studies and at the beginning of my master's degree. A new contradiction emerged: feminists around me were always in favor of repression. Indeed, before I had friends who were critical of repressive institutions, the only discourse I had ever heard aligned with carceral feminism: perpetrators of sex crimes must be put in prison. They must be punished for their actions, and they must serve as an example so that women and children can be safe. In this scenario, prison is described as the obvious solution to sexual violence. However, I was not in favor of repression, which led me to wonder, was I still a feminist? I had come to understand that incarceration is often used to alienate people who do not fit the status quo of whiteness, cis-hetero-patriarchy, and middle-class status. Thus, racialized, queer, disabled, and poor people are direct targets of criminalization.

I wanted to explore this idea further in my master's degree, thinking that I could finally openly criticize and question heteronormativity, the status quo, and the punitive meaning of "justice," all of which are imposed on us from birth. But I quickly hit a wall. The criminology department at the Université de Montréal is no less conventional at the graduate level and the vast majority of my colleagues did not question the dominant discourse. It was then that I understood that if I wanted to engage in research using a critical criminological framework it would have to be a do-it-yourself (DIY) project. Luckily, my coauthors helped pave the way and encouraged me to go for what I wanted to see. I also discovered the department's few critical professors. However, it is extremely disappointing to note that my thesis would have been only the third devoted to queerness and the first to adopt a queer abolitionist lens.[17]

With other queer people, I found the sense of community I was look-ing for growing up, other people who also felt marginalized and alienated from societal norms. The state, police, prison, and repressive institutions contribute to violence against queer communities. These institutions rob us of what makes us *us*. They try to eliminate the sense of community that has kept us resisting for decades, but we are fighting back. Abolition-ism is the path to the liberation of marginalized people who are punished for not being middle-class white cis hetero men—including us queers.

CONCLUSION: ABOLITIONISM IS PART OF US

Turning Points

For us, queerness is intimately linked to abolitionism. We grew up expe-riencing various forms of social exclusion, discrimination, and interper-sonal as well as structural violence. We refer to these experiences as *turning points*. From coming out, to victimization, to hospitalization, to fear of calling the police, to the police murder of George Floyd, and to the punitive management of the COVID-19 pandemic, we have experi-enced these turning points as situations of exclusion and discrimination. These have collectively been grafted onto each other in our understand-ing of life and society.

Our experiences with justice, whether in the hospital, in the shelter, or in court, have been marked by exclusion. For each of us, entry into the criminology department quickly became a vector of injustice. In our attempts to understand our confinement, our victimization, and social control of those whom we are supposed to help, we have encountered a department that others us and that reproduces social inequalities in its practices and discourses. This department has few tools and ambitions to conduct the work of improving our living conditions and those of our communities. Instead, it promotes science that produces discourse about us—marginalized groups—while taking care to position itself very far from us.

This feeling has been further exacerbated during the ongoing pan-demic, which echoes community knowledge stemming from the AIDS epidemic. When life-threatening and mass disabling illness exacerbates social inequalities and state violence, and when this same illness is min-imized as something of the past by governments and institutions, it is especially important to bring abolitionist and queer perspectives into our practices and research.

Care and Community

Our stories highlight the importance of community and allyship within the university setting. Being queer teaches you the importance of chosen family, while abolitionist praxis emphasizes the importance of care and community in undoing and responding to violence and control. Through our respective journeys within criminology, we have found each other and critical allies who have allowed us to improve our understanding of the penal system. We are grateful for this research community, which has provided mentorship, trust, and support.

Queer and abolitionist theories are more than abstract knowledges to us. They cross through our lives, our identities, our communities, and the relationships we build, into and out of university walls. Our friends, our lovers, our colleagues, and our elders are targeted by the criminal legal system. Thus, abolitionism is linked to our living conditions, to our identities, and to our experiences of social life. We cannot consider it as simply a school of thought. *Abolitionism is part of us* as queer and trans people. And to us, abolitionism is the only possible horizon for the liberation of marginalized communities.

Toward a Queer, Abolitionist Anticriminology

As closing thoughts, we ponder what a queer, abolitionist criminology can entail. Moving forward, criminology departments *could* hire queer abolitionist scholars, engage with queer and abolitionist theories, and instill practices that take these into account, such as divesting from campus police. Students and faculty *could* center the violence the criminal legal system directs toward queer bodies.

Yet we doubt it would be worthwhile to reform criminology departments and the discipline to "include" queer abolitionist perspectives. As Kitossa and Tanyildiz remind us, the urge for racial diversity within the university setting is a neoliberal trap.[18] From a queer standpoint, diversity, equity, and inclusion initiatives stink of assimilationism. "Including" queer and trans bodies, politics, and theories, or making these more visible, is not the same as changing our material conditions for the better, nor is it the same as making the university setting less oppressive. For trans people especially, increased visibility often leads to increased victimization; this has certainly been the case for Alexis, including in the university setting.[19] Additionally, the university has often been a site of epistemic violence for queer and trans people, as this is where research pathologizing us has historically been conducted and where the validity of our existence is currently getting dissected by gender-critical scholars. Having more queer and trans scholars in criminology departments is not the be-all and end-all path to our liberation.

Instead, the logical conclusion to a queer, abolitionist criminology may be to . . . abolish criminology. Indeed, criminology is a violent discipline that aims to normalize racism, colonialism, genocide, and more while delivering "ever finer and finer gradations for pain delivery."[20] The discipline is thus fundamentally and irreparably compromised. Indeed, conventional criminology's core tenets have not meaningfully changed despite the development of minority criminologies.[21] Although there is no singular path toward abolishing criminology, Kitossa and Tanyildiz suggest that this anticriminology project includes exposing and critiquing the discipline and the university setting as state-sponsored rackets that reinforce white, imperial, colonial, and capitalist projects.[22]

We would add that a queer, abolitionist anticriminology does not need to be limited to the ivory tower, nor to other institutional settings. As all three of us ponder leaving academia, we wonder what that means for the work we have been doing these past years. Yet the answer is obvious: although queer criminology can be framed as activism, abolitionism and queer liberationism are both grassroots movements at their core.[23] True to queer legacies of mutual aid and community organizing, we have all been involved in community-run abolitionist projects and organizing. Whether that is writing letters to incarcerated queer folks, supporting queer and trans justice-involved pals and strangers, or running public education initiatives, we have been *doing* queer, abolitionist anticriminology all along. And this work has arguably been more disruptive and effective than anything we've done in academia. At the end of the day, publishing peer-reviewed manuscripts that will be read by only a handful of critical scholars is not enough to change the world.

Back to the streets it is.

NOTES

1. F.-Dufour, Villeneuve, and Martel, "Portrait de la criminologie québécoise des dix dernières années selon le courant, la méthodologie et l'appartenance institutionnelle des auteurs"; Marcoux Rouleau, Melouka, and Pérusse-Roy, "Whose Criminology? Marginalised Perspectives and Populations within Student Production at the Montreal School of Criminology."

2. Marcoux Rouleau, Melouka, and Pérusse-Roy, "Whose Criminology? Marginalised Perspectives and Populations within Student Production at the Montreal School of Criminology."

3. Collins, "Learning from the Outsider Within: The Sociological Significance of Black Feminist Thought."

4. Walker et al., "Experiences of Trans Scholars in Criminology and Criminal Justice."

5. Hayes and Jeffries, "Romantic Terrorism: An Auto-ethnographic Analysis of Gendered Psychological and Emotional Tactics in Domestic Violence"; Zempi, "Researching Victimisation Using Auto-ethnography: Wearing the Muslim Veil in Public."

6. Marcoux Rouleau, "Lessons from Insiders: Embracing Subjectivity as Objectivity in Victimology."

7. Warner, *Never Going Back: A History of Queer Activism in Canada.*

8. Bauer and Scheim, *Transgender People in Ontario*, *n* = 433; JusticeTrans, *2STNBGN Perspectives on Access to Justice: A Legal Needs Assessment*, *n* = 703.

9. Sudbury, "Maroon Abolitionists."

10. Giallombardo, *Society of Women: A Study of a Women's Prison.*

11. Sykes, *The Society of Captives: A Study of a Maximum Security Prison.*

12. Haggerty and Bucerius, "The Proliferating Pains of Imprisonment."

13. R. v. Torres Wicttorff, No. 500-01-139945-163 (QCCQ October 20, 2017).

14. Marcoux Rouleau, Melouka, and Pérusse-Roy, "Whose Criminology? Marginalised Perspectives and Populations within Student Production at the Montreal School of Criminology."

15. *Câlisse* is a Québécois swear word. It references the Catholic chalice.

16. Sedgwick, "Queer and Now."

17. For example, Marcoux Rouleau, Melouka, and Pérusse-Roy, "Whose Criminology? Marginalised Perspectives and Populations within Student Production at the Montreal School of Criminology."

18. Kitossa and Tanyildiz, "Anti-Blackness, Criminology and the University as Violence Work: Diversity as Ritual and the Professionalization of Repression in Canada."

19. Koch-Rein, Haschemi Yekani, and Verlinden, "Representing Trans: Visibility and Its Discontents."

20. Kitossa and Tanyildiz, "Anti-Blackness, Criminology and the University as Violence Work: Diversity as Ritual and the Professionalization of Repression in Canada," 56.

21. Kitossa and Tanyildiz, "Anti-Blackness, Criminology and the University as Violence Work: Diversity as Ritual and the Professionalization of Repression in Canada"; Marcoux Rouleau, Melouka, and Pérusse-Roy, "Whose Criminology? Marginalised Perspectives and Populations within Student Production at the Montreal School of Criminology."

22. Kitossa and Tanyildiz, "Anti-Blackness, Criminology and the University as Violence Work: Diversity as Ritual and the Professionalization of Repression in Canada."

23. Ball, "Queer Criminology as Activism."

CHAPTER 5

A Radical Vision for Prison Abolition

JENNIFER M. ORTIZ, THE COLLEGE OF NEW JERSEY

The United States has the largest reported prison population in the world and many communities live under constant surveillance and fear of law enforcement. Killings by police are rampant. Court processes are often unfair, coercive, and overly punitive. Jail and prison conditions are often unsafe and inhumane.

—Human Rights Watch

INTRODUCTION

In recent years, citizens of the United States have witnessed atrocities within the criminal legal system, including the public executions of unarmed persons and the horrid state of the American penal system. Witnessing the cruelty that exists within criminal "justice" has given rise to a renewed call for abolition, a concept that for decades has existed only in the margins of criminological research. Although abolition has been discussed in activist circles for nearly one hundred years, the public, including most academics, remain uninformed about the true meaning of abolition.[1]

The notion of abolishing correctional systems may stir fear in some people. When most people hear the phrase *prison abolition*, they likely envision a chaotic world filled with violent criminals preying on the innocent. This view arises from years of pro–criminal justice propaganda that leads many to believe the criminal legal system is the only thing standing between them and violence.[2] However, decades of research have shown that the criminal legal system does not prevent crime, allows most crimes to go unsolved, and often causes secondary victimization among crime victims.[3] Despite these systemic failings, many people still hold fast to the possibility of prison reform because they cannot fathom a world without the current system of punishment. I once belonged to that camp.

This chapter begins with an autoethnographic reflection on my personal journey from reformer to abolitionist. The chapter then introduces the reader to prison abolition by presenting research-based arguments and by addressing common myths associated with abolition. I conclude the chapter with my vision for a world without prisons.

FROM REFORMER TO ABOLITIONIST

Like many people living in the United States, I once held a fascination with the criminal legal system that emerged from years of exposure to television programming.[4] Moreover, I was raised in East New York Brooklyn in the 1980s and 1990s, which was the height of the crack cocaine epidemic. I witnessed firsthand the corruption within the New York Police Department (NYPD), the detrimental impact incarceration had on my family, and the many forms of oppression experienced by the most marginalized in our society.[5] My interest in becoming part of the criminal justice system stemmed from a desire to change the many injustices I witnessed. I wanted to reform the system and achieve true justice.

My journey from reformer to abolitionist began during my undergraduate career. As an undergraduate, I naively wanted to become an NYPD officer so I could single-handedly reform policing. I was determined to become an officer and root out corruption from *within* the system. During my first semester of college, I read about police culture and the Blue Wall of Silence that indoctrinates officers into an us-versus-them mentality and allows officer misconduct to go unpunished.[6] I quickly learned that reform was not possible because the policing system actively works to maintain the status quo. My interests shifted toward helping people accused of crimes by becoming a criminal defense attorney. Law classes taught me about our "assembly line justice" system, where defense attorneys and prosecutors work together to extract plea bargains from desperate people.[7] As a criminal defense attorney, I would become just another cog in a cruel machine. Despite this knowledge, I remained determined to create change within the criminal legal system.

After completing graduate-level policy courses, I realized that I could help more people by becoming a data analyst and using my skills to support existing reform efforts rather than trying to be a one-woman reform army. While pursuing my doctorate, I worked as the research director for the New York State Permanent Commission on Sentencing. I conducted statistical analyses and prepared reports that were used to support proposed legislative bills. This position allowed me to meet with state officials and nonprofit organizations who were tasked with reforming sentencing laws in New York. I thought I had finally found the path to true reform. For the next four years, I watched as career politicians argued against data or flat-out ignored proposed legislation because it did not fit their political agendas. In the years I worked with the commission, the state legislature passed no meaningful sentencing reform. Four years of work resulted in no changes to the system. I became painfully aware that laws are not based on data or justice; laws are enacted by career politicians whose only concern is reelection. No data or reports could sway people whose only interest was career advancement. Systemic-level change was a pipe dream because the system reinforces itself.[8]

Being married to a formerly incarcerated man made me painfully aware of the cruelties people experience after being released from prison.[9] Upon completing my doctorate, I shifted my research focus to reentry after incarceration. I began working directly with formerly incarcerated people by volunteering for the Kentucky-based, reentry nonprofit organization Mission Behind Bars and Beyond. I attended parole meetings, visited halfway homes, and helped recently released people navigate the complexities associated with entering society after incarceration. I watched as people suffering from mental health issues and substance use disorders, who had spent years caged in cells, were released to a society that disdained them. I visited a halfway house where people were sleeping in the crawl space under the home. There were mentally ill people detoxing from medication because they had no means to acquire prescriptions. The state compounded these issues by charging these individuals for their freedom through parole and court fees, which left them unable to afford food or housing. Moreover, the public treated the formerly incarcerated as social pariahs by systematically denying them employment and housing. What I witnessed was cruelty of the worst kind.[10]

These firsthand experiences, coupled with the knowledge I acquired through my education and employment, shifted my mindset from reform to abolition. If a system does not allow for reform, then the system is not broken; it is designed to create the conditions it produces.

The injustices that people in the system experience are not collateral, as criminologists often refer to them, they are intentional.[11] In other words, the oppression experienced by people in the criminal legal system is not a by-product of well-intentioned efforts. The system functions to create and sustain inequality. Once I saw the criminal legal system through that lens, the only option left to consider was creating a new system, one worthy of including *justice* in its name.

PRISONS IN THE UNITED STATES

While most people cannot envision a world without prisons, modern prisons have existed for approximately two hundred years, or less than 1 percent of the length of time humankind has existed on earth. Modern penitentiaries emerged in the 1800s and were rooted in Quaker beliefs about penance through silence and engagement with the Bible.[12] The most notable of Quaker penitentiaries is Eastern State Penitentiary (ESP) in Pennsylvania, which opened in 1829. ESP utilized a solitary confinement model meant to allow the individual to reflect and communicate with God.[13] These extended periods of solitude and silence often led to severe mental health issues and self-injury.[14] After an 1842 visit to ESP, English writer Charles Dickens wrote,

> I am persuaded that those who designed this system of Prison Discipline, and those benevolent gentlemen who carry it into execution, do not know what it is that they are doing. . . . I hold this slow and daily tampering with the mysteries of the brain to be immeasurably worse than any torture of the body; and because its ghastly signs and tokens are not so palpable to the eye . . . and it extorts few cries that human ears can hear; therefore, I the more denounce it, as a secret punishment in which slumbering humanity is not roused up to stay.[15]

Dickens's quote captures two points that remain true today: (1) prison is inhumane torture and (2) most people remain blissfully unaware of its true cruelty. Although the ESP model was eventually abandoned and new models emerged, each subsequent design included its own forms of mental and physical torture. Today's prisons are no different.

The United States has the largest incarcerated population and the sixth-highest incarceration rate in the world, despite having only 4.4 percent of the world's population.[16] As of 2023, there are 1.9 million people incarcerated in the United States and 3.7 million people on community supervision who may experience incarceration through parole and probation violations.[17] These people are controlled by a complex correctional system consisting of varying prison models, security levels, and confinement levels. Prisons can range from minimum security camps, where the incarcerated can freely associate with each other and have freedom to move within the facility, to super-maximum-security fortresses where the incarcerated have no human contact and no freedom of movement (e.g., ADX Florence). People at all levels of incarceration experience horrific conditions that are traumatic and run counter to rehabilitative practices.

Mass incarceration causes overcrowding, scarcity of resources (space, food, etc.), and unsafe living conditions within prisons.[18] These conditions place incarcerated people in constant competition with one another for what limited resources exist.[19] For example, food is a major commodity in prisons because there are no national standards to regulate nutritional value or minimum caloric intake requirements.[20] States are allowed to dictate what food they provide to their incarcerated population with no federal oversight. A state can even decide to serve food that is not "intended for human consumption."[21] Thus, the state creates competition between incarcerated people for the most basic necessity of life, which subsequently contributes to violence in prisons.[22]

Further contributing to violence and victimization within prisons are mental health issues and substance use disorders. The deinstitutionalization movement of the 1960s and 1970s led to the shuttering of many mental health facilities in the United States. Society shifted its view of mental illness from a health problem to a criminal justice problem.[23] Subsequently, people who were previously treated at mental health hospitals were funneled into the criminal legal system. According to the Department of Justice, two in five incarcerated persons have a history of mental illness, 63 percent of whom receive no treatment during their incarceration.[24] Thus, jails have become the largest mental health providers in the United States, while simultaneously being unfit to treat mental illness.[25] Most mental health treatment within jails and prisons consists of prescription medication, with minimal assistance from mental health providers.[26] Moreover, correctional facilities often respond to mental health–related behavior with extended stays in solitary confinement.[27] The lack of proper mental health treatment in prisons coupled with the traumatic effect of incarceration can cause deterioration of a person's mental health, as well as increasing the likelihood of victimization.[28] Mental health issues in prisons are exacerbated by substance use disorders (SUD). According to the National Institute on Drug Abuse, "85% of the prison population has an active substance use disorder or were incarcerated for a crime involving drugs or drug use."[29] Treatment for SUD in prison is not comprehensive and is often difficult to access due to overcrowding and high demand. Furthermore, drug use often continues in prison through the black market.[30]

The issues caused by mass incarceration are evident in the abuse, death, and violence that plagues our prison system. Because resources are limited and reporting abuse is often an arduous task, correctional staff physically and sexually abuse incarcerated persons, deny them access to medical care, deprive them of food, place them in solitary confinement, and even murder them without consequence.[31] Physical victimization rates within prisons are high, with one in three incarcerated men and one in four incarcerated women reporting being victimized. The rates of sexual victimization are one in ten for incarcerated men and one in four for incarcerated women.[32] Thus, the state bears responsibility for much of the violence and drug use in prisons because they have created an environment that necessitates the use of both for survival.

The abuse experienced by incarcerated people, combined with a prevalence of mental health issues and SUD, leads to self-destructive behavior. Research indicates that self-injury is a weekly occurrence in 85 percent of prisons, suicide rates in prisons have reached record levels, and drug- and alcohol-related deaths rose 611 percent between 2001 and 2018.[33] Contributing to these rising death tolls is the role correctional officers play in the prison black market. Research and investigations have uncovered state and federal correctional officers smuggling drugs and other contraband.[34] The state further contributes to mental health and substance use disorders by utilizing solitary confinement to address rule violation, despite extensive research that shows the detrimental effect of isolation and sensory deprivation.[35]

PRISON ABOLITION MOVEMENT: WHAT IS PRISON ABOLITION?

The prison abolition movement has existed for nearly a hundred years and came to prominence in the United States during the 1960s and 1970s when activists expressed concerns about the ever-growing penal state. The 1971 Attica Prison Uprising forced society to bear witness to the cruelty that existed within the US prison system. During this uprising, men incarcerated at Attica Correctional Facility in New York took control of the prison to protest against their inhumane treatment, which included appalling medical care, rampant racism, and being locked in their six-by-nine-foot cells for fourteen to sixteen hours per day.[36] After four days of negotiation, New York Governor Nelson Rockefeller ordered armed police officers to breach the prison, which left 39 incarcerated people and officers dead and another 128 wounded.[37] These deaths led to public demands for an investigation and improved conditions within the prison. The Attica Prison Uprising was a pivotal moment for the Prisoner's Rights Movement and the Abolition Movement. Campaigns against inhumane prison conditions coordinated by incarcerated people and supported by people on the outside emerged throughout the 1980s.[38] Although the abolitionist movement waned in popularity in subsequent decades, the 2020 social uprisings in response to the police killing of unarmed persons gave rise to a new call for abolition.

Central to the Abolition Movement is the inclusion of incarcerated people's voices in decision-making and policy advocacy. For example, Black & Pink, an abolitionist LGTBQIA+ organization comprised of incarcerated and "free world" members, produces a newsletter and operates a pen pal program that serves to promote and share incarcerated voices. Through these programs, "free" members can share incarcerated members' views in public policy hearings. Incarcerated people's voices are further amplified through prison radio shows, like *Calls from Home*, and writing outlets, like the *Journal of Prisoners on Prisons*.[39] Centering the voices of incarcerated persons provides abolitionists on the outside with ideas and goals rooted in the lived experiences of those directly impacted by the carceral system.

Prison abolitionists do not all agree on the goals of abolition. Some argue that prisons need to experience major reform to achieve crime control, while others argue that we need a mass reduction in our use of incarceration by thinking beyond the prison as punishment.[40] Still others argue that the prison complex is corrupt to its core and must be dismantled.[41] The underlying thread that weaves these views together is the belief that the current system is rife with problems.

My vision for prison abolition requires the dismantling of our punishment system by providing social welfare, educational, and treatment programs to address the inequality that contributes to crime. As we develop a more equitable society, crime will naturally decline, and we can develop new approaches to lawbreaking that will prioritize rehabilitation and equity. Moreover, the existing prison population will decrease through decarceration strategies until we achieve a world without prisons.[42]

THE CASE FOR ABOLITION

While abolition may seem like a radical concept, there are logical arguments and research that support the need to radically transform our societal views of punishment and justice. The primary arguments for abolition are rooted in four main points. The prison system (1) does not reduce crime or increase safety, (2) does not utilize education and treatment to rehabilitate, (3) does not address underlying causes of criminality, and (4) exacerbates existing social problems. This section presents reasons to support prison abolition that incorporate these four main points.

Reason 1: Prison Doesn't Work

Two main goals of punishment are deterrence and rehabilitation. Deterrence refers to a punishment's ability to stop someone from reoffending. Our current national and state-level recidivism data indicate that prison fails to achieve deterrence. Within three years of release from state prison, 68 percent of people will be rearrested. The rearrest rate increases to 79 percent five years after release.[43] The major cause of these high recidivism rates is the scarcity of rehabilitative programming in prisons.

State prisons are not required by federal mandate to offer rehabilitative programming that can address the underlying causes of a person's engagement in crime. Where programming is available, it is often underfunded or grant dependent, which affects the quality of programming and the number of persons who can participate in a program.[44] By failing to provide programming that addresses the underlying causes of crime, the prison system fails to rehabilitate, which contributes to the staggeringly high recidivism rates in the United States. Moreover, prison environments are not conducive to the mental health treatment, educational programming, and vocational skills training that many incarcerated people require.[45]

Reason 2: Crime Is a Consequence of Society's Structure

To move our mindsets toward abolition, we must reflect on our individual biases and how they influence our view of people who break the law. Media in the United States depict crime as the result of individual choice.[46] If an individual breaks the law, we are told to view them as evil or morally corrupt, while ignoring the role of structural and societal-level factors.[47] We hold these beliefs despite extensive research that demonstrates the impact of macro-level factors (e.g., poverty rates) on criminality.[48]

Research indicates that increasing equality in a society can reduce crime. Studies have consistently found a link between high levels of economic inequality and engagement in crime.[49] Economic inequality is evident in the United States through our education system. Funding for public schools is largely dependent on the property values around the school.[50] The higher the property values, the higher the property taxes, which increases the overall funding a school receives. This link between property values and education means that the quality of a child's education depends on the real estate market rather than ensuring that every child receives the best education possible. From an early age, economic inequality begins to self-perpetuate. Put simply, a child who is born into a poor neighborhood begins life at a significant disadvantage to a child who is born into a rich neighborhood because they receive lower-quality education as a result of less funding.[51]

Receiving lower-quality education in childhood leads to lifelong negative consequences. Students who attended underfunded schools are less prepared for college and are less successful in the adult labor market compared to students from wealthy areas.[52] Thus, it is not a matter of chance that poor children are incarcerated and institutionalized at higher rates than wealthy children. The link between inequality and crime is evident in the incarcerated population. People born into lower-income families are more likely to experience incarceration.[53] Statistics reveal that the incarcerated population is less educated, has less work experience, earned less income prior to their incarceration, and will earn less over their lifetime compared to people who have never experienced incarceration.[54] Thus, economic inequality and incarceration form a vicious cycle. If society is genuinely interested in reducing crime and increasing public safety, our attention should shift toward increasing equity in society.

Reason 3: Incarceration Is Morally Reprehensible

A primary argument in favor of abolition is rooted in morals. As discussed earlier, prisons have been criticized since their establishment. The American Civil Liberties Union (ACLU) and the Global Human Rights Center identified violations of "the most fundamental human rights to life and dignity" within the American correctional system, including the use of solitary confinement.[55] Over the past one hundred years, research has proven that humans are social animals and that solitude and sensory deprivation can cause severe psychological and physical issues.[56]

Incarceration should also be condemned because of its connection to slavery.[57] Following the abolition of slavery, many states established race-based laws known as Black Codes. These laws allowed for the arrest and imprisonment of newly freed slaves, who were then forced to labor on plantations as punishment for their crimes. The advent of Black Codes and the subsequent War on Drugs has enshrined a criminal legal system that disproportionately impacts people of color.[58] These laws and policies caused a "blackening" of prisons, whereby the incarcerated population shifted from predominately white (70 percent) in 1950 to predominately Black and Latino (70 percent) by 1989.[59]

Today, people of color are more likely than white individuals to be stopped by the police, be searched by the police, experience physical force by the police, be killed by the police, be arrested for a petty offense, be denied bail, be falsely accused of a crime, and receive longer sentences, including the death penalty.[60] This research illustrates how racism is built within the structure of the criminal legal system. We must see these disproportionate impacts as the product of a system created to control people of color rather than the product of a few bad actors.[61] Since racism is woven into the foundation of our punishment system, the only way to eradicate racism is to dismantle the system and lay a new foundation.

Reason 4: Incarceration Is Counterproductive

Incarceration exacerbates the underlying conditions that contribute to crime, including mental health. As mentioned earlier, a significant portion of the incarcerated population suffers from mental health issues. The experience of incarceration is traumatic and leads to deterioration of mental health.[62] People who are in mental health crisis will experience violence at the hands of officers who are trained to use force to address misbehavior and may not recognize that the individual is in crisis. Even if the officers do identify the crisis, there may be no psychiatric or psychological staff on duty, which leads to the overuse of solitary confinement.[63] When staff are present, the quality of care varies by state because prison health care is "not regulated in the same way hospitals and clinics are regulated in the community."[64]

Incarceration also worsens economic disadvantage. Because criminal records are publicly available in the United States, the government enables discrimination against the formerly incarcerated. People with criminal records are less likely to obtain employment,[65] earn lower hourly wages, and have lower lifetime earnings.[66] Being incarcerated also leads to lowered employability, due to gaps in employment history, lack of work experience, and lack of education.[67] Ability to find housing is limited by housing restrictions, criminal background checks, and the stigma associated with having a criminal record.[68] Moreover, the psychological and social issues that emerge from incarceration make successful reintegration into society nearly impossible.[69] Thus, incarceration is not the solution to crime.

ENVISIONING A WORLD WITHOUT PRISONS

The vision of a world without prisons varies across abolitionists. This chapter presents merely one vision of prison abolition, with the goal of inspiring readers to envision their own views of abolition.

Improving Social Conditions

If economic inequality contributes to criminality, then logic follows that equality would result in law-abiding behavior. The primary way to increase equality in society is to radically transform our social welfare system, beginning with the establishment of housing, health care, and education as basic human rights that every person receives simply by being a member of society. Educational funding for schools should be based on student population size, not property taxes. Providing the same amount of funding per student allows students to have equal chances of success in school.

Free universal health care for all citizens would alleviate the medical bills that currently account for 66.5 percent of all bankruptcies in the United States.[70] Moreover, the ability to see a doctor free of cost would lead more people to seek help *before* medical conditions worsen and become more difficult to treat. Our society would also benefit from developing a free public health system that includes outpatient mental health clinics, ninety-day inpatient substance abuse treatment, and supervised injection sites, which have been proven to reduce overdoses and increase access to treatment for SUD.[71] By providing free, comprehensive substance use treatment, we can meet the goal of rehabilitation by reverting substance use back to a medical approach. To truly view substance use disorder as a medical issue, we must begin by decriminalizing drug use so that it is no longer an arrestable offense. Instead, officers would take people who are high or possess drugs to designated treatment locations.[72] With well-funded substance use treatment centers, we would avoid addressing substance use through arrests and lengthy incarcerations that are counterproductive.[73] Over time, decriminalization, coupled with wide availability of treatment, would lead to a reduction in drug use and potentially a reduction in social stigma surrounding substance users.[74]

Schools and the public health system would work in conjunction to address reproductive health, utilizing both educational and medical approaches. These approaches would reduce teen pregnancy rates and delay child-rearing, which would increase economic success.[75] To further ensure children's ability to succeed, we should provide parents with a monthly stipend to ease the financial burden of having children and provide income-based childcare, which currently accounts for 8–19 percent of median family income *per child* in the United States.[76] Lastly, employers would be required to offer a minimum of six months of paid parental leave. Research indicates that the first six months of life are vital for the parent-child bond, which subsequently affects child development.[77] Parents should be able to support their child's development without fear of losing their employment. Collectively, these social support systems would allow for increased social equality and opportunities for success.

To achieve a strong social support system, society must implement strong business regulations, including restricting the CEO-to-worker total compensation ratio to a maximum of 150 to 1. This means that if the minimum wage was $20 per hour, a CEO could not receive more than $3,000 per hour in total compensation. By implementing an income ratio, we will reduce economic inequality and ensure that corporate profits translate into shared economic success. Addressing economic inequality would also require raising the minimum wage to $20 per hour, or a minimum salary of $42,000 per year.

This new social structure would require that everyone in the system contribute meaningfully, especially corporations and the wealthy. Corporate tax rates should return to pre-Reagan-era levels. The corporate tax rate today is 22 percent, less than half the rate in 1980 (46.2 percent). Increasing corporate taxes allows society to fund a strong social welfare network. While some will argue that we are "punishing" the wealthy for being successful, the reality is that corporations will benefit from a more educated and healthier society. Individual income taxes would be based on a sliding scale, where the highest earners pay higher tax rates, including capital gains taxes, than lower-income individuals, similar to existing structures in Canada.

In addition to the increased revenue from corporate taxes and individual taxes, a strong social support system will result in cost savings. If the United States abolished the prison system, we could reinvest the $80 billion we spend annually on incarceration into social welfare programs and treatment centers that would provide care *before* a person violates a law or engages in deviant behavior, which would reduce crime.[78] A reduction in crime would lead to additional cost savings by reducing the aggregate costs associated with crime.[79] Society would also benefit from additional tax revenue, because people who break the law would no longer be stigmatized and socially excluded, which would increase labor market participation, thereby increasing tax revenue and strengthening the economy.[80] The strengthening of the social support system within the United States would benefit everyone by creating a society rooted in community and rehabilitation rather than individualism and retribution.

Addressing Violations of the Law

A primary concern many people have with abolition is the notion that people will "get away" with crime. While people would no longer go to prison, they would still face consequences for their actions. The goal of consequences is not retribution or revenge; it is rehabilitation and restorative justice through medical, psychological, and therapeutic means. Providing evidence-based rehabilitative treatment and programming to people who violate the law will reduce their engagement in crime.[81] The specific responses to crime would be based on the offense type. Since drug offenses would be decriminalized, violations of the law would fall into two main categories: nonviolent and violent crimes. Approaches to both offense types will center restorative justice and trauma-informed care.

Restorative justice is a set of principles and practices that approach crime as a violation of relationships and communities. This approach to crime focuses on the harm caused by the act, rather than focusing on the violation of a law. Moreover, "restorative justice practices work to address the dehumanization frequently experienced by people in the traditional criminal justice system."[82] Rather than focusing on punishment or retribution, restorative justice focuses on the need to (1) address the harm committed, (2) hold the responsible party accountable, and (3) increase community safety through providing rehabilitative programming. A key component of restorative justice is the acknowledgement that all persons, including those who commit crimes, are deserving of respect and assistance. Restorative justice centers the victim and the community by ensuring they are part of the process, rather than bystanders watching the state hand down punishments.[83] This approach acknowledges that the offender has a responsibility to address the harm they committed, rather than merely languishing in a cell for an arbitrarily decided length of time.

Trauma-informed care (TIC) is an approach to treatment that assumes all individuals have experienced trauma during their lifetime.[84] Beginning with this assumption shifts the provider's focus to the harm caused *to* the individual rather than the harm caused *by* the individual. In doing so, the provider can identify and address the underlying causes of criminality, rather than focusing on just the criminal act committed. TIC coupled with restorative justice practices can create a paradigm shift that prioritizes treatment for all parties affected by the criminal act over punishment. How these approaches work within the criminal legal system would depend on the offense type.

Nonviolent and property crimes are the most common offense types in the United States. According to the Federal Bureau of Investigation (FBI), there are 2,109.9 property crimes for every one hundred thousand people living in the United States, with the most common offenses being larceny, burglary, and motor vehicle theft.[85] Property crimes are motivated by financial need, and therefore, the best approach to these offenses is to address economic inequality.[86] The development of a stronger social safety net, as described earlier, will reduce overall engagement in property crimes[87] but will not eliminate them. To address property crimes, we should utilize existing restorative justice practices, including mediation and financial compensation to the victim. Research indicates that the public and property crime victims are willing to participate in mediation.[88] Victims would also have access to free trauma-informed therapy through the universal health care system. Financial compensation to the victim would be based on the market value of the property affected. Payments on this debt would be based on a person's income, which would ensure the individual is able to make payments without facing an extreme financial burden. In the current criminal legal system, judges include victim's compensation or restitution as part of criminal sanctions; however, few victims ever receive payment because of most defendants' inability to pay.[89]

To address the issue of inability to pay compensation, society should invest in ensuring that people who commit offenses no longer experience the conditions that contributed to their engagement in property crimes. Thus, treatment should include employment readiness training, educational assistance, and therapeutic care to address underlying trauma. By addressing the underlying causes of property crime, we can reduce recidivism, thereby increasing public safety.[90] Providing employment readiness training and educational programming can also increase a person's ability to financially compensate a victim for their losses. Moreover, many property offenses are motivated by substance use, which would be approached through medical treatment, as described earlier in this chapter.[91]

Existing funds allocated for prison development and expansion can be diverted to develop programming in the community. Grassroots efforts can be mobilized to educate the public and government officials about the harms associated with new prisons and jails. For example, in response to a proposed new jail in San Francisco, several grassroots organizations created the No New SF Jail Coalition. The coalition successfully lobbied the San Francisco Board of Supervisors to reallocate the $80 million to provide mental health and substance use services. Although this victory was short-lived because California required the money be used for a jail or returned to the state, this grassroots campaign offers a glimpse into the potential for reallocation of funds away from the criminal legal system and toward community-based care.

Utilizing restorative justice and trauma-informed care to address property crimes may be easy for people to accept because the harm associated with these offenses is often less severe. Conversely, the idea of not incarcerating people who commit violent crimes can be less palatable because of fear and desire for revenge. However, within a restorative justice framework, even people who engage in violent crimes deserve respect and assistance. Operating from a place of anger or a desire for retribution does nothing to address the harm caused by the individual's actions. For example, research indicates that incarcerating a person or sentencing them to death does not provide closure to victims.[92]

The violent crime rate in the United States is 379.4 crimes per one hundred thousand people, which includes murder, rape, assault, and other crimes that stir public outrage and fear.[93] The approach to these crimes must be more intensive than that for property offenses, while remaining rooted in behavior modification (e.g., cognitive behavioral therapy) that operates through a trauma-informed lens.[94] A trauma-informed lens allows us to explore the underlying causes of a person's engagement with violence by exploring the psychological, social, and environmental factors that influenced the individual. To address violent crimes, society should establish facilities that provide treatment based on the offense type. For example, people who commit sex offenses should enter facilities that focus on sex offenses and urges by identifying and treating the underlying cause of their criminality. The length of stay in a treatment facility would depend on needs assessments; however, there would need to be regulatory limits on the length of stay to ensure these facilities center treatment, not control.

Existing psychological treatments are proven to reduce recidivism and alter decision-making processes among persons convicted of violent offenses and should be utilized in these new proposed treatment facilities.[95] The specific treatment needs would be determined by medical staff with expertise in the psychological and social causes of crime, not based on financial limitations or bureaucracy. Care would be individualized and trauma informed. The goal would not be to incapacitate and dehumanize the individual through rituals of degradation, but rather to restore the individual by moving toward a place of healing.[96] Treatment should also include voluntary participation from the victim, community-offender restoration, and other transformative justice practices.

MYTHS ABOUT PRISON ABOLITION

The above vision for prison abolition provides the reader with a general framework for developing a society that moves closer to the goal of true justice. My goal in developing this framework was to help dispel some of the myths associated with abolition, myths created by the media and politicians who have a strong desire to maintain the status quo—myths that are rooted in conjecture, not fact.

Myth 1: Abolition Means Anarchy

Abolition and anarchy are two terms that are often misunderstood and used interchangeably as a fear tactic. While notions of abolition are rooted in anarchist thought, the terms are not synonymous. Anarchism is a political theory that questions authority and how power is constructed.[97] Anarchist thought asserts that no governments should exist because all governments allow for "domination of one class by another."[98] While prison abolition emerges from anarchist perspectives, most modern prison abolitionists do not call for the dismantling of our government. Instead, prison abolitionists call for altering our views of punishment to allow for the dismantling of prison systems. The vision presented in this chapter is not chaotic; it is a vision of humanizing care for those in need.

Myth 2: Abolition Will Increase Crime

Prison abolition would *decrease* crime by addressing the social conditions that cause most crimes. Research demonstrates that a strong social safety net reduces crime.[99] High-quality education and work readiness training reduce the onset of crime and recidivism.[100] Addressing mental health issues, especially those that arise from traumatic experiences, could also reduce law violations. If the United States were to increase economic equality, we could decrease our crime rate and bring it in line with other countries, like Canada and Sweden.[101]

Myth 3: Abolition Means People "Get Away" with Crimes

A common belief about abolition is that people who violate the law would face no consequences. This belief is rooted in our deeply held belief that justice is about retribution. Prioritizing retribution when addressing crime has contributed to the inhumanity that exists within our current legal system. To achieve true justice, we must shift our perspectives away from punishment and toward rehabilitation. Within a restorative or transformative justice framework, the most effective and appropriate approaches to crime are rooted in healing. People who violate the law would still face consequences for their actions; however, the goals of these consequences would be to address the harms caused by the law violation and the underlying conditions that led to the violation.

CONCLUSION

Research indicates that the United States has the longest prison sentences in the world; however, only 28 percent of US citizens believe prison sentences are too long.[102] These findings are indicative of American culture. Many US citizens believe that the criminal legal system's purpose is retribution through lengthy incarcerations or capital punishment.[103] Media promulgates this view by portraying crime as being the result of individual-level failings.[104] These deeply held beliefs allow society to feel justified in utilizing prison to address crime while ignoring the role of economic inequality and other structural-level factors.

Prison abolition requires us to fundamentally alter our views of and approaches to addressing criminal acts. Crime is the result of inequality within society, not individual-level failings. Research indicates a strong relationship between economic inequality and engagement in crime.[105] Thus, approaches to crime must prioritize addressing inequality. Criminal acts should be addressed using transformative justice and trauma-informed practices that provide humanizing responses to heal and restore all parties.

This chapter provided a view of abolition that diverged from the myths propagated by the media and politicians. Research presented in this chapter illustrates that the correctional system is failing and needs to be dismantled to achieve justice. While abolitionist writings often focus on theoretical arguments in supporting abolition, this chapter attempted to shift the conversation beyond theory and toward praxis by providing a vision for a world without prisons. As the movement toward abolition continues to grow in years to come, we must never forget that justice is only possible through collaboration. It is my sincere hope that this chapter sparks discussion and debates about prison abolition across multiple academic fields and moves the debates beyond conjecture and toward justice.

NOTES

Epigraph: Human Rights Watch, "Criminal Justice."

1. Washington, "What Is Prison Abolition?"

2. Kappeler and Potter, *The Mythology of Crime and Criminal Justice.*

3. Parsons and Bergin, "The Impact of Criminal Justice Involvement on Victims' Mental Health"; Baradaran Baughman, "How Effective Are Police? The Problem of Clearance Rates and Criminal Accountability"; Lee, Eck, and Corsaro, "Conclusions from the History of Research into the Effects of Police Force Size on Crime—1968 through 2013: A Historical Systematic Review."

4. Robinson, *Media Coverage of Crime and Criminal Justice.*

5. See Ortiz, "From East New York to the Ivy Tower: How Structural Violence and Gang Membership Made Me a Critical Scholar."

6. Skolnick, "Corruption and the Blue Code of Silence."

7. Zeidman, "Eradicating Assembly-Line Justice: An Opportunity Lost by the Revised American Bar Association Criminal Justice Standards."

8. Ortiz and Jackey, "The System Is Not Broken, It Is Intentional: The Prisoner Reentry Industry as Deliberate Structural Violence."

9. Montalvo and Ortiz, "Perpetual Punishment: One Man's Journey Post-incarceration."

10. See Ortiz and Jackey, "The System Is Not Broken, It Is Intentional: The Prisoner Reentry Industry as Deliberate Structural Violence."

11. Kirk and Wakefield, "Collateral Consequences of Punishment: A Critical Review and Path Forward."

12. Schmid, "'The Eye of God': Religious Beliefs and Punishment in Early Nineteenth-Century Prison Reform."

13. Dolan, *Eastern State Penitentiary*.

14. Prison Discipline Society, *Thirteenth Annual Report of the Board of Managers of the Prison Discipline Society*.

15. Dickens, *American Note for General Circulation and Pictures from Italy*, 83.

16. Prison Policy Initiative, "United States Profile."

17. Ortiz and Wrigley, "The Invisible Enclosure: How Community Supervision Inhibits Successful Reentry"; Sawyer and Wagner, "Mass Incarceration: The Whole Pie 2023."

18. Simon, *Mass Incarceration on Trial: A Remarkable Court Decision and the Future of Prisons in America*.

19. MacDonald, "Overcrowding and Its Impact on Prison Conditions and Health."

20. Santos and Iaboni, "What's in a Prison Meal?"

21. Bolden, *Out of the Red: My Life of Gangs, Prison, and Redemption*, 89.

22. Ifeonu, Haggerty, and Bucerius, "Calories, Commerce, and Culture: The Multiple Valuations of Food in Prison."

23. Parsons, *From Asylum to Prison: Deinstitutionalization and the Rise of Mass Incarceration after 1945*.

24. Bronson and Berzofsky, *Indicators of Mental Health Problems Reported by Prisoners and Jail Inmates, 2011–12*.

25. Fuller et al., *Emptying the "New Asylums": A Beds Capacity Model to Reduce Mental Illness behind Bars*; Torrey et al., *More Mentally Ill Persons Are in Jails and Prisons than Hospitals: A Survey of the States*.

26. Bronson and Berzofsky, *Indicators of Mental Health Problems Reported by Prisoners and Jail Inmates, 2011–12*.

27. Siennick et al., "Revisiting and Unpacking the Mental Illness and Solitary Confinement Relationship."

28. Blitz, Wolff, and Shi, "Physical Victimization in Prison: The Role of Mental Illness"; DeVeaux, "The Trauma of the Incarceration Experience"; Goomany and Dickinson, "The Influence of Prison Climate on the Mental Health of Adult Prisoners: A Literature Review."

29. National Institute on Drug Abuse, "Drug Fact: Criminal Justice," 4.

30. Carpentier et al., "The Global Epidemiology of Drug Use in Prison."

31. Shapiro and Hogle, "The Horror Chamber: Unqualified Impunity in Prison"; Jacobs, "Prison Power Corrupts Absolutely: Exploring the Phenomenon of Prison Guard Brutality and the Need to Develop a System of Accounta-

bility"; Vaughn and Smith, "Practicing Penal Harm Medicine in the United States: Prisoners' Voices from Jail"; Bach, "Defining 'Sufficiently Serious' in Claims of Cruel and Unusual Punishment"; Reiter et al., "Psychological Distress in Solitary Confinement: Symptoms, Severity, and Prevalence in the United States, 2017–2018."

32. Wolff, Shi, and Siegel, "Patterns of Victimization among Male and Female Inmates: Evidence of an Enduring Legacy."

33. Wang and Sawyer, "New Data: State Prisons Are Increasingly Deadly Places"; Applebaum et al., "A National Survey of Self-Injurious Behavior in American Prisons."

34. Ross, "Deconstructing Correctional Officer Deviance: Toward Typologies of Actions and Controls."

35. Reiter et al., "Psychological Distress in Solitary Confinement: Symptoms, Severity, and Prevalence in the United States, 2017–2018."

36. Zinn, *A People's History of the United States.*

37. Thompson, *Blood in the Water: The Attica Prison Uprising of 1971 and Its Legacy.*

38. Herzing and Piché, *How to Abolish Prisons: Lessons from the Movement.*

39. Herzing and Piché.

40. Davis, *Are Prisons Obsolete?*; Knopp et al., *Instead of Prisons: A Handbook for Abolitionists.*

41. Shelby, *The Idea of Prison Abolition.*

42. See Knopp et al., *Instead of Prisons: A Handbook for Abolitionists.*

43. Alper, Durose, and Markman, *2018 Update on Prisoner Recidivism: A 9-Year Follow-up Period (2005–2014).*

44. Ortiz and Jackey, "The System Is Not Broken, It Is Intentional: The Prisoner Reentry Industry as Deliberate Structural Violence."

45. Daniels, *Building a Trauma-Responsive Educational Practice: Lessons from a Corrections Classroom.*

46. Surette, *Media, Crime, and Criminal Justice: Images, Realities, and Policies.*

47. Robinson, *Media Coverage of Crime and Criminal Justice.*

48. Clear, *Imprisoning Communities: How Mass Incarceration Makes Disadvantaged Neighborhoods Worse.*

49. Itskovich and Factor, "Economic Inequality and Crime: The Role of Social Resistance"; Kennedy et al., "Social Capital, Income Inequality and Firearm Violent Crime"; Messner, "Poverty, Inequality, and the Urban Homicide Rate: Some Unexpected Findings."

50. Leachman et al., *Most States Have Cut School Funding, and Some Continue Cutting.*

51. Morgan and Amerikaner, "Funding Gaps 2018: An Analysis of School Funding Equity across the U.S. and within Each State."

52. Duncan et al., "The Importance of Early Childhood Poverty"; Contreras and Oropeza-Fujimoto, "College Readiness for English Language Learners (ELLs) in California: Assessing Equity for ELLs under the Local Control Funding Formula."

53. Looney and Turner, *Work and Opportunity before and after Incarceration*.

54. Taylor, "Adult Earnings of Juvenile Delinquents: The Interaction of Race/Ethnicity, Gender, and Juvenile Justice Status on Future Earnings"; Looney and Turner, *Work and Opportunity before and after Incarceration*; Wolf Harlow, *Education and Correctional Populations*; Pettit and Gutierrez, "Mass Incarceration and Racial Inequality"; Rabuy and Kopf, "Prisons of Poverty: Uncovering the Pre-incarceration Incomes of the Imprisoned."

55. American Civil Liberties Union, *Captive Labor: Exploitation of Incarcerated Workers*.

56. Haney, "Restricting the Use of Solitary Confinement."

57. Wacquant, "The New Peculiar Institution: On the Prison as Surrogate Ghetto."

58. Alexander, *The New Jim Crow: Mass Incarceration in the Age of Colorblindness*.

59. Wacquant, "The New Peculiar Institution: On the Prison as Surrogate Ghetto."

60. Shatz, Pierce, and Radelet, "Race, Ethnicity, and the Death Penalty in San Diego County: The Predictable Consequences of Excessive Discretion"; Pierson, Simoiu, and Overgoor, "A Large-Scale Analysis of Racial Disparities in Police Stops across the United States"; Kramer and Remster, "Stop, Frisk, and Assault? Racial Disparities in Police Use of Force during Investigatory Stops"; Ross, Winterhalder, and McElreath, "Racial Disparities in Police Use of Deadly Force against Unarmed Individuals Persist after Appropriately Benchmarking Shooting Data on Violent Crime Rates"; Stevenson and Mayson, "The Scale of Misdemeanor Justice"; Arnold, Dobbie, and Yang, "Racial Bias in Bail Decisions"; Rizer, "The Race Effect on Wrongful Convictions."

61. Alexander, *The New Jim Crow: Mass Incarceration in the Age of Colorblindness*.

62. Goomany and Dickinson, "The Influence of Prison Climate on the Mental Health of Adult Prisoners: A Literature Review."

63. Reiter et al., "Psychological Distress in Solitary Confinement: Symptoms, Severity, and Prevalence in the United States, 2017–2018."

64. Canada et al., "Multi-level Barriers to Prison Mental Health and Physical Health Care for Individuals with Mental Illnesses," 2.

65. Pager, "The Mark of a Criminal Record."

66. Taylor, "Adult Earnings of Juvenile Delinquents: The Interaction of Race/Ethnicity, Gender, and Juvenile Justice Status on Future Earnings."

67. Pettit and Gutierrez, "Mass Incarceration and Racial Inequality."

68. Roman and Travis, "Where Will I Sleep Tomorrow? Housing, Homelessness, and the Returning Prisoner."

69. Ortiz and Jackey, "The System Is Not Broken, It Is Intentional: The Prisoner Reentry Industry as Deliberate Structural Violence."

70. Himmelstein et al., "Medical Bankruptcy: Still Common despite the Affordable Care Act."

71. Potier et al., "Supervised Injection Services: What Has Been Demonstrated? A Systematic Literature Review"; Simpson et al., "A National Evaluation of Treatment Outcomes for Cocaine Dependence."

72. See Collins, Lonczak, and Clifasefi, "Seattle's Law Enforcement Assisted Diversion (LEAD): Program Effects on Recidivism Outcomes."

73. Pew Charitable Trusts, *More Imprisonment Does Not Reduce State Drug Problems: Data Show No Relationship between Prison Terms and Drug Misuse.*

74. Queirolo et al., "Explaining the Impact of Legal Access to Cannabis on Attitudes toward Users."

75. Hoffman and Maynard, *Kids Having Kids: Economic Costs and Social Consequences of Teen Pregnancy.*

76. Landivar, Graf, and Rayo, *Childcare Prices in Local Areas: Initial Findings from the National Database of Childcare Prices.*

77. Plotka and Busch-Rossnagel, "The Role of Length of Maternity Leave in Supporting Mother–Child Interactions and Attachment Security among American Mothers and Their Infants."

78. DeVuono-Powell et al., "Who Pays? The True Cost of Incarceration on Families."

79. See Anderson, "The Aggregate Cost of Crime in the United States."

80. Bell, "The Long Shadow: Decreasing Barriers to Employment, Housing, and Civic Participation for People with Criminal Records Will Improve Public Safety and Strengthen the Economy."

81. Lipsey and Cullen, "The Effectiveness of Correctional Rehabilitation: A Review of Systematic Reviews."

82. Zehr, *The Little Book of Restorative Justice*, 12.

83. Menkel-Meadows, "Restorative Justice: What Is It and Does It Work?"

84. Fallot and Harris, "A Trauma-Informed Approach to Screening and Assessment."

85. Gramlich, "What the Data Says (and Doesn't Say) about Crime in the United States."

86. Sutherland et al., "Motivations, Substance Use, and Other Correlates among Property and Violent Offenders Who Regularly Inject Drugs."

87. Swanson and Belden, "The Link between Mental Illness and Being Subjected to Crime in Denmark vs the United States: How Much Do Poverty and the Safety Net Matter?"

88. Gabbay, "Justifying Restorative Justice: Theoretical Justification for the Use of Restorative Justice Practices."

89. Haynes, Cares, and Barry, "Reducing the Harm of Criminal Victimization: The Role of Restitution."

90. Swanson and Belden, "The Link between Mental Illness and Being Subjected to Crime in Denmark vs the United States: How Much Do Poverty and the Safety Net Matter?"

91. Sutherland et al., "Motivations, Substance Use, and Other Correlates among Property and Violent Offenders Who Regularly Inject Drugs."

92. Bandes, "Victims, Closure, and the Sociology of Emotion."

93. Gramlich, "What the Data Says (and Doesn't Say) about Crime in the United States."

94. Levenson and Willis, "Implementing Trauma-Informed Care in Correctional Treatment and Supervision."

95. Papalia et al., "A Meta-Analytic Review of the Efficacy of Psychological Treatments for Violent Offenders in Correctional and Forensic Mental Health Settings."

96. Goffman, *Asylums: Essays on the Social Situation of Mental Patients and Other Inmates*.

97. Fiala, "Anarchism."

98. Bakunin, *Statism and Anarchy (Gosudarstvennost' i anarkhiia)*, 178.

99. Swanson and Belden, "The Link between Mental Illness and Being Subjected to Crime in Denmark vs the United States: How Much Do Poverty and the Safety Net Matter?"

100. Eggleston and Laub, "The Onset of Adult Offending: A Neglected Dimension of the Criminal Career"; Uggen, "Work as a Turning Point in the Life Course of Criminals: A Duration Model of Age, Employment, and Recidivism."

101. Swanson and Belden, "The Link between Mental Illness and Being Subjected to Crime in Denmark vs the United States: How Much Do Poverty and the Safety Net Matter?"

102. Gramlich, "U.S. Public Divided over Whether People Convicted of Crimes Spend Too Much or Too Little Time in Prison"; Kazemian, "Longest Sentences: An International Perspective."

103. Pew Research Center, "Most Americans Favor the Death Penalty despite Concerns about Its Administration."

104. Surette, *Media, Crime, and Criminal Justice: Images, Realities, and Policies*.

105. Buonanno and Vargas, "Inequality, Crime, and the Long Run from Slavery"; Itskovich and Factor, "Economic Inequality and Crime: The Role of Social Resistance."

PART TWO

Roots of Oppression

Unearthing Queer Criminalization

CHAPTER 6

Dismembering the Powermonger

A BlaQueer Feminist Approach to Abolition

TONIQUA C. MIKELL, UNIVERSITY OF MASSACHUSETTS
DARTMOUTH

A powermonger is a person who abuses power in a tyrannical or irresponsible fashion. Of course, the inhumanity of the criminal legal system effectively disqualifies the metaphor of "a person." However, the legal system is a para-lifelike entity. It is not a stagnant, autonomous being independent of sociopolitical influence. Thus, the criminal legal system as a Powermonger is best understood as an entity made up of independent yet interdependent elements (e.g., police, courts, prisons) that function to carry on the activities of society—racist, imperialist, patriarchy—through tyrannical social control. Throughout this piece, I develop an understanding of the Powermonger as a parasitic entity that is humanlike in form and functions with the singular goal of self-preservation. Readers will see the necropolitical criminal legal–established pattern of existence that uses the power of police, courts, and incarceration to dictate who is worthy of life or deserving of death.[1]

THE POWERMONGER: DEATH EMBODIED

This chapter rewrites the body politic into a metaphor to present the criminal legal system as a brute—a violent creature—that exists and functions in the form of an undead human body. I illustrate the criminal legal system as the Powermonger—a parasitic entity whose body is weaponized to intentionally brutalize and kill Black people, particularly Black women, across all gender and sexuality spectrums. A necropolitical entity, the Powermonger is sustained by the control and disposal of those perceived to be furthest away from white, cisgender, able-bodied, heteronormative, patriarchal conformity. The carceral state, through its unilateral control of mortality, is predicated on and sustained by the destruction and desecration of human life and bodies. Thus, I employ the visual of the Powermonger as an insatiable anthropomorphic creature to encourage readers to visualize the criminal legal system as an entity that must be dismembered for the life, safety, and freedom of all people.

Rooting this chapter in Black Feminist Hauntology and necropolitics, I present the Powermonger as a creature that draws its death force from the life, land, and resources of marginalized communities.[2] Building upon Foucault's notion of biopower/biopolitics,[3] Mbembe presents necropolitics/necropower to "account for the various ways weapons [of war, violence, and control, i.e., conquest] are deployed in the interest of maximum destruction of persons [who pose threats to the civilized sovereign] and the creation of *death-worlds*—forms of social existence in which vast populations are subjected to conditions of life conferring upon them the status of the *living dead*."[4] Drawing from Black Feminist Hauntology's transcendent-shape-shifting, I shift the burden of death *from* marginalized communities who are devoured to be *placed back* on to the shoulders of the being that spreads it.[5] Per Saleh-Hanna, "At its core, transcendent-shape-shifting requires an intimate understanding of powerlessness and conquest to garner viewpoints that shape-shift out of ideological conquest (subjugation) and into knowledge of self and power residing beyond colonial propaganda. Transcendent-shape-shifting requires we un-fetishize[6] our relationship to colonized, enslaved and imprisoned bodies, and turn our critical lens upon the bodies of colonizers, slavers, and imprisoners."[7]

By locating, naming, decapitating, and dismembering the Powermonger, BlaQueer Feminist Abolition is transcendent-shape-shifting.[8] Where Mbembe would argue that the Powermonger forces the socially constructed "other" into *death-worlds* and subjects us to an existence as *living dead*,[9] I engage with criminal legal institutions as parts and systems of a necrotic being clinging to life by maintaining homeostasis.[10] I offer a BlaQueer feminist narrative of social institutions that have continued to live as they require death. It is the Powermonger that is the living dead and *we* are the living whom it renders dead.

As external threats to survival become apparent, the Powermonger's individual parts have immune-type responses to restore balance.

Through the deployment of necropower, specifically, the weaponization of state control, the Powermonger finds ways to renew itself through the repair of broken body parts. In truth, this renewal of life and longevity is dependent on stealing life to repair a disrupted status quo. Like the zombie of science fiction and folklore that is driven to consume for survival, so too is the Powermonger. The Powermonger seeks not to fix the harm it has caused or return the strength it has drawn from the shattered souls and bodies of enslaved and colonized peoples. Instead, the Powermonger is replenished and renewed through increasingly violent consumption of oppressed peoples, particularly the consumption of Black, Indigenous, people of Color [POC], and/or queer women and femmes.[11] Liberation of global siblings within state-victimized communities requires dismemberment of the Powermonger.

I begin this discussion with a narrative of the lifetime of the Powermonger's body parts, each representing an institution of the criminal legal system that has survived by evolving the methods of de facto and de jure control of Black, Brown, and Indigenous folks, women, and 2SLG-BTQIA+ peoples.[12] The foundation of this analogy starts with the head of the Powermonger, which represents "Racist-Imperialist-Patriarchy [R.I.P.]," the values that form and support tyrannical social control.[13] The head of the Powermonger is the source of its existence and it is that which must be completely removed for the permanent death of the Powermonger. For without decapitation, the individual parts continue drawing death to sustain life. The torso of the Powermonger is seen by society as jails and prisons—including the arms as extensions of those systems—which have upheld R.I.P. through the weaponization of captivity and surveillance. Within the torso, the courts are built upon the heart of the Powermonger pumping criminalized others through its body, drawing its life from the death of the people. Lastly, the police function as legs mobilizing the Powermonger, making it capable of fight-or-flight when threatened. These parts represent the roles and renewals that have existed over time and continue to sustain the Powermonger. I conclude this chapter by discarding the parts of the Powermonger's body and reiterating that the necrotic creature [the criminal legal system] must be dismembered [abolished]. Most importantly, it must be decapitated [disconnected from R.I.P.], thereby severing necropower [carceral and state-sanctioned violence] from notions of justice and freedom. Only after the Powermonger's dismemberment may the colonized, racialized, and oppressed find peaceful rest in this life or the next.

DECAPITATION: RACIST-IMPERIALIST-PATRIARCHY [R.I.P.]

In this section I discuss why abolition requires a prioritization of R.I.P. decapitation. Decapitation is necessary first to disrupt the rememory of the intergenerational, institutional structural violence that is R.I.P.[14] I engage with Saleh-Hanna's rememory as being "persevered in institutions, branded upon their violently structured bureaucracies and practiced upon by the bodies of the colonized by the bodies of the colonizers."[15] It is the rememory within the head of the Powermonger that motivates the chase for homeostasis. The criminal legal system does not exist without R.I.P. systems of power. The head harbors the structures of R.I.P. and must be decapitated. It is the values rooted in the colonization of Indigenous lands and people, violent exploitation of enslaved African labor, and sexual control of women that controls the Powermonger head, thus dictating the actions of the body parts. For the Powermonger to die, decapitating R.I.P. from normative standards of justice, or even legality, must be the first step of dismemberment. It is here, at the head, that abolition must be initiated. As Saleh-Hanna writes, "The very existence of the criminal justice system is predicated upon protecting and enforcing R.I.P. conditions that fuel the R.I.P. structures of power through which it was born. Because the criminal justice system is wholeheartedly a European colonial invention, it diligently represents white power cultures and interests."[16]

For the Powermonger, its head is where messages that support white supremacist capitalist patriarchy are the instinctual default. The creature's survival is driven by those instincts. Actual or anticipated changes to the environment threaten the Powermonger. Blalock's racial threat theory provides support for this dynamic.[17] When the white power majority perceives that they are being threatened economically, politically, and/or symbolically by the mere presence of Black people, whites weaponize their power and implement racialized methods of social control.[18] The Powermonger's R.I.P. brain interprets the social advancement of nonwhite, nonmale, nonelites as threats to white habitus and signals the body to reestablish homeostasis to guarantee its survival.[19] Those threats, real or perceived, create "all-encompassing negative feelings evoked by perceptions of change to orthodox society," or habitus angst, often leading to violence targeting marginalized groups.[20]

Responses to threat, and in turn habitus angst, manifest as increased social controls, disenfranchisement, and death. The Powermonger has weaponized these mechanisms of necropower since the early formation of the United States. For example, early versions of the Declaration of Independence cited Britain's encouragement of arming enslaved Africans who could and should then integrate with Native Americans.[21] In other words, Britain's shifting views of slavery jeopardized the very cornerstone of colonial white male elitism, thus motivating the war for colonial independence.[22] The genocide of Native Americans during the Indian Removal Act of 1830 was a policy choice in response to threats posed to western expansion of the United States.[23] Poll taxes and literacy tests were white supremacist policy responses to formerly enslaved Black men gaining the right to vote after the Civil War.[24] The criminalization of immigration and xenophobic legislation, historically and presently, has been a response to migrants' threat to the economic prosperity and job security of [white] Americans,[25] and perceptions of external un-American threats to internal American ways of life have been used to justify US imperialism and neocolonialism.[26] These "threats" create a narrative that, as Saleh-Hanna states, "insists that danger resides within the bodies and actions of the colonized when in reality dangerousness is endemic to white supremacy."[27] The Powermonger is a brute that inflicts violence upon racialized others who dare to interfere with white entitlement.[28] The extraction of people and resources from life-preserving land, cultures, and kinship based on misdirected notions of civility and barbarism is the necropower wielded by the United States.

While Black, Indigenous, and POC liberation has been one of the more obvious contributors to habitus angst, women's liberation and 2SLGBT-QIA+ rights are also part of this matrix.[29] R.I.P. institutions prioritize cisgender-heteronormative [cis-het] relationships, with particular emphasis on men's *entitlement* to women's bodies, reproductive capacity, and labor.[30] Tarana Burke's #MeToo movement, originally coined in 2006, directly challenges the patriarchal narrative that women exist to service the predatory natures of rapacious men. Accountability for men's role in the perpetuation of rape culture continues to be warped into expressions of masculinity.[31] That is, patriarchy mandates hegemonic masculinity, especially in the form of sexual aggression from straight men upon women.[32] Therefore, being "MeToo'ed" threatens men's access to being appropriately masculine, as though men are blocked from masculinity if they cannot sexually assault and harass women with impunity.

The rise of rejection killings—men killing women after being rejected during romantic or intimate pursuit[33]—is a direct consequence of patriarchal entitlement. Being blocked from open access to women, which they feel entitled to, breeds habitus angst in cis-het men and leads to deadly violence.[34] This is particularly true for Black [cisgender] women[35] and transgender women of Color.[36] The parallel arcs of the #MeToo movement and violence against uninterested women intersects with a R.I.P. sociopolitical climate that continues to view women's bodies as the property of men.

The repeal of *Roe v. Wade* (1973) and *Planned Parenthood v. Casey* (1992) via the decision of *Dobbs v. Jackson Women's Health Organization* in 2022 cannot be viewed as an isolated act of conservative politicking. It did not happen by accident and did not happen in a vacuum. Women have been increasingly more public about prioritizing our sexuality and pleasure, decisions to remain unmarried and child-free, and openly supportive of consenting sex workers. In fact, the validation of sex work, rise of the pro-hoe era, and fall of slut-shaming have been hallmarks of Fourth Wave Feminism. Therefore, policies aimed at curtailing women's sexual freedoms and autonomy have become the antithesis of modern feminist activism. This should not surprise men and certainly does not surprise women. Homeostasis within the Powermonger's body needs women to be under the control of the carceral state, and by extension, under the control of [white] men.

The body will go in the same direction the head goes. The Powermonger's body will also follow its head. As this chapter will show, the various iterations of policing, incarceration, convictions, and court outcomes, and other colonial expansions of power—legitimized through policy choices made by "democratically" elected representatives—are all examples of how the head of the Powermonger leads the individual parts of the whole back into homeostasis. BlaQueer feminist abolition acknowledges that white supremacist capitalist patriarchy is the ultimate influencer for the way criminal legal institutions are weaponized for the preservation of whiteness and patriarchal dominance. Therefore, in the first step of dismemberment, the head must be removed and discarded away from the other pieces of the body. The separation of white supremacy's influence from justice must be immediate and absolute, "for without the death of these pillars, colonialism will thrive in a variety of manifestations and increasingly horrific apparitions."[37]

DISMEMBERMENT: HOMEOSTASIS KILLS US

In this section, I engage with Black Feminist Hauntology's structural shape-shifting to illustrate the Powermonger's quest for homeostasis.[38]

Through this framework, I map how institutions of oppression and control do not get reformed but simply *re*-formed under evolving standards of [alleged] social and public decency. For "the criminal justice system provides the language and tools whereby the unspeakability of slavery can be uttered."[39] And, as required by R.I.P. ideologies, these modernized institutions remain committed to the structure and systems of power that feed on the bodies of those whom society deems not only worthy of death but explicitly *un*worthy of life.

The Torso: Confinement and Surveillance

While it is the function of the brain that sends signals throughout the body on how to respond to stimuli, including threats, most of our vital organs are in the torso. It is that area of the human body that does most of the work to keep the body alive. The same is true of the Powermonger's body. The structure of the spine, ribs, and internal organs in the torso is what holds the body upright. Thus, it is the very existence of prisons that supports the carceral state. The capacity to punish is necropower; specifically, incarceration is a weapon of the power-majority used to coerce the powerless into conformity through the exclusive control of state-sanctioned violence and captivity. Warehousing, removing, destroying, and ultimately discarding the life of those deemed undesirable is the most proximate goal of maintaining the status quo. For the Powermonger, the physical proximity of the torso to the head is a literal depiction of the metaphor, whereby captivity is directly connected to the source of racist-imperialist patriarchy.

Echoing Stanley and Smith, "Prison abolition must be one of the centers of trans and queer liberation struggles."[40] (Therefore, conversations around abolition as liberation for women and femmes of the Global Majority and BlaQueer peoples must confront the realities of the Eurocentric, hypermasculine, anti-Black, heteronormative systems of control that inform the structures of punishment, specifically, the prison.[41] At its most basic, R.I.P. depends on (re)enforcement of conventional gender roles and sex scripts.[42] The prison seeks to accomplish this by making captivity highly gendered and sexualized. The significance of gendered and sexualized values of punishment is that, despite every racial demographic being overrepresented in prisons except for whites,[43] it is explicitly white masculinity (and femininity) that is setting the standard by which every other gender and sexuality is measured.[44] This is the goal of the Powermonger. Criminalizing or otherwise perpetuating a narrative that paints Black, Indigenous, and 2SLGBTQIA+ people as violent or inferior validates the perceived threats to white supremacist capitalist patriarchy that the Powermonger neutralizes through captivity, sexual violence, and death. BlaQueer feminist abolition of the Powermonger recognizes that this perpetual cycle of captivity and death as punishment for Blackness, homosexuality, or simply challenging white male elitism is intricately rooted at the plantation.[45] Through this lens, chattel slavery shape-shifts across time to take the form of penitentiaries to warehouse Black Americans, central city stakes upon which to burn lesbians, witches and heretics, and ICE[46] detention centers to cage immigrants.

The arms, as they reach out from the torso of the body, serve as representative extensions of the carceral state. Probation, parole, and other versions of community supervision are often touted as alternatives to prison because they allow folks to stay in the community, thus preserving prosocial community relationships.[47] However, equally important are the impacts of chronic and constant surveillance.[48] Nationwide, 45 percent of admissions into state prisons are for probation/parole or technical violations.[49] That is, their reentrapment in the legal system is related to violations of conditional freedom, not the commission of new crime. In this regard, recidivism is attributed not to overt repeating of criminal activity, but instead to overpolicing and hypersurveillance.

Even seemingly neutral or supposedly positive social institutions serve the interests of a white supremacist capitalist patriarchal Powermonger. Government welfare programs[50] and financial systems,[51] health care,[52] education,[53] and family services[54] have all been weaponized to control and eliminate the lives of those who seek out these resources for support. When we understand the salience and reach of these punishing systems, we can visualize the structural shape-shift of the Powermonger's torso, whereby jails and prisons are used to house the poor, state-run insane asylums are used to store *lunatics* and dangerous madmen, and conversion camps become repositories for LGBT youth, with devastating impacts on their mental health.[55] These institutions of state necropower aid in and expedite the death of those sentenced to encounter them.

The Heart: Courts

The public views criminal courts as the neutral part of the legal system. There's a general *mis*understanding that the prosecutor and defendant are opposing teams, and the judge and jury are the referees who ultimately determine the winner. This is a dangerous yet widely held farce. BlaQueer feminist abolition vehemently proclaims from the victimized shoulders of our ancestors that courts are not spaces of neutrality. Without question, it is the power to accuse, decide guilt, and label behavior as "crime" and people as "criminals" that serves as a weapon of totalitarian [tyrannical] control.[56] Therefore, criminal courts have a vested interest in the preservation of R.I.P. As the court systems are assumed finders of fact and truth, it is the judiciary's rendering of guilt that ultimately reinforces the necropower of the state. Court outcomes validate police actions, initiate prison violence, assign suffering, and authorize death. The heart of the Powermonger is where the process of trial and conviction happens. It is the organ where people are quite literally filtered and pumped into the various carceral systems of captivity, surveillance, and state-sanctioned violence.[57]

Make no mistake, the criminal court system is but one chamber of the Powermonger's heart. The necropower of the courts is not limited to criminal-legal sentencing contexts. The Supreme Court of the United States—the highest court in the land and final authority on determinations of legality—is not neutral. SCOTUS judges are appointed by presidents who seek to have their own political ideologies prioritized from the bench, a position that extends beyond the term of the presidency and through the lifetime of the judge. The same is true at most state levels of government. The people on the bench do not get there through neutrality. The virtual lifetime appointment of judges and minimal oversight of both judges and attorneys make the courts a fertile ground in which to grow unchallenged, unchecked white supremacy. The court actors who supposedly represent the interests of the people are accountable only to the Powermonger, and the Powermonger expects the delivery of souls and requires consumption of bodies.

The Legs: Police

The legs ensure that the Powermonger has the means to move to safety when threatened. When the white supremacist brain sends signals that homeostasis has been disrupted, a fight-or-flight response is triggered. When animals, including humans, are threatened, the fight-or-flight response is implemented to tell the body what is needed for self-preservation. Does survival require us to physically overcome the threat (fight) or is our best option to run away (flight)? The legs of the Powermonger carry out the fight-or-flight. The police are how the Powermonger moves to safety, either through fighting the threat or fleeing from it.

To be clear, the Powermonger does not possess the capacity to access the freeze component often seen within discussions of fight-or-flight responses. A tyrannical brute would never acquiesce in defeat to perceived threats. BlaQueer feminist abolition recognizes that police are the boots on the ground doing the work of the Powermonger's survival.[58]

The legs of the Powermonger are tasked to either physically overtake or kill the threat or move the creature to safety. Situating the police away from *public safety* and toward *law and order* is a fight response. When the Powermonger is in *fight* mode, the results are deadly: citizens in need of government assistance or mental health care are murdered (e.g., Margaret LaVerne Mitchell in 1999; Shereese Francis in 2012; Brianna Grier in 2014); those who dare to travel freely are killed (e.g., Sandra Bland in 2015; Mya Hall in 2015); and peaceful protests for the right to exist encounter the full weight of police *necro*power (e.g., civil rights demonstrations in the 1960s; twenty-first-century Black Lives Matter movements; 2024 student activism for Palestinian Liberation). The Powermonger in *fight* mode seeks only to neutralize and eliminate threats through swift deadly violence, with devastating, disproportionate impacts on Black women.[59]

In *flight* mode, understand that we do not see police fleeing away from a disrupted status quo, but instead moving toward new methods of survival. For example, under chattel slavery, the legs of the Powermonger were slave catchers. Following emancipation, when chattel slavery was no longer the method by which homeostasis was maintained, lynch mobs were extralegal yet state-supported responses to violations of Black Codes and Jim Crow legislation, in other words, to restore order.[60] Whether it was on the plantation or as the strange fruit of the poplar tree,[61] the message of Black folks as fit only for bondage was maintained through the structural shape-shifting of the Powermonger's legs.[62] To be clear, even though lynch mobs were technically acts of illegality, they were a highly visible transition stage from slave patrols in the antebellum South through to the days of modern policing.[63] Those who evaded the hangman almost certainly found themselves returned to the plantation under the loophole of the Thirteenth Amendment. The only difference now is that the overseers have been renamed prison guards.[64]

By viewing police through a BlaQueer feminist lens, we see that the twenty-first-century Powermonger's boots on the ground have shapeshifted into soldiers of the state. Through this narrative, the increased militarization of local police agencies positions officers and citizens as combatants of war. BlaQueer feminist abolition sees R.I.P. values in policing as intranational warfare, bringing the imperialist battlefield to the front door of expendable citizens.

DISCARD: VANQUISHING THE POWERMONGER

The violent Powermonger is a brutish creature made up of independent yet interdependent elements and utilizes tyrannical social control to carry out social values of imperialism, white supremacy, capitalism, heterocentrism, and patriarchy. Imperialism is about global control by a singular superpower. White supremacy upholds extermination of the Global Majority racialized as Black, Brown, or "of Color." Capitalism prioritizes amassing exorbitant amounts of money and concentrating it within the hands of a powerful few. Patriarchy is cisgender-heterosexual male dominance over women, the gender-variant, or queer peoples. While the Powermonger's size and strength are context specific, it would not be unreasonable to view the Powermonger of the United States as merely an Americanized warrior in a larger military of imperialist global superpowers advancing the Global North's exploitation of the Global South. Future engagement with BlaQueer feminist abolition should seek to name international Powermongers and call for their decapitation and dismemberment as well.

In understanding the Powermonger, societies worldwide must disengage with ideas that the criminal legal system is the penultimate source of justice by confronting the reality that it draws its death force from misogyny, racism, and heterocentrism. We must separate and destroy the evidence of structures that have allowed this system to pull itself back together throughout history under the guise of reform. In truth, institutions of punishment and control have simply undergone a process of structural shape-shifting. Dismembering the Powermonger's body is necessary because such a creature cannot coexist alongside liberty and justice for all. History has proven this and continues to repeat itself.

To end the cycle of R.I.P. abuse, the message of this chapter is the dispossession of power from the Powermonger.[65] I present a BlaQueer feminist approach to abolition—over reform—and the complete dismemberment of the criminal legal body, whereby alleged systems of accountability, public safety, and justice are decapitated from R.I.P. values and ideologies. The dead Powermonger creates fertile ground from which wild seed justice can take root.[66] From the abolished flesh of the Powermonger, I see the rising mother goddess Anyanwu,[67] who "is relational and holds within herself all that is needed for a good life and well-being."[68] BlaQueer feminist abolition envisions Anyanwu with her legs of change in constant motion to balance the needs of humanity, the land, and the nonhuman animals with whom we share the planet. Her torso is a place of embrace, where community prevails in firm defiance of colonial standards of isolation and detention. And, most importantly, Anyanwu's head holds ancestral knowledge of Wild Seed Justice that knows justice as "a practice that extends access to our truest selves and collective freedoms."[69] As a society, we are in a colonial coma, and until we wake up from it, R.I.P. institutions of violence and control will flourish.[70] Global *elites* will continue to prosper, and the Global *Majority* will continue to suffer. Once the Powermonger has been vanquished, Black women and femmes will find respite in the embrace of Anyanwu. We then open ourselves to the possibilities of a world that does not depend on necropolitical domination but instead finds promise in the opportunities for freedom to grow.

NOTES

1. Mbembe, "Necropolitics."
2. Mbembe, "Necropolitics"; Saleh-Hanna, "Feminist Hauntology: Rememory the Ghosts of Abolition?"
3. Foucault, *Society Must Be Defended: Lectures at the Collège de France, 1975–1976.*
4. Mbembe, "Necropolitics," 176.
5. See also Césaire, *Discourse on Colonialism.*
6. Farley, "The Black Body as Fetish Object."
7. Saleh-Hanna, "Feminist Hauntology: Rememory the Ghosts of Abolition?," 19.
8. Saleh-Hanna, 19.
9. Mbembe, "Necropolitics."
10. Biologically, homeostasis is a "state of balance among all the body systems needed for the body to survive and function correctly" (National Cancer Institute, "Homeostasis").
11. I do not use the term *BIPOC* [Black, Indigenous, people of Color] because Black and Indigenous peoples have experiences [in the United States] that cannot be compared to those of other racialized groups [i.e., people of Color]. As such, I hold space for the specific harm inflicted upon descendants of enslaved Africans who are racialized as Black, as well as the survivors of the genocides committed upon Indigenous peoples.
12. Two-spirit, lesbian, gay, bisexual, transgender, queer/questioning, intersex, asexual, and other gender, and sexual spectrum identities.
13. Saleh-Hanna, "An Abolitionist Theory on Crime: Ending the Abusive Relationship with Racist-Imperialist-Patriarchy [R.I.P.]."
14. Saleh-Hanna.

15. Saleh-Hanna, "Feminist Hauntology: Rememory the Ghosts of Abolition?," 9.

16. Saleh-Hanna, "An Abolitionist Theory on Crime: Ending the Abusive Relationship with Racist-Imperialist-Patriarchy [R.I.P.]," 427.

17. Blalock, *Toward a Theory of Minority-Group Relations*.

18. See also Blumer, "Race Prejudice as a Sense of Group Position"; Bobo, "Prejudice as Group Position: Microfoundations of a Sociological Approach to Racism and Race Relations."

19. Bonilla-Silva, Goar, and Embrick, "When Whites Flock Together: The Social Psychology of White Habitus."

20. Isom, *Gratuitous Angst in White America: A Theory of Whiteness and Crime*.

21. Ortiz, *An African American and Latinx History of the United States*.

22. Ortiz.

23. Dunbar-Ortiz, *Not a Nation of Immigrants: Settler Colonialism, White Supremacy, and a History of Erasure and Exclusion*; Dunbar-Ortiz, *An Indigenous Peoples' History of the United States*.

24. African American Pamphlet Collection, *To the Colored Men of Voting Age in the Southern States*.

25. Golash-Boza, *Deported: Immigrant Policing, Disposable Labor, and Global Capitalism*; Hernández, *Migrating to Prison: America's Obsession with Locking Up Immigrants*.

26. Feagin and Ducey, *Racist America: Roots, Current Realities, and Future Reparations*; Jouet, *Exceptional America: What Divides Americans from the World and from Each Other*; Treitler, *The Ethnic Project: Transforming Racial Fiction into Ethnic Factions*.

27. Saleh-Hanna, "Feminist Hauntology: Rememory the Ghosts of Abolition?," 24.

28. Isom, *Gratuitous Angst in White America: A Theory of Whiteness and Crime*.

29. Collins, *Black Feminist Thought: Knowledge, Consciousness, and the Politics of Empowerment*.

30. Isom, *Gratuitous Angst in White America: A Theory of Whiteness and Crime*.

31. Brownmiller, *Against Our Will: Men, Women and Rape*.

32. Connell and Messerschmidt, "Hegemonic Masculinity: Rethinking the Concept"; Messerschmidt, *Crime as Structured Action: Gender, Race, Class, and Crime in the Making*.

33. Tylka, "Getting to Tarasoff: A Gender-Based History of Tort Law Doctrine."

34. Isom, *Gratuitous Angst in White America: A Theory of Whiteness and Crime*.

35. Violence Policy Center, "When Men Murder Women: An Analysis of 2020 Homicide Data."

36. Human Rights Campaign, "Tools for Equality and Inclusion."

37. Saleh-Hanna, "Feminist Hauntology: Rememory the Ghosts of Abolition?," 27.

38. Salch-Hanna, 27.

39. Saleh-Hanna, 5.

40. Stanley and Smith, *Captive Genders: Trans Embodiment and the Prison Industrial Complex*, 12.

41. Davis, *Are Prisons Obsolete?*

42. Davis et al., *Abolition. Feminism. Now.*

43. Isom, *Gratuitous Angst in White America: A Theory of Whiteness and Crime.*

44. Messerschmidt, "The Salience of Hegemonic Masculinity."

45. Hard labor had long been a viable sentence for punishment for free [white] people but would not be any different than the conditions of slavery. At the time of the founding, Thomas Jefferson suggested banishing enslaved peoples out of the colonies as punishment (Davis, *Are Prisons Obsolete?*). During this time, cut off from family and resources, this would almost certainly be a death sentence.

46. ICE is the acronym for U.S. Immigration and Customs Enforcement.

47. Latessa and Lovins, *Corrections in the Community.*

48. Butts and Schiraldi, *Recidivism Reconsidered: Preserving the Community Justice Mission of Community Corrections.*

49. Council of State Governments Justice Center, "Confined and Costly: How Supervision Violations Are Filling Prisons and Burdening Budgets."

50. Desmond, *Poverty, by America.*

51. Baradaran, *Color of Money: Black Banks and the Racial Wealth Gap*; Robles, Leondar-Wright, and Brewer, *The Color of Wealth: The Story behind the US Racial Wealth Divide.*

52. Roberts, *Killing the Black Body: Race, Reproduction, and the Meaning of Liberty.*

53. Morris, *Pushout: The Criminalization of Black Girls in Schools.*

54. Roberts, *Torn Apart: How the Child Welfare System Destroys Black Families—and How Abolition Can Build a Safer World.*

55. Green et al., "Self-Reported Conversion Efforts and Suicidality among US LGBTQ Youths and Young Adults, 2018"; Human Rights Campaign, "Tools for Equality and Inclusion."

56. Krafft, "Marxist Criminology Abolishes Lombroso, Marxist Criminology Abolishes Itself."

57. Browne-Marshall, *She Took Justice: The Black Woman, Law, and Power—1619 to 1969.*

58. My use of the term *police* is not limited to local and state agencies. I am also including federal agencies tasked with so-called law enforcement, that is, the Federal Bureau of Investigation, U.S. Customs and Border Patrol, the Drug Enforcement Agency, the Central Intelligence Agency, and so on.

59. Crenshaw and Ritchie, *Say Her Name: Resisting Police Brutality against Black Women*; Ritchie, *Invisible No More: Police Violence against Black Women and Women of Color*; Weissinger, Mack, and Watson, *Violence against Black Bodies: An Intersectional Analysis of How Black Lives Continue to Matter.*

60. Hadden, *Slave Patrols: Law and Violence in Virginia and the Carolinas.*

61. See "Strange Fruit" written by Abel Meeropol (1937) and performed by Billie Holiday (1939) at https://www.youtube.com/watch?v=ky7tzqQZAGE.

62. Saleh-Hanna, "An Abolitionist Theory on Crime: Ending the Abusive Relationship with Racist-Imperialist-Patriarchy [R.I.P.]."

63. Anderson, *White Rage: The Unspoken Truth of Our Racial Divide*; Hadden, *Slave Patrols: Law and Violence in Virginia and the Carolinas.*

64. Saleh-Hanna, "Feminist Hauntology: Rememory the Ghosts of Abolition?"

65. Saleh-Hanna, "An Abolitionist Theory on Crime: Ending the Abusive Relationship with Racist-Imperialist-Patriarchy [R.I.P.]."

66. Saleh-Hanna, "A Call for Wild Seed Justice."

67. Anyanwu is the primary protagonist in *Wild Seed* (1980) by Octavia E. Butler.

68. Saleh-Hanna, "A Call for Wild Seed Justice," 20.

69. Saleh-Hanna, 24.

70. Absolon, *Kaandossiwin: How We Come to Know: Indigenous Re-Search Methodologies.*

CHAPTER 7

"At Any Given Point in Your Life, You Can Be Wrong about Everything"

Queer and Trans Perspectives, Community Care, and the Abolitionist Imagination

MAX OSBORN, VILLANOVA UNIVERSITY

STATE VIOLENCE, QUEER LIBERATION, AND COMMUNITY CARE

Queer communities and resistance to state violence have gone hand in hand for as long as carceral institutions have targeted and surveilled us—which is to say, as long as such institutions have existed. In 1970, the advocacy collective Street Transvestite Action Revolutionaries (STAR), newly founded by Sylvia Rivera and Marsha P. Johnson, began providing housing assistance and material support to queer and trans youth and sex workers.[1] The same year, STAR issued a manifesto outlining its goals for liberation, among them "the immediate end of all police harassment and arrest of transvestites and gay street people, and the release of transvestites and gay street people from all prisons and all other political prisoners."[2] Two decades later, during the peak of the US AIDS crisis, marchers in New York City's pride parade distributed copies of an anonymous pamphlet titled "Queers Read This," positioning queer resistance as part of a broader project of liberation. "We must fight for ourselves (no one else is going to do it)," the piece reads, "and if in that process we bring greater freedom to the world at large then great."[3]

Queer and trans communities have long understood that the state and its institutions—including police and prisons—were not created to serve us, nor do they protect us. Rather, these institutions reinscribe social norms that create gendered and racialized hierarchies of power, producing "security for some populations and vulnerability for others."[4] Or, as French queer theorist Guy Hocquenghem put it, "We know that society is afraid of everything that comes from the deepest parts of ourselves, because it needs to classify in order to rule. Identify in order to oppress."[5] Queerness, with its fluidity and flexibility, poses a direct threat to those systems of classification and to the rigidity of formal gender roles. Those who occupy visibly ambiguous positions vis-à-vis gender and sexuality—those who are unclassifiable and unidentifiable, whose ambiguity comes from "the deepest parts of ourselves"— therefore become targets for institutional surveillance, enforcement, and harm. Rather than being resigned to a perpetual position of vulnerability and exclusion, queer liberation activists have urged us to push back against it. "Our difference, our otherness, our uniqueness can either paralyze us or politicize us," states the "Queers Read This" manifesto.[6] "Hopefully, the majority of us will not let it kill us."

Within the context of a newly energized movement for racial, gender, and economic justice, queer and trans scholars and activists have continued to integrate abolitionist principles into theory and practice. In the introduction to a 2022 special issue of *GLQ*, Marquis Bey and Jesse Goldberg wrote that their goal was to "push analyses of queer liberation and abolition past the observations that prisons disproportionately or especially harm queer people toward seriously, rigorously imagining and working toward liberatory futures without prisons, police, or the tyranny of colonial gender systems."[7] They positioned queerness as "not merely a non-het, non-cis 'identity' but a political posture subversive of normativity, hegemony, and power."[8] In this framing, rather than simply naming and repairing harms done to vulnerable people, embracing queerness *necessarily* means striving to eliminate the oppressive hierarchies of racial capitalism and carcerality altogether.

As abolitionists emphasize, abolitionism not only entails dismantling harmful systems, but replacing them with healthier, sustainable alternatives—another practice long embraced by queer communities, as well as Black and Indigenous communities, sex workers, and other communities who have been harmed, excluded, and neglected by the state and its institutions.[9] Hil Malatino writes that "queer and trans care webs" often arise in direct response to institutional abandonment: "It would be foolish to deny that some of what binds us to one another is directly tied to the affective and practical disinvestment of the people and institutions we've needed—or been forced—to rely upon for survival. We have learned to care for one another in the aftermath of these refusals."[10] Queer community care takes many forms, from STAR's protection of street youth to the coalition-building and medical advocacy undertaken during the AIDS crisis, to grassroots support groups, to crowdfunding campaigns for gender-affirming surgeries. Research on peer support within queer and trans communities suggests that in addition to providing material needs, these networks serve as important buffers against identity-related stressors, such as interpersonal stigma, gender-based violence, and discrimination when seeking medical care.[11]

The findings presented in this chapter are drawn from a larger interview project on LGBTQIA+ people's interactions with police and access to formal and informal resources. Although I did not initially set out to examine prison and police abolitionism, and did not prepare questions focused on those topics, I soon found that they came up organically as people recounted experiences with police and were subjects many interviewees had thought deeply about. This brought me to consider the following questions:

1. How do queer and trans people begin engaging with police and/or prison abolition?
2. What connections do queer and trans people draw between LGBTQIA+ identity and abolitionism?

In 2020, I conducted forty-two interviews with LGBTQIA+ adults in New York City. Given the study's focus on experiences with policing, interviewees were required to have interacted with law enforcement in some capacity, though the extent and type of this contact varied across the sample. I advertised the study by posting recruitment messages in online spaces catering to LGBTQIA+ communities, including some that were specific to the NYC area. Some interviewees also referred friends and acquaintances for participation. Since many queer and trans people exhibit justifiable skepticism about participating in research conducted by people outside these communities, I openly stated my own positionality as a queer nonbinary trans person during the recruitment process.[12]

Interviews took place remotely, most via videoconferencing, although a few people spoke by phone due to technological issues or personal preference. Interviews ranged from 27 to 112 minutes and included questions about LGBTQIA+ identity, visibility, and presentation; personal safety and risk across contexts; police encounters; help seeking;

and access to formal and informal support. Interviewees received fifty dollars as compensation. After transcribing the interviews, I used a modified grounded theory approach for analysis, engaging in close readings of text, identifying meaningful segments, and generating descriptive codes.[13] As a feminist qualitative researcher, I rely on *standpoint theory*, the understanding that knowledge is generated from personal experience, and therefore one's social position inevitably shapes one's interpretations of the world.[14] Researchers drawing on this theory often assume that people from marginalized groups, who have been established as outsiders or "others," can articulate particularly valuable viewpoints on power and oppression due to their own positionalities.[15] In other words, queer and transgender people, historically subjected to increased surveillance and enforcement by police and the prison industrial complex, should offer distinct, useful perspectives on these institutions.

The forty-two LGBTQIA+ participants ranged in age from twenty-one to fifty-six years (mean = 30.6). Rather than presenting preset demographic response options, I asked participants to describe their gender, race/ethnicity, sexual orientation, and current occupation in their own words. This approach allows for increased autonomy and the collection of data on specific identities that the researcher may not have anticipated.[16] Note that when a particular person is described below, their own self-selected identity labels for gender, race, and sexual orientation are used. Participants were also asked whether they considered themselves to fall within the category of transgender and/or nonbinary.

Participants described their genders in twenty-five unique ways. In addition to five (11.9%) cisgender men and six (14.3%) cisgender women, thirty-one (73.8%) people self-identified as trans and/or nonbinary. Grouped into broader categories, nine people (21.4%) were trans men and/or transmasculine, seven (16.7%) were trans women and/or transfeminine, eleven (26.2%) indicated a nonbinary identity not framed in terms of masculinity or femininity, and four (9.5%) described genders not covered by any of the above categories. When describing race/ethnicity, participants used twenty-four unique terms; grouped more broadly, nineteen (45.2%) were white, ten (23.8%) were mixed-race/multiracial, five (11.9%) were Black, five (11.9%) were Asian, and three (7.1%) were Latinx and/or Hispanic. Participants used nineteen distinct descriptors for sexual orientation, the most common being pansexual (seven, or 16.7%), gay (seven, or 16.7%), and queer (six, or 14.3%). Occupations ranged widely in terms of field and level of professional training (e.g., retail worker, graduate student, psychotherapist, tech company employee). Around a quarter of participants (eleven, or 26.2%) were without formal employment; some engaged in volunteer work, community organizing, and/or underground economies such as sex work.

FINDINGS

Not all the queer and trans people I spoke with self-identified as abolitionists. However, those who either explicitly described themselves that way or who expressed abolitionist sentiments, such as a refusal to engage with police, shared how they came to feel alienated from police and the carceral system as potential sources of help, their engagement in community care networks as a preferred alternative, and how their queer and trans identities impacted the development of their abolitionist values.

Dissatisfaction with Police Response

Overwhelmingly, whether abolitionist-identified or not, interviewees expressed dissatisfaction with police officers' handling of crises and requests for help. Attitudes toward police ranged from strongly negative to ambivalent, with very few exceptions. Among the most widespread criticisms were (1) ineffective response, (2) secondary victimization, and (3) disproportionate response. Taken together, negative experiences with police and the carceral system appeared to dissuade interviewees from further engagement with these systems.

Ineffective response encompassed officers' inability to respond in an appropriate and timely fashion to requests for support. This might include lengthy response times following 911 calls or a failure to show up altogether. For example, Olivia, a twenty-two-year-old white bisexual cisgender woman, called police after an altercation with a neighbor who pounded on her door and screamed threats at her. After waiting an hour and a half, she called again, only to be told by the dispatcher, "Oh well, they'll get there when they get there." Police also refused to take complaints seriously, dismissing civilians' concerns as irrelevant or failing to take requested action. Victims of violence reported that police actively discouraged them from seeking further help. In Olivia's case, when officers finally arrived, they told her there was nothing else to be done since her neighbor hadn't physically harmed her. Other interviewees described police refusing to intervene or offer protection in situations of physical assault, stalking, and intimate partner violence.

Interviewees also encountered bureaucratic obstacles when dealing with police. When Ben, a twenty-nine-year-old white pansexual trans man, was assaulted while biking across the Manhattan Bridge, which connects Manhattan to Brooklyn, police declined to investigate because they could not determine the borough in which the assault had taken place and therefore could not decide which precinct to assign the case to. In other instances, police failed to file paperwork or follow up about reported incidents, leading interviewees to conclude that seeking help from law enforcement was a waste of time. Notably, those who fell into this camp included victims of serious violent crimes as well as more minor incidents.

Another major concern was *secondary victimization*, meaning instances in which police inflicted additional harm on survivors attempting to seek help, exacerbating the initial trauma.[17] Multiple interviewees called 911 to report a dangerous situation, only to end up being penalized themselves when police arrived; these responses included being physically threatened or restrained, interrogated as suspects rather than victims, and taken into custody. These experiences compounded the existing harm interviewees had suffered, while also driving home their lack of agency. A common refrain was that civilians asking for help were treated as nuisances or potential criminals, rather than legitimate victims.[18] Those treated this way became disillusioned with police as a source of help, like Pax, a twenty-five-year-old white nonbinary person who called for assistance dealing with an abusive, intoxicated family member. When the officers arrived, they found Pax in the midst of a panic attack, while their family member remained calm. Since Pax was the person who appeared agitated, the officers decided to transport them to the hospital to be placed under an involuntary psychiatric hold, threatening to forcibly restrain and handcuff them if they refused to cooperate. "From that moment on," they said, "not that I ever had faith in the police, but [. . .] that solidified my hatred in the police. Because I had never felt more betrayed in my life."

Lastly, interviewees described police engaging in *disproportionate responses* to so-called "quality-of-life" offenses, such as loitering, open container violations, hopping the subway turnstile, and remaining in a public park after it had closed for the evening. "All I see them do, practically, is like hassle homeless people and respond to stupid shit," commented Ruth, a twenty-nine-year-old white queer trans woman. Rooted in "broken windows" and order maintenance approaches to public safety, aggressive crackdowns on minor disturbances in communal spaces often culminated in police using or threatening arrest and/or physical force against civilians.[19] Nicole, a thirty-year-old white gender-variant dyke, had lived in neighborhoods predominantly populated by people of color and where there was "a massive police presence *all* the time." They explained, "I saw multiple people getting incorrectly, unlawfully arrested, you know, when you're standing outside and you're watching them and you're filming them and there's just fucking nothing you can do." After watching these situations unfold repeatedly, Nicole concluded that calling the police was neither a safe nor a helpful thing to do, and could often make a bad situation worse.

Police Violence and Discrimination

Interviewees repeatedly cited the recent *protest movement* against police violence, as well as further violence committed by police at those demonstrations, as having amplified their distrust in law enforcement. Some had directly witnessed or been subjected to harm in this context. "Most people I know are very targeted and heavily surveilled by the police," explained Kavitha, a twenty-one-year-old Indian-American nonbinary/genderqueer person who regularly participated in protests. "We've all been brutalized by them multiple times. I've had friends who have broken limbs and bashed faces and like, ended careers. All sorts of shit." Similarly, Ari, a twenty-eight-year-old white, Jewish, queer nonbinary person, noted that the 2020 uprising marked "the closest proximity I've had to really violent police behavior." Among other incidents, Ari's friends had nearly been injured after police deliberately drove a vehicle into a crowd of protesters. This action, which risked seriously harming or killing unarmed civilians, illustrated how police used violence not in self-defense, but as a form of control and retaliation. As a white person, Ari had grown up insulated from the immediate impact of these harms, but developed a deeper understanding of police violence via community ties with people of color: "I think also, being very close to my roommate who is Black, and hearing about their experiences with police, has um . . . I wouldn't say it's like shifted. My opinions on police were already there. But it's definitely like hammered stuff in, or been stuff that . . . like, even knowing how bad it all is, was still shocking to me."

Lauren, a twenty-six-year-old white bisexual nonbinary person, had also reevaluated their understanding of police after witnessing police violence at protests. "I think in the past they've been more of a neutral fact of life than anything," they said. "You just kind of acknowledge they're there and don't think much about it. And that is something that I never had to think about, because I've always been privileged." As they attended more protests and became more involved in anti-carceral organizing spaces, Lauren had more cause to consider how their own past levels of risk and fear around police differed from those of their friends and colleagues of color.

In addition to direct experiences, interviewees formed opinions about police via what they learned from the media. Kymir, a twenty-five-year-old Black pansexual transmasculine person, saw a video from a protest in Buffalo, New York, in which two officers pushed an elderly man to the ground, fracturing his skull.[20] "It kind of like got me to a place, I'm like, your oath is to protect and serve," Kymir explained. "I'm sorry, I'm like—I don't have any words. It was just like, *that* one incident just made me realize that they're not here to protect people like me, or just like regular day-to-day people." Pax, the nonbinary person whom police had hospitalized after they called for help, recalled seeing videos of officers "plowing into people with trucks," pepper-spraying journalists, and throwing a protester to the ground so forcefully that she hit her head and had a seizure. "It's gotten to the point where I see no difference between the NYPD and the KKK," Pax said, adding that they considered the police to be a "modern lynch mob." Like Kymir, Pax sarcastically invoked the NYPD's motto of "protect and serve": "I don't feel like the cops are there to protect and serve people. They are gonna protect and serve people wearing *red fucking hats*. And if *that* doesn't tell you the problem with the New York Police Department, then I don't know what does. Because they are political. They are political in and of themselves. Their very purpose is to—their very core purpose is to criminalize Black and brown people." Multiple people asserted that the core function of police was not to protect "people," but rather specific groups of people—namely, wealthy white people with right-wing politics.

By contrast, interviewees emphasized that police disproportionately directed violence toward people of color and people in poor neighborhoods. Interviewees who were themselves people of color had learned at a young age, through their own experiences and those of their family members, that police could not be relied upon to help their communities. Lin, a twenty-six-year-old Vietnamese nonbinary person whose parents were refugees, was taught growing up that police were "never an option" and should not be called upon even in times of crisis. Mateo, a twenty-three-year-old Hispanic man of trans experience, recalled seeing his father get pulled over while driving in an obvious instance of racial profiling, which "made [him] question" the function of policing, even as a young child. "They exist to criminalize poor people," stated Ruth, a twenty-nine-year-old white queer transgender woman. "And they exist to enforce class barriers. . . . There's nothing that a poor person could do to get their sympathy. But at the same time, there's nothing that a rich person could do to lose it." These concerns are similar to those articulated by abolitionist scholars like Dean Spade, who argue that institutions like the criminal legal system, though appearing ostensibly neutral, reinforce delineations between social ingroups and outgroups, "who deserves protection and who is a threat."[21] Those who fall outside the norm, whether by virtue of race, class, gender, sexuality, or other marginalized identities, are cast as dangerous or disposable and are therefore excluded from the "life chances" that such institutions make possible for more privileged members of society.

Targeted violence on the basis of gender or sexuality surfaced as a pervasive concern. For example, Cookie, a fifty-year-old Puerto Rican and Black trans woman, referred to an incident featured in the local news, in which plainclothes officers grabbed an eighteen-year-old trans woman off the street at a protest, dragged her into an unmarked van, and drove away, an act criticized by a city council member as being "more like provocation than public safety."[22] Both the unpredictability of police actions and the fact that the protester was trans appeared particularly salient to Cookie, who now feared attending protests because of incidents like that. Some interviewees related direct experiences of anti-queer and anti-trans police violence, including officers using queerphobic and transphobic slurs, profiling queer and trans people—particularly trans women of color—for sex work and "quality-of-life" infractions, repeatedly strip-searching trans women as a form of sexual punishment, and beating queer and trans protesters, in some cases severely enough to cause long-term injuries.

These repeated experiences of police violence, both direct and vicarious, negatively impacted interviewees' trust in policing as an institution. As one person put it,

> I don't want anyone calling the police on me or my friends ever again. . . . After the last few months, it's—it's more clear than ever. More than ever. Like just how much law enforcement wants us dead and gone. . . . Anything mildly supporting [policing] now is now just abhorrent to me. So I, I can't anymore. . . . This is a core belief of mine now. It was before, but now even more than ever. . . . A police officer is not going to *help* me. You know? They won't. They don't—pretend like they are, but they won't. And so um, none

of us in this house are doing any of that anymore. (Christina, twenty-six, female, Mexican/Puerto Rican/Italian, queer/lesbian)

Besides her own exposure to police violence at protests, Christina had watched a roommate become traumatized by the police's aggressive, unsolicited response to a call for mental health assistance. After this incident, she and her housemates, all of whom were also queer, made alternate plans for future crisis situations, including lining up multiple potential options for car rides to the hospital so that they could avoid calling an ambulance in the future. "Because of just my experience legal observing, I just overall really don't trust the police that much," explained Tyler, a twenty-four-year-old white queer transmasculine person who attended protests to witness and record instances of misconduct. "I've seen them arrest my friends who are legal observers and shouldn't be arrested. . . . So because of that, and also my work with my nonprofit, which does not call the police on people, I am—unless absolutely necessary, I will not call the police."

Community Care and Mutual Aid

Lack of trust in carceral institutions to resolve crises meant that interviewees often came to rely on others in the queer and trans community for help and support. Consistent with previous literature, interviewees turned to informal support networks after becoming disillusioned with formal resources, including police.[23] This meant relying on friends, biological or chosen family, or neighbors for immediate needs. Some interviewees became active in neighborhood mutual aid or swap groups; others participated in forms of care work that are often criminalized, such as sharing medication with people who lacked health care access, or sex workers trading safety tips for dealing with clients.

"I have friends who are doctors, I have friends who are lawyers," explained Kavitha, an Indian-American genderqueer person, when asked about the resources and support systems they had access to. "I have friends who are engineers. I don't see myself *needing* to call any sort of preestablished community other than my own." In a major medical crisis they might go to the hospital, they conceded, but otherwise they avoided engaging with most formal institutions unless absolutely necessary, preferring to call on community members whenever possible. On principle, Kavitha refused to engage with police even in the event of an emergency.

Nicole, a white gender-variant dyke, similarly described themself as living "outside of formalized resources and formalized institutions." The advent of the COVID-19 pandemic, however, had placed significant strain on their ability to function this way. "I have realized this year, with the pandemic," they explained, "how many informal networks and webs I've built and am a part of that have collapsed." At the time we spoke, Nicole had become active in local mutual aid projects, such as food distribution, but found themself frustrated at the loss of in-person connection. "I guess I have a lot of informal ways of going about community building," they said. "But it's also deeply . . . it relies upon community impact, like being in a room together." Despite the new challenges presented by the pandemic, Nicole ultimately still found comfort in the way that queer people devised new and creative ways of connecting with each other in periods of crisis. "I don't think that will go away soon," they concluded. Nicole's experience corresponds with research demonstrating that the pandemic exacerbated existing resource access issues among LGBTQIA+ communities.[24]

Despite the increased logistical, economic, and emotional burdens precipitated by the pandemic, the value of community care stood in stark contrast to the perceived inefficacy of police and other institutions. Lin, a twenty-six-year-old Vietnamese nonbinary person, participated in mutual aid work during the pandemic: "The fact that there are people distributing food, water, medication, all this stuff, the things that the police are supposed to do to protect and serve the people—I'm like, so we didn't need the police after all. We just needed the community to back each other up." Lin also asserted that "institutions are already doing a roundabout way of trying to take care of you. . . . Why would I trust in somebody that hasn't been able to help me? . . . Why wouldn't I lean on the people that are in the same here and now that I am? Like my neighbors. My friends. Lovers. Whoever."

Echoing other interviewees, Lin reoriented the NYPD's motto of "protect and serve" to encompass what they considered true protection and service: helping fellow community members meet their immediate needs. Similarly, Cookie, a Puerto Rican and Black trans woman, said that in a crisis, "I wouldn't call the cops 'cause they're very transphobic," but would seek out a trusted friend she'd known for thirty years. "She's also trans," Cookie added. "If I'm in trouble or something. I run to her house. Even if I need a plate of food, you know? For rough times, in need, she's the one that I run to. Somebody that identifies same thing I identify." This insistence on relying on people "in the same here and now," who might share a queer or trans identity—community peers rather than out-side authorities—speaks to the degree to which queer people felt alien-ated from and failed by formal resources, as well as the importance of establishing mutual and nonhierarchical forms of trust and caregiving. Queer or trans identity was not the sole basis for the formation of com-munity; interviewees also mentioned cultural background, neighbor-hoods and physical proximity, and common political goals as points of connection and were quick to point out disparities in privilege and oppor-tunity among queer social circles. However, queerness—and more spe-cifically, shared experiences of exclusion and discrimination *because* of one's queerness—emerged as a powerful unifying force that solidified interviewees' commitment to helping each other.

When discussing these support networks, interviewees situated them-selves within a lineage of queer and trans community care. Nicole, a white gender-variant dyke, described mutual aid as "our legacy," with noninstitutional resource-sharing practices "passed on within genera-tions of queer people." Annie, a thirty-year-old white and Chinese queer cisgender woman, characterized her queer friends as especially "invested in building community support, and kind of doing the work internally as well, to think about conversations around accountability and safety." Interviewees referred both explicitly and implicitly to AIDS activism, often in relation to the care work being enacted in the context of the COVID-19 pandemic. In both instances, grassroots efforts emerged in the absence of institutional support, with queer and trans people forced to rely on each other rather than on formal systems of care.[25] "Because [the queer community] have done it before, they're like okay, we could do it again," said Taz, a twenty-four-year-old Latinx trans masc/fluid person. "Because they were already doing it beforehand, it was very easy to continue it in a new way."

Queer and Trans Identity and Abolitionism

In addition to explaining their reasons for mistrusting police, interview-ees discussed their involvement in abolitionist advocacy. For some, anti-carceral organizing spaces provided safe environments in which to try out new aspects of their identities. "My [abolitionist] organizing com-mittees have been just, I think, the best incubators for me to explore gender," said Ari, a white, Jewish, queer nonbinary person. In these groups, meetings often began with attendees sharing their names and pronouns, offering repeated convenient opportunities to test-run new iterations of both and see how it felt. "My organizing collective is not explicitly queer in any way," Ari clarified. "But just like so many of us are. And I think like . . . a fourth or a third of us are nonbinary? So that's just been kind of like a beautiful thing."

In Ari's case, abolitionist activism helped facilitate a more open and expansive understanding of their gender identity. For others, however, queerness and transness opened the door to abolitionist thought rather than the other way around, with some interviewees framing their embrace of abolitionism as a direct result of their exploration of gender and sexuality. Shay, a twenty-nine-year-old white trans nonbinary pansexual person, admitted to having "nightmares" about what their life might have been like if they had never questioned their gender. This alternate-universe version of themselves, they imagined, would likely be living in a heterosexual marriage with children, closeted even to themself and restricted to male-coded clothing and hobbies: "I mean honestly [my perspective on police] wouldn't have ever shifted if I weren't queer. You know? . . . I don't think I would be as—at the front of this new education in my life, if it wasn't because I was trans. . . . Or even just queer. I feel like if you're not challenging your beliefs by [. . .] the core of your identity not congealing with what we're told and how we're told to be and how we're told to act, you wouldn't question it."

In this framing, it is not simply that queerness or transness directly prompts an exploration of beliefs. More specifically, the experience of being othered for one's queer or trans identity prompts reassessment of conventional understandings of the world, as well as a desire to challenge unjust or oppressive structures. As Shay came to understand their identity and selfhood as being at odds with the prescribed gender roles set out for them, they found themself interrogating the validity and necessity of other social structures and institutions that they had previously taken for granted:

> People just need to be put in a position to where they're like, wait, what is *really* keeping me from being happy and healthy and thriving? Oh, it's rules created by *other people*. It's nothing—like it has nothing to do with me. Other people are telling me that I'm, you know, I can't have this job because I want to dress how I want to dress. Or because I have tattoos on my fingers. . . . Or I'm not allowed to use this bathroom, I have to use that bathroom. Or like whatever it may be. People made those rules. People.

For Shay, any system centered around "rules created by other people" could and *should* be questioned—and having already engaged in this type of questioning related to gender, they could more easily imagine pushing back against other sets of rigid, normative expectations. This framing puts Shay and other interviewees in conversation with abolitionist scholars such as Angela Davis, who expressed a similar sentiment during a 2020 panel discussion: "I don't think we would be where we are today, encouraging ever larger numbers of people to think within an abolitionist framing, had not the trans community taught us that it is possible to effectively challenge that which is considered the very foundation of our sense of normalcy. . . . If it is possible to challenge the gender binary, then we can certainly effectively resist prisons, and jails, and police."[26]

One central talking point that abolitionists often raise is that the carceral institutions that we take for granted are relatively new inventions in the course of human history, and that since they were originally designed and created by society, they can be dismantled the same way. However immutable they may seem, systems of criminal punishment are, at their core, simply "rules created by other people."

As with mutual aid, interviewees positioned their own involvement in anti-carceral organizing as part of a long-standing tradition. Christina, a mixed-race queer woman, explained her own place in the global and historical abolitionist movement as follows:

> My point is we should abolish the police. . . . And I mean *literally* that, and I don't want people to twist my words around and be like, she didn't mean it. I mean it. We're gonna defund them, and then we're gonna slowly wean off society out of all of it. And then the military complex is gonna—and the prison industrial complex is gonna happen next, too. . . . It isn't a wack job idea. Being a society that no longer needs a terrorist police organization should be a *goal*. And was considered a goal in like the late '60s, early '70s. We have imagined this world, and people in other places in the United States and Europe and South America, all over, have already started, you know, making changes to experiment with a truly, a truly equitable society where people's needs are being met, and we don't need to involve the state or the carceral system. And I'm done with it. I'm done with it. And everyone is done with it.

Despite her assertion that "everyone is done with" policing—at least within her own social circles—Christina recognized that some might perceive abolition as a "wack job idea." She also indicated concern about the potential for abolitionist principles or slogans to be misinterpreted or diluted as they gain public attention—a common point of frustration among abolitionist organizers.[27] Drawing parallels between her own activist work and movements from other times and places appeared to be a way to shore up her own stance and establish it as part of an intellectual lineage. Her statement about imagination and experimentation also echoes the phrasing of fellow abolitionists like Mariame Kaba, who has said, "We need a million experiments. A bunch will fail. That's good because we'll have learned a lot that we can apply to the next ones."[28] According to this experimental framing, the work of abolitionism requires both long-term ambition and short-term creativity.

Interviewees also described what being an abolitionist meant in terms of everyday practice. For Lauren, a twenty-six-year-old white bisexual nonbinary person, one of the first steps toward embracing abolitionism meant reckoning with one's prior complicity in upholding criminal legal institutions. "If you acknowledge that there's problems with the police system, then you acknowledge that you have been [. . .] a problem if you've called the police, or if you've trusted the police," they reasoned. Claiming responsibility must be coupled with a willingness to develop alternate conceptions of safety and harm. "You have to change your way of thinking entirely," Lauren added. "And you have to realize that at any given point in your life, you can be wrong about everything." Their phrasing echoes that of abolitionist scholar Ruth Wilson Gilmore, who writes that "abolition requires that we change one thing: everything."[29] As interviewees explained, they had already *had* multiple opportunities to reevaluate their understandings of themselves and the world, and to make radical life changes based on these shifts in perception. Incorporating abolitionism into that new worldview was in many ways a natural next step in that process.

CONCLUSION

In *Cruising Utopia*, José Esteban Muñoz wrote that "the future is queerness's domain. Queerness is a structuring and educated mode of desiring that allows us to see and feel beyond the quagmire of the present. The here and now is a prison house. . . . Queerness is essentially about the rejection of a here and now and an insistence on potentiality or concrete possibility for another world."[30] Muñoz's invocation of the present as a carceral institution is neither casual nor accidental, but a reflection of the degree to which policing, surveillance, and institutional violence pervade experiences of being queer in the world. Through these experiences, many queer and trans people come to recognize that, as Eric A. Stanley writes, "racialized anti-trans/queer violence is not antagonistic to the democratic state; it is among its foundations—a minor claim that demands the end of the world."[31] Stanley also notes the "shared tactics of survival" that emerge among people designated by the state as disruptive, pathologized, or criminalized and which constitute alternative modes of being in community.[32]

The queer and trans people I spoke with expressed dissatisfaction with currently available options for crisis response services, particularly those involving police, which often caused further harm without addressing underlying problems. At best, interviewees repeatedly articulated, police were unhelpful and ineffective; at worst, they actively and deliberately caused harm to marginalized communities. Importantly, many of these negative experiences with law enforcement related directly to the policing of gender and sexuality, and the ways in which queer and trans people were frequently singled out by police for disproportionate scrutiny and enforcement. Being treated as inherently suspicious, deviant, or potentially criminal as queer people prompted a renewed interest in, and solidarity with, other marginalized groups who had been treated similarly. Many interviewees who were themselves members of some of these groups—such as immigrants, disabled people, and people of color—had long since divested from the idea that police were a viable resource to be called upon in times of crisis. Meanwhile, queer and trans people from more privileged backgrounds found that their interactions with police prompted a clearer understanding of what economically disadvantaged neighborhoods and communities of color endured on a continuing basis. These experiences had caused many to entirely reevaluate their perceptions of policing as an institution and of what public safety meant to them in the first place.

Distrust of police often prompted an intention to divest from criminal legal system resources, which also meant turning *toward* each other and toward community-centered sources of support. Participants connected their investment in alternate, noncarceral forms of crisis response with an explicitly queer and trans political lens, noting that exploring and expressing their identities had opened their minds to abolitionist viewpoints and encouraged them to develop broader understandings of harm, care, safety, and support than those offered by formal institutions. Ari, an organizer, drew some of the most explicit connections between their gender journey and their abolitionist one. "Mutual aid, abolition," they mused. "I guess there's like a common creativity that I see [. . .] both to build a world without police, and with transformative justice. And to envision and figure out your gender once you've sort of like knocked off the binary. There's I guess this generative element to both."

Queer and trans people are used to inhabiting worlds of our own making, whether by design, by affinity, or by necessity. The same qualities that mark us as targeted "others" also provide lenses through which to envision alternate futures. Having first reimagined ourselves—sometimes once, sometimes many times over—we can reimagine the systems that surround us. It is important, of course, to resist the temptation to romanticize community support systems as being inherently purer, gentler, and free from abuses of power. Queer and trans communities are hardly immune from harmful behavior. We cause hurt; we struggle with our own trauma; we are insensitive; we screw up; we lash out. But we keep trying. Our support networks, built in response to state violence and institutional abandonment, must allow space for imperfections, experimentation, and the acknowledgment and repair of harm. As we open ourselves to the possibilities that we may have been "wrong about everything" we previously took for granted, we will continue to discover opportunities to grow.

NOTES

1. Feinberg, "Street Transvestite Action Revolutionaries."
2. Cohen, *The Gay Liberation Youth Movement in New York: An Army of Lovers Cannot Fail*, 37.
3. Queer Nation, "Queers Read This," New York, 1990, https://archive .qzap.org/index.php/Detail/Object/Show/object_id/184.
4. Spade, *Normal Life: Administrative Violence, Critical Trans Politics, and the Limits of Law*, 5.
5. Hocquenghem, *Gay Liberation after May '68*, 91.
6. Queer Nation, "Queers Read This," New York, 1990, https://archive .qzap.org/index.php/Detail/Object/Show/object_id/184.
7. Bey and Goldberg, "Queer as in Abolition Now!," 160.
8. Bey and Goldberg, 159.
9. Bassichis, Lee, and Spade, "Building an Abolitionist Trans and Queer Movement with Everything We've Got."
10. Malatino, *Trans Care*, 2.
11. Hudson and Romanelli, "'We Are Powerful People': Health-Promoting Strengths of LGBTQ Communities of Color"; Sherman et al., "Trans* Community Connection, Health, and Wellbeing: A Systematic Review."
12. Perry, Thurston, and Green, "Involvement and Detachment in Researching Sexuality: Reflections on the Process of Semistructured Interviewing"; Vincent, "Studying Trans: Recommendations for Ethical Recruitment and Collaboration with Transgender Participants in Academic Research."

13. Charmaz, *Constructing Grounded Theory: A Practical Guide through Qualitative Analysis*; Saldana, *The Coding Manual for Qualitative Researchers*.

14. Hartsock, "The Feminist Standpoint: Developing the Ground for a Specifically Feminist Historical Materialism."

15. Collins, "The Social Construction of Black Feminist Thought"; Thompson, "Feminist Methodology for Family Studies."

16. Cameron and Stinson, "Gender (Mis)Measurement: Guidelines for Respecting Gender Diversity in Psychological Research."

17. Orth, "Secondary Victimization of Crime Victims by Criminal Proceedings"; Williams, "Secondary Victimization—Confronting Public Attitudes about Rape."

18. See Goodmark, *Imperfect Victims: Criminalized Survivors and the Promise of Abolition Feminism*, for a recent exploration of how survivors of harm are often criminalized.

19. Vitale and Jefferson, "The Emergence of Command and Control Policing in Neoliberal New York."

20. Alsharif and Levenson, "Buffalo Police Officers Who Pushed 75-Year-Old during Black Lives Matter Protest Cleared of Wrongdoing."

21. Spade, *Normal Life: Administrative Violence, Critical Trans Politics, and the Limits of Law*, 75.

22. Gilbert, "New York Police Grabbed a Trans Protester and Threw Her into an Unmarked Van."

23. Rengifo, Slocum, and Chillar, "From Impressions to Intentions: Direct and Indirect Effects of Police Contact on Willingness to Report Crimes to Law Enforcement."

24. Gamio Cuervo et al., "'Solidarity and Community on Our Terms and through Our Lens': Community Care and Shared Trauma for Transgender and Nonbinary Peer Supporters during the COVID-19 Pandemic."

25. Gamio Cuervo et al., "'Solidarity and Community on Our Terms and through Our Lens': Community Care and Shared Trauma for Transgender and Nonbinary Peer Supporters during the COVID-19 Pandemic"; Gould, *Moving Politics: Emotion and ACT UP's Fight against AIDS*.

26. Dream Defenders, "Sunday School: Abolition in Our Lifetime."

27. See, for example, the mildly exasperated-sounding title of Mariame Kaba's *New York Times* op-ed: "Yes, We Mean Literally Abolish the Police."

28. Mariame Kaba, "We Need a Million Experiments. A Bunch Will Fail," Twitter, June 15, 2020, https://twitter.com/prisonculture/status/1272548582139330566.

29. Gilmore, *Change Everything: Racial Capitalism and the Case for Abolition*.

30. Muñoz, *Cruising Utopia: The Then and There of Queer Futurity*, 1.

31. Stanley, *Atmospheres of Violence: Structuring Antagonism and the Trans/Queer Ungovernable*, 114.

32. Stanley, 120.

CHAPTER 8

Queer against the Law

AMANDA M. PETERSEN, INDEPENDENT SCHOLAR

I write this in a historic moment when, like many moments past, anti-LGBTQ+ rhetoric, legislation, and violence are making headlines.[1] And once again, like many moments past, these efforts both derive from and result in the idea that LGBTQ+ people are criminally dangerous, especially to children. In response, LGBTQ+ people and allies are staunchly denying that queer and trans people are "pedophiles, "groomers," or "predators," situating such rhetoric as offensive and inflammatory. This urge to draw a clear discursive and political distinction between being an LGBTQ+ person and being someone who has harmed (or wants to harm) children is one that makes sense to me. However, when I analyze such denials alongside a radical, abolitionist politics, their impact becomes troubling. Indeed, in this chapter, I argue that these denials not only fail to move us closer to queer and trans liberation, but result in the reconstruction of the criminal Other.

I begin this chapter with a brief, US-focused overview of the historic and ongoing criminalization of LGBTQ+ people, with a focus on the labeling of LGBTQ+ people as harmful to children. I then examine the ways that LGBTQ+ people, allies, and advocacy organizations have worked to delegitimize the conceptual linkage between queerness and criminality through an embrace of the respectable queer family and a rejection of the dangerous criminal. Next, I trouble these counter-narratives through a reading of Cathy Cohen's iconic theorization of a radical queer politics, ultimately arguing that queer liberation will never be achieved through the creation of, and distancing from, a criminal Other.[2] Via Cohen, I close by offering a radical queer politics for the present moment—one that embraces carceral abolitionist ethics and rejects criminalization in all its forms, instead working to destroy the laws (both formal and informal) that control, confine, and degrade life.

THE LAW AGAINST QUEERNESS

While queer sex and "transing" gender have been long frowned upon in the Western world, the conceptual linkage between queerness and criminality that emerged in the twentieth century ultimately led to the still-present criminalization—both conceptually and factually—of LGBTQ+ people.[3] This criminalization of queerness has perhaps been no more evident than in the discourse and politics of sexual violence, especially child sexual abuse. Indeed, child sexual abuse has long been "homosexualized," or associated with queer sexuality, leading to a string of moral panics and the further stigmatization, victimization, and imprisonment of LGBTQ+ people.[4] Of course, efforts to link child sexual abuse and queerness are not politically innocent but are used to justify the cultural norms, social practices, and discriminatory laws that marginalize and stigmatize LGBTQ+ people.

The "Eulenburg Affair" of early 1900s Germany, which involved a conspiracy theory that Prince Philipp Eulenburg and a band of traitorous, gay "pederasts" had emperor Kaiser Wilhelm II under their political control, is described as "the first gay panic of the modern era."[5] This relatively specific and localized framing of queer people as necessarily traitorous and conniving saboteurs quickly took on international appeal, ultimately informing the "Lavender Scare" of the late 1940s to mid-1970s in the United States, which sought to purge LGBTQ+ persons from government employment. Writer Richard Beck goes so far as to argue that the homophobic sex panics of World War II, and beyond, were rooted in the idea that the desire to abuse children was inherent to gay sexuality.[6]

The mid-century also saw the emergence of "sexual psychopath" laws across various Western countries, including Australia, Canada, and the United States.[7] These laws were rooted in the idea—which emerged in the intersecting fields of psychology, psychoanalysis, and psychiatry—that particular "sex offenders" were sexually immature and lacked control over their sexual behavior. Among them were "homosexuals," whose sexual deviancy was theorized to be caused by childhood sexual abuse. Given this, they were caught in a period of "arrested development" and thus would seek sexual relationships with children rather than adults. As such, "homosexuals" and other "perverts" targeted by sexual psychopath laws were given indeterminate sentences to be either incapacitated or subject to long-term "treatment." Thus, even when an LGBTQ+ person may not have engaged in sexual violence, they too were confined under these laws in an attempt to remove them from society and cure them of their perversity.

The criminalization did not stop there. Anti-sodomy laws, or laws against nonprocreative sex, have existed throughout US history.[8] While early US laws focused less on same-sex sex (and more on other sex practices deemed immoral, disgusting, predatory, and polluting, and thus a threat to the White Christian family), the rhetoric associated with anti-sodomy laws shifted in the mid-1900s, targeting "predatory homosexuals" who were supposedly tempting and debasing children. As such, legal scholar William Eskridge Jr. argues that throughout the 1900s, "homosexuality became synonymous with sodomy."[9] And while there is little evidence that anti-sodomy laws (whether or not explicitly criminalizing same-sex sex) were widely prosecuted, they were used to justify police surveillance and harassment of gay bars, cruising spots, and other queer spaces.[10] Further, these laws turned LGB people into a "criminal class," whose sexual practices were not only seen as immoral but illegal, inviting additional forms of stigmatization, violence, and discrimination.[11] While deemed unconstitutional in the United States, laws specifically criminalizing "consensual same-sex sexual acts" still exist in many parts of the world.[12]

As lawmakers in the United States were busily criminalizing queer sex and LGB people, they also took aim at cross-dressers (i.e., anyone who wore clothing inconsistent with gendered expectations). Indeed, between the 1840s and 1980s, at least seventy jurisdictions in the United States passed laws banning cross-dressing, likely in an attempt to—among other goals—dissuade "gender deviance," punish "homosexuality," and "impose upper-class white Christian morality on the new urban masses," while reifying the gender binary, racial classification, and class standing.[13] Because of these laws, cross-dressers, especially those who were non-White, became subject to the same, if not worse, police surveillance, harassment, and violence as LGB people.[14] The legacy of these laws lives on, for example, in anti-drag laws and the targeted criminalization of trans women of color, especially those who do sex work.[15]

As federal employment bans, gay sodomy laws, cross-dressing laws, and "sexual psychopath" laws faced legal challenges and waned in the mid- to late-1900s, the gay panic linking queerness and pedophilia took on a new target—this time in the context of schools and childcare settings. Perhaps most famously, in the late 1970s, singer Anita Bryant led the local-turned-national "Save Our Children" campaign against a law that would ban various forms of anti-LGB discrimination in Dade County, Florida. Among other discriminatory beliefs and claims, Bryant asserted that people with public LGB identities should be denied employment in K–12 schools, rooting her argument in the idea that "militant homosexual" teachers who "flaunt their deviant lifestyle" would be "promoting sin" to their students.[16] Further, Bryant argued that "homosexual" teachers would use the classroom to "recruit the youth of America" and "encourage more homosexuality by inducing pupils into looking upon it as an acceptable life-style."[17] Or worse yet, Bryant asserted that "a particularly deviant-minded teacher could sexually molest children."[18] Beyond this, Bryant was known to draw linkages between being "so-called-gay," bestiality, child pornography, and other forms of commercial sexual exploitation of children.[19] The subsequent and related 1980s moral panic over satanic child sexual abuse in day care facilities was driven, in part, by these same beliefs—that queer people are predisposed to pedophilia or are otherwise a danger to children.[20]

These interrelated narratives are still alive and well in the United States. Currently, for example, LGBTQ+ people in the United States are subject to a series of state-level laws aimed at banning people from performing in drag; reading books by or about LGBTQ+ people; acknowledging the existence of LGBTQ+ people, teaching about LGBTQ+ issues, or offering gender-inclusive sexual education in K–12 schools; accessing gender-affirming medical care (or *any* medical care); being a gender-affirming parent; playing sports, using a restroom, or using a locker room while trans; updating gender information on government documents; or making civil rights claims.[21] Many of these anti-LGBTQ+ laws and policies—branded as "anti-grooming bills" by their proponents—are rooted in, and productive of, the idea that LGBTQ+ people and their allies are "groomers," "predators," and "pedophiles" who are "sexualizing" children with the ultimate goal of (at best) recruiting them into becoming LGBTQ+ or (at worst) sexually abusing them.[22] Further, recent laws aimed at banning trans people from using public restrooms or locker room facilities are fueled by the idea that trans people—especially trans women—are duplicitous and sexually violent.[23] No doubt, this association grows from *and* produces a wide range of television and film media portraying trans people as violent, conniving, and unhinged.[24]

QUEERS AGAINST CRIMINALS

In response to these panics and their associated outcomes, many LGBTQ+ people, allies, and advocacy organizations have worked to refute the conceptual linkage between queerness and criminality. I've noticed four approaches used to achieve this.

The first strategy is to make salient the queer/criminal narrative, and then frame this narrative—with its accusations of "grooming" and labels such as "groomers," "pedophiles," or "predators"—as deeply offensive. For example, Evan Wolfson, a civil rights lawyer and key activist in the movement for marriage equality, considers "grooming" claims to be defamatory and "despicable," arguing that they are "a classic trope of dehumanization and fear that has been used against gay people decade after decade after decade."[25] He goes on to encourage us to "think about the calumny against gay people throughout most of our lifetimes: that gay people somehow are molesting kids, or after kids, or predatory." Similarly, journalist Matthew Rozsa cites the work of Gillian Frank, a scholar of religion and sexuality, to argue that the groomer narrative "associates one's opponents with the worst evil that humans are capable of committing" and renders them "monsters."[26] The Anti-Defamation League refers to claims of pedophilia and "grooming" as "false and malicious," noting that such claims "demonize" LGBTQ+ people and subject them to increased violence and marginalization.[27] Indeed, they argue that "painting the LGBTQ+ community as child predators and criminals will lead to continued harassment and violence against a community already suffering from hate speech, harassment and violence by extremists and bigots."

Second, and relatedly, some people and organizations draw a binary distinction between LGBTQ+ people and "pedophiles," "groomers," and "predators." In other words, LGBTQ+ people and "criminals" are framed as two mutually exclusive and antagonistic groups. For example, writer and journalist John Paul Brammer argues that "the LGBTQ+ community has long been maliciously associated with pedophiles" and "sexual predators."[28] Through pluralization, he constructs a social class of "pedophiles" and "sexual predators" that exists alongside and in opposition to LGBTQ+ people. Rooted in this same logic, we see explicit rebukes such as "We are not groomers," "We are not pedophiles," and "We are not rapists."[29] In countries where queer sex and the expression of trans identity are criminalized, we see similar proclamations that "We are not criminals."[30]

Third, it has become common for journalists and organizations to disrupt the rhetoric of the queer or trans pedophile by pointing to studies showing that LGBTQ+ people abuse children at similar, or even lesser, rates than non-LGBTQ+ people.[31] Unlike the aforementioned binary distinction between LGBTQ+ and "groomer," "pedophile," or "predator," this research-based approach frames LGBTQ+ as equally criminal (or perhaps slightly less criminal) than non-LGBTQ+ people. So, while these critics acknowledge that LGBTQ+ people *do sometimes* abuse children, a new binary is introduced: criminals and noncriminals, or those who are "sexual predators" and those who are not.

Fourth, advocacy organizations have used media campaigns and communications tools to normalize LGBTQ+ people and families. For example, some contemporary organizations are taking a page from the marriage equality playbook by producing and distributing heartwarming videos of close-knit, upper- and middle-class families with children, or videos featuring military families.[32] For example, a video produced by GLAAD features a White, seemingly middle-class family doing things like jumping on a trampoline, playing music, and lighting fireworks as the mother narrates in defense of her trans son. Importantly, she reassures the viewer that "my family's just like yours."[33]

The normalizing approach is also taken in a series of instructional guides by the Movement Advancement Project.[34] The organization educates readers on how to combat negative perceptions of LGBTQ+ people—particularly related to dangerousness—through conversation starters and counter-messaging that emphasize "shared values," such as safety and fairness. Like popular video campaigns, Movement Advancement Project's messaging focuses on the normalcy and respectability of LGBTQ+ people and families. They build upon this counter-messaging by working to create distance between LGBTQ+ people and "offenders," advocating for the detection and punishment of these "offenders." For example, their guides promote the following messaging:

> We all know LGBTQ people. They're our family, our friends, our co-workers, our neighbors. When we stop and think about the people in our lives, we know how baseless and offensive these anti-LGBTQ smears are—and how much they hurt people we know and care about.[35]

> Safety and privacy in restrooms is important for all of us. That's why we already have laws in place that make it illegal to harm or harass people, or invade their privacy. These laws are used to prevent assault, keep people safe, and hold offenders accountable. Updating our nondiscrimination laws won't change that.[36]

Title IX is vitally important when it comes to girls' sports. If we want to support girls' sports, we should be providing more funding and more opportunities to play, and also creating stronger laws to protect female athletes from harassment and abuse—not banning transgender youth from participating in school sports with their peers.[37]

The experience of schools across the country has shown that student abuse of these policies simply does not happen. Students cannot pretend to be transgender in order to engage in misconduct. And if someone abuses any school policy to harm another student or invade their privacy, schools can and will stop such behavior as part of their legal obligation to provide a safe learning environment for all students.[38]

While the work people and organizations are doing to resist current attacks on LGBTQ+ autonomy, health, and civil rights is vital, and while efforts to reject the association between queerness and criminality are certainly understandable, I will use the rest of the chapter to push back on some of these approaches and envision a more liberatory resistance strategy. To do this, I read this counter-messaging alongside the radical and visionary work of Black feminist scholar and activist Cathy Cohen.

COHEN'S RADICAL QUEER POLITICS

Written in the latter quarter of the long 1990s—which saw the reclamation of the term *queer*, the emergence of queer theory in the academy, the height of the AIDS epidemic, radical queer activism related to the AIDS epidemic, and, unfortunately, a (new) assimilationist strain of queer activism—Cathy Cohen's now-canonical *Punks, Bulldaggers, and Welfare Queens: The Radical Potential of Queer Politics?* poses important questions about queer politics, its failures, and its liberatory potential.[39] Her critique is, in many ways, as germane today as it was in 1997.

Cohen's critique is rooted, in part, in radical theorizations of gender and sexuality from the early years of what is now considered queer theory, as well as from early, radical queer politics. Cohen highlights the ways these early theorists and activists destabilized the cultural and discursive production of inherent and stable categorizations of sexuality. Importantly, Cohen notes that queer theory brought forth a paradigm shift, in which the sexual subject was no longer understood as stable and natural, but one "constructed and contained by multiple practices of categorization and regulation that systematically marginalize and oppress those subjects thereby defined as deviant and 'other.'"[40] Cohen describes the alignment between this body of theory and early queer politics, which used confrontation and public displays of gender-fuckery to challenge the various forms of heteronormative power that produce and police such subjects and render them "invisible and at risk."[41] Through this rejection of such normalizing power, both in the academy and in the streets, Cohen argues that queer politics held the promise of also rejecting single-axis political organizing by building solidarity with "all those deemed marginal and all those committed to liberatory politics."[42] For Cohen, however, this potential was never realized on a large scale. Cohen critiques the dominant queer politics that emerged in the 1990s for its failure to engage in "a truly radical or transformative politics," and she offers at least four critiques in this regard.[43]

First, Cohen contends that dominant queer politics took on an assimilationist agenda, striving for inclusion within, and replication of, oppressive systems and institutions. This involved prioritizing a strategy of civil rights attainment while ignoring the ideological, political, and economic systems that led to the denial of those rights in the first place. Additionally, Cohen argues that assimilationism relies on apologizing for, disidentifying with, or rebuking behaviors, people, and relationships deemed sexually deviant, while taking on the norms of dominant heterosexuality. For Cohen, such a strategy works to uphold, rather than undermine, the status quo, which necessarily advantages only the already-most-privileged queer people.

Second, Cohen demonstrates that dominant queer politics came to define the struggle for queer liberation through a binary opposition between queerness and heterosexuality, and between queer people and straight people. In this sense, queer politics positioned itself against both heterosexuality and heterosexual people rather than heteronormativity and the totality of forces that render all people "who stand on the outside of the dominant constructed norm of state-sanctioned white middle- and upper-class heterosexuality," regardless of their sexual orientation, vulnerable to oppression and exploitation.[44] Further, Cohen argues that by focusing solely on sexual orientation as a point of alliance and as a political issue, queer politics created an antagonistic binary, effectively positioning all queer people as power*less* and all heterosexual people as power*ful*.

Third, Cohen points out the way that much of queer politics relies on single-axis identity politics, eschewing analyses of other forms of oppression such as racism, sexism, and capitalism in the lives of both queer and heterosexual people. In this sense, nonradical queer politics foregoes an intersectional analysis of oppression, resulting in—among other problems—a failure to recognize how heteronormativity often interacts with multiple systems of oppression to reduce the life chances of both queer and straight people.[45] Cohen offers numerous examples—both historic and contemporary—of the ways heteronormativity intersected with racism, sexism, and class discrimination to frame certain heterosexual people and relationships as undesirable or deviant. These include restrictions that barred enslaved couples from marrying; bans on interracial marriage; prosecution of women suspected of using drugs while pregnant; forced sterilization of women of color; stigmatization of single, young, and/or Black mothers using welfare assistance; and stigmatization of Black sexuality, broadly. Given this broad range of examples, Cohen asks whether it is perhaps "*most* of us" who are "truly on the outside of heternormative power."[46] However, by constructing an antagonistic binary between queer and straight, dominant queer politics rendered invisible the ways power actually operates on *all* of us, whether through privilege or marginalization.

For each of these reasons, Cohen argues that queer activists failed to build coalition with other identity-based activist groups, simultaneously limiting the political power of queer people and obscuring the oppression of many straight people of color. It was not the case, however, that a critique of this dominant politics did not exist at the time and would only develop at some point in the future. Cohen goes on to demonstrate that an analysis that addressed each of these critiques *already* existed among LGBTQ+ activists of color, Black feminists, and radical Black activists and theorists. Within these radical communities, heteronormativity was understood to not only impact queer people, but to interact with racism, sexism, and capitalism to prohibit or stigmatize a range of relationships, including heterosexual relationships. And what these communities of color already knew, but dominant queer politics failed to realize, is that those defined as most marginal, no matter their sexual orientation, become vulnerable "to be used either as surplus labor in an advanced capitalist structure and/or seen as expendable, denied resources, and thus locked into correctional institutions across the country."[47]

RETHINKING ANTI-ANTI-GROOMER RHETORIC

Cohen's critique of dominant queer politics provides an analytic framework for interrogating (and then dismantling) the common and perhaps intuitive denial-based responses to the conflation of LGBTQ+ identity with pedophilia, sexual trickery, and other forms of interpersonal violence.

To begin, Cohen's work has direct applicability to what I identify as pro-LGBTQ+ denials related to the establishment of new binaries, whether that be a binary of criminal and queer, or one of predator and nonpredator. Pro-LGBTQ+ media sources have recognized the claims of criminality as politically motived, used primarily by right-wing figures and organizations to restrict, devalue, and erase the lives of LGBTQ+ people.[48] For example, rhetoric linking queerness and criminality has been referred to in the media as "talking points,"[49] a "long-standing trope,"[50] "one of the oldest narratives in the homophobic playbook,"[51] and as having "absolutely nothing to do with preventing child sexual abuse."[52] However, I have yet to find a source where these attack-related terms are deconstructed in their own right and not simply condemned for their weaponization against LGBTQ+ people. In other words, terms such as "pedophile," "groomer," "predator," "offender," "criminal," and the like are taken as legitimate but misdirected labels.

There are at least two problems with this. First, to deny such claims, especially without denouncing the assumption of a class of criminal Others, is to implicitly frame the anti-LGBTQ+ activists' argument as a sound one: that there is a class of criminal Others preying on children whom we must guard ourselves and our families against. While child sexual abuse obviously occurs, and is indisputably harmful, ongoing moral panics related to child sexual abuse are not politically neutral. Indeed, in addition to their relationship to anti-LGBTQ+ rhetoric and criminalization, anti-child-abuse panics are shaped by the intersection of—at the very least—attempts to affirm the White, heterosexual family; the political and psychic desires to obscure heteronormativity and its embedded violences; efforts to construct an internal national enemy; denial of intrafamilial violence; anxiety about changing sexual, social, and familial norms; and an attempt to undermine women's liberation efforts.[53] For these reasons, queer theorist Kevin Ohi[54] argues that "an antihomophobic project," rather than distancing itself from—and in so doing, legitimizing—these moral panics, "should work to understand how all sexual oppressions are linked and related."[55] In our current context, we might ask, for example, how the oppression of LGBTQ+ people is related to sexual violence inside families, or how gender policing also contributes to sexual violence.

Second, and relatedly, not only are we failing to critique these terms in their own right, but we are reapplying the labels on those *we* consider the criminal Other. This establishes "our" common enemy as the "criminal," one who is fundamentally unlike "us." Of course, in the United States and other nation states colonized by Europe, this common enemy has always been non-White and has often been poor, disabled, LGBTQ+, undocumented, or otherwise marginalized and oppressed. When we try to escape the criminal classification without also condemning it, we do precisely what Cohen warns against—normalizing the most privileged individuals and families and attempting to assimilate into a White, middle- or upper-class, heteronormative society. As we work to slough off these labels, we leave in our wake those we consider the actual evil monsters,[56] the actual demons,[57] and the actual predators.[58]

Further, à la Cohen, when we reconstitute the criminal Other, we erase the reality that sexual violence is *always* contextualized by homophobia, transphobia, racism, sexism, ableism, class exploitation, and other forms of oppressive power. Thus, we fail to recognize how these forces act upon the lives of people who use sexual violence, opting instead to simply label them as evil, psychopathic monsters who live outside the bounds of the human. Put differently, we fail to see the humanity of people who use sexual violence by ignoring the various forms of trauma and oppression that contextualize their use of violence. At the same time, we hide the ways that all of us have used, or are capable of using, violence as a resource. As a result, we limit our ability to rigorously theorize sexual violence and other forms of gender-based violence and to work toward solutions that address the root causes of interpersonal harm. Additionally, we frame ourselves as morally superior, respectable, and beyond reproach, and others as morally depraved, irredeemable, and worthy of punishment. When these binaries—of criminal and queer, and predator and nonpredator—are rejected, we are given the opportunity to interrogate how the labels of "groomer," "predator," "pedophile," and so on have become a (thus far) productive strategy of dividing, controlling, and confining us.

For Cohen, a rejection of the queer/straight binary was not simply a matter of ethics, but fundamental to the coalitional struggle against heteronormativity and the heterosexist violence that flowed from it. Regarding our current matter, adherence to the queer/criminal and non-predator/predator binaries encourages a single-axis identity politics based on the needs and desires of the most socially acceptable LGBTQ+ people and families. It leaves out LGBTQ+ people who have used violence, as well as those who are undocumented, do sex work, use drugs, or are homeless. It leaves out LGBTQ+ people whose gender presentations upset expectations around the gender binary, medical transition, and "passability."

However, as Cohen and others highlight, pro-LGBTQ+ organizing rooted in a radical politics has always allied with other liberatory movements. This has been especially true in the context of anticarceral activism. For example, writer Hugh Ryan documents the ways that the Women's House of Detention in New York City became an organizing hub for these intersecting movements in the 1960s and 1970s, arguing that "the Women's House of Detention was the place where Black liberation, women's liberation, and gay liberation came together to battle the carceral state."[59] Ryan profiles, for instance, the way women incarcerated in the House of D (as it was known) participated in the anti-police Stonewall Rebellion by chanting and throwing burning materials through the window[60] or cared for Afeni Shakur as she stood trial while pregnant. Oppositely, he discusses how the Gay Liberation Front was born of efforts to protest the incarceration of members of the Black Panther Party at the House of D. Similarly, historian Regina Kunzel highlights queer, anticarceral organizing happening on the opposite coast: "At a 1975 rally in support of the San Quentin Six, Bay Area gay liberation activist Karen Turner pledged her movement's support for the struggles of all prisoners, 'because we understand that the system that has created and maintained prisons as a method of social control is the same system that oppresses us on the outside who have the least vested interest in this social system.'"[61]

Likewise, Kunzel discusses the work of Mike Riegle, the founder of *Gay Community News*'s Prisoner Project in 1975: "Incarceration, Riegle claimed, could be understood as an 'intensified version of what we *all* have gone through. . . . *All* of our lives are profoundly affected by the pressure of a legal code and a justice system and social attitudes that push us hard in the direction of conformity, in sexual things especially.' By supporting lesbian and gay prisoners, he wrote, 'we help our community understand that the same system that puts people in prison also organizes the oppression in their lives.'"[62] Kunzel argues that this period of radical solidarity building largely petered out in the 1980s as new leaders in LGBTQ+ advocacy organizations began to disidentify with prisoners and the prisoner rights movement. These new leaders saw prisoner rights work as controversial and divisive, shifting their focus to a quest for respectability, social acceptance, and the attainment of civil rights.

And while this tradition of intersectional, anticarceral, LGBTQ+ activism has regained some momentum in recent decades—including among artists, scholars, criminalized survivors, and radical LGBTQ+ organizations—dominant queer politics has continued to maintain distance from the incarcerated and criminalized, especially those who are not LGBTQ+.[63] For Kunzel, this distance was, and remains, lamentable not only for the lost opportunities for radical organizing but for the ways LGBTQ+ activists and organizations work to police queerness, ultimately upholding, rather than undermining, the heteronormative values that lead to their oppression in the first place. These same urges inform the anti-anti-groomer rhetoric of LGBTQ+ people and allies today, sabotaging our efforts to build truly liberatory frameworks and coalitions.

QUEER AGAINST THE LAW, OR, A RADICAL QUEER POLITICS FOR THE PRESENT MOMENT

Following her critique of *dominant* queer politics, Cohen offers a vision of a *radical* queer politics: "I envision a politics where one's relation to power, and not some homogenized identity, is privileged in determining one's political comrades. I'm talking about a politics where the nonnormative and marginal position of punks, bulldaggers, and welfare queens, for example, is the basis for progressive transformative coalition work. Thus, if there is any truly radical potential to be found in the idea of queerness and the practice of queer politics, it would seem to be located in its ability to create a space in opposition to dominant norms, a space where transformational political work can begin."[64]

Here, we see Cohen imagining a future politics where solidarity is built on shared marginal status rather than identity categories. For Cohen, this is important in rejecting binary notions of power and identity, but also practical in the sense of building movements capable of responding to the interconnected sites of power. How might we take inspiration from, or build upon, Cohen's politics for our present moment?

At the very least, we must refuse to criminalize others, whether in name or in concrete boxes. Queer and trans liberation will never be achieved by identifying, classifying, stigmatizing, and punishing the "actual predators." The violence against LGBTQ+ people will not stop because we have adequately convinced right-wingers and transphobic leftists that our sexuality and gender are not deviant *but* that sexual deviants certainly lurk among us. Indeed, a liberatory movement rooted in a radical, abolitionist queer politics is not a movement against anyone at all. It is a movement against cisheteronormativity, racism, capitalism, ableism, nationalism, fatphobia, xenophobia, carcerality, and every social, political, economic, and cultural structure that improves the life chances of some of us at the expense of others. When we forget this, we distance ourselves from the most marginalized and despised—including those who have used violence.

However, when we embrace (or at least accept) proximity, we can find affinity with those who have harmed others, including those who have caused profound harm. Doing so encourages us to ask what systems and structures shape both our lives and to seek common cause to tear them down. We do not need to say "but we are unlike *them*." Instead, we can say we *are* like them because the world attempts to deny each of our abilities to live meaningful lives and build healthy communities. We can direct our anger and rage at the systems that destroy us rather than one another. We can see that we live in a world that hates both of us and sees us as sinful, monstrous, and irredeemable. Indeed, when we let go of the urge to point the finger at others, we can acknowledge criminalization as a political issue worthy of coalition building. We can ask, together, what are the systems, hierarchies, ways of thinking, and traumas that inform our interpersonal relationships, that engender interpersonal violence, and that lead us, collectively, to eschew accountability and embrace avoidance? This is the true work of violence prevention, as it is these systems, hierarchies, ways of thinking, and traumas that are at the root of violence—including sexual violence.

When we address the root causes of violence rather than searching for someone else to criminalize—to make an internal enemy—we honor and participate in the legacy of solidarity between LGBTQ+ people, prisoners, and other radical organizers. Conversely, when we distance ourselves from criminality by attempting to place the label elsewhere, we fail to recognize, and even celebrate, the ways queers have always broken the law to both resist and survive life in a cisheteronormative world. Further, when we refuse distance, we can stop denying our own capacity to do harm, refusing to make ourselves virtuous for the sake of acceptance into a society that would prefer we not exist. In doing this, we refuse to integrate into the dominant structures of respectability. Indeed, as many radical queers have argued, the point is not integration but to overthrow the intersecting systems of oppression that not only constrain the lives of LGBTQ+ people but foster an environment where power and control can show up in any type of human relationship.[65]

For all these reasons, I dream of a queerness that works against all laws that control and confine us—the codified laws that lock us up, degrade our lives, and fail to address the root causes of violence; the cultural laws that have us pointing fingers at one another rather than at violent systems and structures; the social laws that break us down into good and bad, innocent and guilty, worthy and unworthy, and respectable and deviant; the internalized laws that tell us we must hide who we are and what we have done in order to belong. I want us to tear down the laws that foster every type of violence, not just anti-LGBTQ+ violence, and not just interpersonal violence. In this sense, of being against the law, the conceptual linkage between queerness and criminality is not one to run from but one to embrace.

NOTES

1. American Civil Liberties Union, "Mapping Attacks on LGBTQ Rights in U.S. State Legislatures"; Anti-Defamation League and GLAAD, "Year in Review: Anti-LGBTQ+ Hate & Extremism Incidents"; Center for Countering Digital Hate and Human Rights Campaign, *Digital Hate: Social Media's Role in Amplifying Dangerous Lies about LGBTQ+ People.*

2. Cohen, "Punks, Bulldaggers, and Welfare Queens: The Radical Potential of Queer Politics."

3. Manion, *Female Husbands: A Trans History.*

4. Angelides, "The Homosexualization of Pedophilia."

5. Kirchick, "The Long, Sordid History of the Gay Conspiracy Theory."

6. Beck, *We Believe the Children: A Moral Panic in the 1980s.*

7. Karpman, "The Sexual Psychopath"; Pratt, "The Rise and Fall of Homophobia and Sexual Psychopath Legislation in Postwar Society"; Sutherland, "The Sexual Psychopath Laws."

8. Eskridge, *Dishonorable Passions: Sodomy Laws in America, 1861–2003.*

9. Eskridge, 6.

10. Eskridge, *Gaylaw: Challenging the Apartheid of the Closet*; Lvovsky, *Vice Patrol: Cops, Courts, and the Struggle over Urban Gay Life before Stonewall*; Lawrence v. Texas, No. 539 (US 558 2003).

11. Leslie, "Creating Criminals: The Injuries Inflicted by 'Unenforced' Sodomy Laws."

12. International Lesbian, Bisexual, Gay, Trans, and Intersex Association, "Legal Frameworks."

13. Capers, "Cross Dressing and the Criminal"; Redburn, "Before Equal Protection: The Fall of Cross-Dressing Bans and the Transgender Legal Movement, 1963–86," 688.

14. Eskridge, *Gaylaw: Challenging the Apartheid of the Closet*; Lvovsky, *Vice Patrol: Cops, Courts, and the Struggle over Urban Gay Life before Stonewall.*

15. American Civil Liberties Union, "Mapping Attacks on LGBTQ Rights in U.S. State Legislatures"; Mogul, Ritchie, and Whitlock, *Queer (In)Justice: The Criminalization of LGBT People in the United States*; Ritchie, *Invisible No More: Police Violence against Black Women and Women of Color.*

16. Kelley, "The Playboy Interview with Anita Bryant."

17. Bryant, *The Anita Bryant Story: The Survival of Our Nation's Families and the Threat of Militant Homosexuality*, 114.

18. Bryant, 114.

19. Bryant, *The Anita Bryant Story: The Survival of Our Nation's Families and the Threat of Militant Homosexuality*; Kelley, "The Playboy Interview with Anita Bryant."

20. Beck, *We Believe the Children: A Moral Panic in the 1980s*.

21. American Civil Liberties Union, "Mapping Attacks on LGBTQ Rights in U.S. State Legislatures."

22. Anti-Defamation League, "What Is 'Grooming'? The Truth behind the Dangerous, Bigoted Lie Targeting the LGBTQ+ Community"; Block, "Accusations of 'Grooming' Are the Latest Political Attack—with Homophobic Origins"; Center for Countering Digital Hate and Human Rights Campaign, *Digital Hate: Social Media's Role in Amplifying Dangerous Lies about LGBTQ+ People*.

23. Crissman et al., "Youth Perspectives Regarding the Regulating of Bathroom Use by Transgender Individuals"; Robertson et al., "We Are Just People: Transgender Individuals' Experiences of a Local Equal Rights Debate."

24. *Disclosure*.

25. Block, "Accusations of 'Grooming' Are the Latest Political Attack—with Homophobic Origins."

26. Rozsa, "Why the Moral Panic over 'Grooming' Is So Effective at Manipulating the Right-Wing Mind."

27. Anti-Defamation League, "What Is 'Grooming'? The Truth behind the Dangerous, Bigoted Lie Targeting the LGBTQ+ Community."

28. Brammer, "Behind the Weird Internet Scheme to Associate Pedophiles with the LGBTQ+ Community."

29. Scarlett, "Doctors Speak to Claims about Gender-Confirming Care"; Siegel, "We Are Not 'Groomers': How Anti-LGBTQ Stereotypes Inhibit Reproductive Justice"; Kindy, "Historic Surge in Bills Targeting Transgender Rights Pass at Record Speed."

30. Not a Criminal Campaign, "Home," March 13, 2023, https://notacriminal.org/.

31. See, for example, Anti-Defamation League, "What Is 'Grooming'? The Truth behind the Dangerous, Bigoted Lie Targeting the LGBTQ+ Community"; Czopek, "Why It's Not 'Grooming': What Research Says about Gender and Sexuality in Schools"; Connecticut Alliance to End Sexual Violence, "Fighting Anti-LGBTQ+ Grooming Rhetoric."

32. Block, "Accusations of 'Grooming' Are the Latest Political Attack—with Homophobic Origins"; Freedom to Marry, "Using Online Video to Make the Case for the Freedom to Marry."

33. GLAAD, "PSA: Protect Our Families."

34. Movement Advancement Project, "Messaging Guides."

35. Movement Advancement Project, *Talking about Anti-LGBTQ School Bills & False "Groomer" Attacks*, 2.

36. Movement Advancement Project, *Talking about Transgender People & Restrooms*, 3.

37. Movement Advancement Project, *Talking about Transgender Youth Participation in Sports*, 2.

38. Movement Advancement Project, *Talking about Transgender Students & School Facilities Access*, 3.

39. Cohen, "Punks, Bulldaggers, and Welfare Queens: The Radical Potential of Queer Politics."

40. Cohen, 438–39.

41. Cohen, 439.

42. Cohen, 440.

43. Cohen, 438.

44. Cohen, 441.

45. Because of this, Cohen ("Punks, Bulldaggers, and Welfare Queens: The Radical Potential of Queer Politics") notes the very term *queer* was one relatively unappealing to LGBT people of color who associated the term with unexamined "class, race, and gender privilege" (p. 451) and alienated LGBTQ+ people of color who did not see the experiences and needs of their families and communities represented in dominant queer politics.

46. Cohen, "Punks, Bulldaggers, and Welfare Queens: The Radical Potential of Queer Politics," 457 (emphasis in original).

47. Cohen, 448.

48. Anti-Defamation League, "What Is 'Grooming'? The Truth behind the Dangerous, Bigoted Lie Targeting the LGBTQ+ Community"; Center for Countering Digital Hate and Human Rights Campaign, *Digital Hate: Social Media's Role in Amplifying Dangerous Lies about LGBTQ+ People*.

49. Alfonseca, "Some Republicans Use False 'Pedophilia' Claims to Attack Democrats, LGBTQ People."

50. Rozsa, "Why the Moral Panic over 'Grooming' Is So Effective at Manipulating the Right-Wing Mind."

51. Romano, "The Right's Moral Panic over 'Grooming' Invokes Age-Old Homophobia."

52. Jenny Coleman, as quoted in Keveney, "Weaponized Grooming Rhetoric Is Taking a Toll on LGBTQ Community and Child Sex Abuse Survivors."

53. Angelides, "The Homosexualization of Pedophilia"; Beck, *We Believe the Children: A Moral Panic in the 1980s*; Chenier, "The Natural Order of Disorder: Pedophilia, Stranger Danger and the Normalising Family"; Ohi, "Molestation 101: Child Abuse, Homophobia, and the Boys of St. Vincent."

54. Ohi, "Molestation 101: Child Abuse, Homophobia, and the Boys of St. Vincent," 196.

55. Ohi, 235.

56. Rozsa, "Why the Moral Panic over 'Grooming' Is So Effective at Manipulating the Right-Wing Mind."

57. Anti-Defamation League, "What Is 'Grooming'? The Truth behind the Dangerous, Bigoted Lie Targeting the LGBTQ+ Community."

58. Brammer, "Behind the Weird Internet Scheme to Associate Pedophiles with the LGBTQ+ Community."

59. Ryan, *The Women's House of Detention: A Queer History of a Forgotten Prison*, 276.

60. The Stonewall Inn was a mere five hundred feet from the prison.

61. Kunzel, *Criminal Intimacy: Prison and the Uneven History of Modern American Sexuality*, 193–94.

62. Kunzel, 195.

63. Walker et al., "Why Don't We Center Abolition in Queer Criminology?"

64. Cohen, "Punks, Bulldaggers, and Welfare Queens: The Radical Potential of Queer Politics," 438.

65. See, for example, Conrad, *Against Equality: Queer Revolution, Not Mere Inclusion*.

CHAPTER 9

(Un)DocuQueer

Trapped within Bodies, Borders, and Systems

KAREN Z. ARMENTA ROJAS, BOISE STATE UNIVERSITY

In the late 1800s, following the railroad boom and the Second Industrial Revolution, demand for cheap labor emerged in the United States. Newly acquired territories invited significant westward migration. Oppression, famine, wars, and collapsing economies worldwide fueled a wave of people seeking better opportunities. This influx of people pressured Congress to regulate the immigration process, which transformed into the Bureau of Immigration, housed within the Department of Commerce and Labor. In the early twentieth century, federal attention shifted to standardizing naturalization procedures, which led to the Independent Bureau of Naturalization, and subsequently, the Immigration and Naturalization Service (INS), which existed within the Department of Justice (DOJ) before 9/11.[1] In November 2002, the Homeland Security Act triggered the most extensive government reorganization since the creation of the Department of Defense (DOD). In 2003, Immigration and Customs Enforcement (ICE) was established, with civil and criminal jurisdiction synergy to enhance public safety and protect national security.[2] ICE has treated immigrants as a security threat—not as human beings.

Ostensibly, ICE has become the poster child for the Department of Homeland Security's (DHS's) inhumane excesses. ICE's primary goal is securing the nation's borders and safeguarding the integrity of the US immigration system, which is a primary focus of ICE officers and agents throughout the country.[3] Immigration enforcement is the largest area of responsibility for Enforcement and Removal Operations (ERO) and is a critical part of the nation's overall safety, security, and well-being.[4] However, placing immigration under the oversight of the national security sector rather than commerce or labor promotes anti-immigration rhetoric with xenophobic and racist undertones. When the United States assumes that refugees and asylum seekers may be terrorists, how is it possible for ICE to fulfill its humanitarian obligations?

Additionally, ERO manages the detention and deportation of unauthorized people in the United States, previously the task of INS. However, instead of contributing to the nation's welfare and safety, the agency has become a political pawn for each administration. Consequently, the government created an agency that routinely changes administration and economic conditions to make US citizens and residents feel safer and improve border control system efficiency.[5]

As one of the United States' premier federal law enforcement agencies, ICE is dedicated to detecting and dismantling transnational criminal networks that threaten US industries, organizations, and financial systems.[6] However, ICE agents have appealed to DHS Secretary Kirstjen Nielsen to overhaul the agency.[7] In 2018, nineteen special agents in charge of ICE's Homeland Security Investigations (HSI) division urged Nielsen to split the agency into separate agencies due to HSI's and ERO's divergent goals and functions. The plea suggests that US arrests and deportations significantly impact transnational crime, which is HSI's largest area of responsibility.[8] Hence, the cruelty perpetrated by zero-tolerance immigration policies is by design. Each actor in the process, from the officers executing warrants to the supervisors approving deportation orders, shares responsibility, spreading it thinly to diminish personal accountability. By desensitizing every actor involved, the process can portray them as human rights violators. Thus, the fundamental goal is to replace xenophobic reasoning with moral reasoning.

The message was clear: immigration policy would be critical to the nation's counterterrorism efforts, as ICE was solely tasked with punitive immigration law enforcement. While ICE's civil enforcement efforts, by its assessment, are unrelated to the DHS's national security mission, the DHS significantly influenced ICE's aggressive tactics. Over the years, ICE has gained a reputation for corruption, abuse, racism, and regular law violations.[9] In addition, inhumane practices, such as separating children from their parents, caging them, and forcing them to defend themselves against trained government lawyers in their nonnative language, are everyday occurrences.[10]

Migration is a gendered process that impacts women, lesbians, gays, bisexuals, transgender, queer/questioning, and two-spirit (LGBTQ2S+) communities differently from heterosexual/cisgender men. *Queer migration* refers to a member of the LGBTQ2S+ communities who crossed an international and/or domestic border(s) without making distinctions based on people's state-conferred legal statuses and militarized practices that discriminate and oppress them. Women and LGBTQ2S+ people migrate for a variety of reasons; most do so to escape gender inequalities (i.e., sexual/gender-based violence). Vulnerability does not affect all migrants, refugees, or asylum seekers equally. Those marginalized due to their country of origin, race, class, ability, religion, gender, and sexuality often encounter the most difficulties throughout their migration.[11] LGBTQ2S+ people face persecution and discrimination from sovereign governments worldwide. Unfortunately, this reality incentivizes LGBTQ2S+ people to seek asylum in the United States and other countries, even those without civil wars and widespread conflict. People seeking asylum and refugee status in the United States face different processes and outcomes, depending on their country of origin and personal circumstances.

Ironically, Western media outlets and government officials declare the arrival and presence of many migrants as evidence of a *migration crisis*. However, it is imperative to reframe the *crisis* rhetoric of borders and prisons—walls and cages—and call it what it is—a global *human* crisis. Older policies and practices endorsed the competing concepts of assimilation and cultural pluralism that arose during an earlier period of mass immigration and genocide. Some migrants were allowed to retain their culture, while others were pressured to assimilate. The way migrants integrated into their communities varied, and those living in sanctuary cities were better positioned to resist assimilation due to protective policies. Assimilation in the United States is often described as a "melting pot."[12] This view stresses how diverse people helped construct the US society and contributed to its culture. The "melting pot" metaphor has been criticized for emphasizing assimilation and not recognizing the importance of diversity.[13]

Alternatively, cultural pluralism emphasizes the importance of diversity and recognizes the coexistence of different groups while maintaining their unique identities. Assimilation involves distinct groups merging socially and sharing a common culture, decreasing group differences over time.[14] In contrast, pluralism exists when groups maintain their identities. In a pluralistic society, groups remain separate, and cultural and social differences are preserved.[15] Assimilation and cultural pluralism are central to understanding immigrant communities and sanctuary cities. Sanctuary cities have adopted policies to protect undocumented immigrants from deportation by limiting cooperation with federal immigration authorities.[16] These policies have faced criticism for conflicting with the assimilation process, and it can be argued that they are necessary to safeguard vulnerable populations.[17]

Early twentieth-century immigration policies and practices codified two tracks: one for admission and settlement by primary migrants from northern and western Europe, structured around hetero-nuclear families with a male breadwinner; and one for migrants from Mexico, Central and South America, and the Caribbean, who were predominantly temporary (seasonal) and exploitable workers who were summoned as needed and quickly dismissed.[18] Current immigration policies derived from past administrative policies, further criminalizing and dehumanizing migrants. These policies include Operation Streamline, which needs, in most cases, the federal criminal prosecution of unauthorized immigrants caught (re)entering the country and government agents acting toward the Central American Caravan.[19] Building on this claim, *if* there is a "migration crisis," it stems from unaddressed conditions that force people to migrate. The impacts of punitive state, supranational, and populist responses include expanding criminalization, detention, and deportation.[20]

This chapter explains why ICE should be abolished, emphasizing the importance of understanding and examining the sexuality of international and domestic migration experiences in the United States, where similar institutions exist in varying forms. A theoretical framework for challenging a colonized gendered binary is discussed, as well as insights into heteronormative and cisnormative immigrant systems. Criminal justice and criminology professionals can benefit from understanding the regulation of queer migration through knowledge and experience. The chapter also emphasizes the significance of understanding the cultural and (de)colonized history of gender within bodies and systems. Overall, it aims to address the experiences of queer migrants and offer policy recommendations for improvement.

#ABOLISHICE

After US President Trump took office in his first term, his administration implemented strict immigration policies (e.g., denying asylum to refugees and separating undocumented children from their families), which prompted the call for ICE abolishment, also known as #AbolishICE. In 2018, #AbolishICE became a public outcry against the Trump administration's zero-tolerance immigration policies. They resulted in the separation and detention of families at the United States–Mexico border. Abolishing ICE in this context proposes that ICE's responsibilities be subsumed by a new immigration agency, pointing out the political rhetoric and beliefs that have led to this inhumane treatment of children and adults. However, holding one agency accountable for the dehumanizing treatment of migrants is no better than whitewashing, an issue rooted in colonialism and systematic racism. The DHS must consider the agency and immigration components (e.g., resource allocations, institutionalized intra-agency policy development, and institutional culture) when formulating and implementing immigration policy.

ICE operations should be questioned not only financially, as the agency continues to succeed at securing funding, but also from the perspective of people of color whose communities are directly affected by human rights violations and arbitrary conditions in detention centers.[21] For example, ICE's mistreatment of detainees has led to an astonishing number of deaths in their custody.[22] In addition, there is an ongoing pattern of gross medical negligence in immigration detention facilities nationwide.[23] However, governmental silence and inaction have turned immigrants and refugees—who have perished in the desert, gone missing, been murdered, or remain in detention purgatory—into mere statistics.

When examining race, Brazilian critical pedagogist Paulo Freire cautioned against the danger of marginalized people becoming oppressors rather than fighting for their freedom.[24] Freire uses his experiences and argues that addressing this issue as an intellectual exercise and merely looking at the systemic problem at the macro level, not the micro level, is problematic. In Southern California alone, 40 percent of ICE agents are Latino, and one in three US Customs and Border Protection (CBP) employees is Latino. During recent years, CBP used its discretion to illegally turn away refugees at US land ports of entry, where "the trap," illustrated in figure 1, effectively pushes migrants and refugees to enter through unsafe and lethal routes.[25] Through discretionary border policing practices, US land ports of entry have become the epicenter of human suffering. Racism has been institutionalized in our immigration enforcement regime, targeting any deviation from the Western norm.[26]

The border is a trap. Begun in 2005, Operation Streamline has criminalized border crossing. Authorized ports of entry, tiny holes shown here as 15-miles wide, turn back asylum seekers, pushing them into the 100-mile-wide border zone, where they are exposed to harsh conditions from both the environment and law enforcement.

| Tiles © Esri — Source: Esri, i-cubed, USDA, USGS, AEX, GeoEye, Getmapping, Aerogrid, IGN, IGP, UPR-EGP, and the GIS User Community

FIGURE 1. Screenshot of "The Trap," a portion of a scholarly activism project mapping the outcomes of the United States' 2018 "zero tolerance policy" for asylum seekers at US ports of entry. Adapted from *Torn Apart/Separados*, vol. 1, by Columbia University, 2018 (https://xpmethod.columbia.edu/torn-apart/volume/1/). Licensed under a Creative Commons Attribution 4.0 International License (CC-BY).

During the writing of this chapter, Operation Lone Star exposed a glimpse into the human cost of Texas's discretionary border policing practices. Following Texas's refusal to remove the floating barrier deployed in July 2023 on the Rio Grande near Eagle Pass, the DOJ sued Texas and its governor, Greg Abbott.[27] During soaring temperatures, the inhumane and unlawful actions by xenophobic Texas governor Greg Abbott involved Texas troopers pushing migrants into the treacherous Rio Grande River and denying them access to drinking water.[28] Abbott's miles of razor wire and buoys meant to deter crossing caused irreparable harm by endangering lives and disregarding human rights and dignity principles. The refusal to process refugees at ports of entry upon arrival, as required by Title 8 of the US Code, violates US international treaty obligations and federal law.[29] The Biden administration should not have been in the punitive business against refugee families for trying to enter the United States to save their lives, knowing CBP's illegal conduct forced refugees to enter the country between ports of entry and without inspection. The federal government cannot create the problem it complains about and then propose a solution that violates human rights. Nevertheless, Texas passed three major anti-immigration laws: Texas Senate Bill 4, House Bill 4, and House Bill 6.

QUEER MIGRATION

Queer migrants refers to members of the LGBTQ2S+ communities crossing an international or domestic border; this term does not discriminate based on people's state-conferred legal statuses.[30] This is because legal status reflects not the types of migrants but the workings of power and knowledge that seek to differentiate migrants, delimit the rights and protections they will be granted or denied, and shape forms of surveillance.[31] By contrast, people from war-torn countries are given more asylum possibilities, work authorization, and residency if they can afford the process and survive the journey. However, this triggers the memories of privileged migrants who fit the narrow spectrum of state-designed family ties, skill sets, large bank accounts (e.g., approximately between $4,000 and 12,000),[32] or protection needs, as possibilities for acquiring legal status have been reduced or heavily priced. As a trans-border student, I witnessed the privilege and vulnerability associated with "proper" documentation and was aware of the visa requirements and financial resources needed that do not guarantee "proper" documentation. US asylum and migration processes are discriminatory because they grant asylum and refugee status to certain groups while denying it to others. Asylum seekers, migrants, and refugees who identify as LGBTQ2S+ are adversely affected. While pursuing my immigration process as an adult, I decided to try the "right way" politicians advocate and change my immigration status postgraduation. Since getting a visa requires proof of vast financial resources, I rely on family and friends' solidarity and support to survive. My plea to turn "hashtag" solidarity into tangible support was met with a tiny fraction of friends' financial, emotional, and/or physical support. As my "allies" distance themselves from their guilt by supporting a privileged immigration system, their solidarity hashtags further disempower me as I continue to wait for an immigration appointment years later. Even though my experience is coated with privilege, thanks to the support of my nuclear family and a few friends, I experienced homelessness, mental health issues, racism, and restrictions to mainstream health services, and still experience unemployment due to my "pending" status.

Stories of human suffering that have reopened old wounds from my interactions with CBP are becoming more common as, in recent decades, the number of LGBTQ2S+ refugees and asylum seekers increases. Volunteering with a nonprofit that offers legal and humanitarian support to refugees, deportees, and other migrants at the United States–

Mexico border, I would be taken back to my childhood, hearing stories of humans trafficked or missing relatives who vanished across the border, never to be seen or heard from again, or those who return home only to disappear at the hands of cartels. The wounds worsened when listening to their experiences, which triggered my memories of racial profiling and excessive force at the hands of CBP agents. When I spoke with LGBTQ2S+ refugees, deportees, and other migrants about their experiences and collected evidence of their (poly)victimization necessary for their case, the parallel between coming out as queer and coming out as undocumented became visibly strained. For transgender and gender-nonconforming (TGNC) people, lacking the resources to express their gender identity while fleeing danger can increase their risk of harm.

A challenge unique to TGNC people is their *aesthetics of survival*. Nef discusses the prevailing misconceptions about transgender women and illustrates the struggle to shape/frame their bodies per patriarchal beauty standards, not because these standards are reasonable or valid, but because they preserve dignity and even save their lives.[33] A robust body of literature exists documenting intersectional oppression in the form of assumptions and stereotypes of sexual assault victims (e.g., rape victims/survivors' clothing or appearance). As a risk-reduction strategy, the aesthetics of survival within the LGBTQ2S+ communities have long been recognized when examining femininity. Embodiment of femininity can be the difference between life and death for trans women but does not account for how colonization and patriarchy are inscribed in their bodies.

Goldberg and Conron estimated 289,700 lesbian, gay, bisexual, and transgender (LGBT-identified) people among the adult undocumented immigrant population, representing approximately 3.0 percent of undocumented adults in the United States.[34] Relative to all undocumented immigrants, LGBT undocumented adult immigrants are predominantly male and younger than all undocumented immigrants.[35] Nearly half (48.3%) of LGBT undocumented immigrants are between the ages of eighteen and twenty-nine, compared with about a fifth of undocumented immigrants (21.9%). Additionally, 61.8 percent of LGBT undocumented immigrants are male, compared to 54.0 percent of adult undocumented immigrants and 42.2 percent of all LGBT adults in the United States. Approximately 75.7 percent of LGBT undocumented adults are Latinx, and 13.6 percent are Asian American or Pacific Islander.[36] Nevertheless, further research is warranted regarding LGBTQ2S+ (im)migrants.

Using data from the Pew Research Center, the 2017 Gallup Daily Tracking survey, and the U.S. Census Bureau's American Community Survey, Shoshana Goldberg and Kerith Conron, scholars associated with the Williams Institute at the UCLA School of Law, estimated the number of LGBT-identified (un)documented adult immigrants and foreign-national residents who were part of a same-sex couple.[37] Goldberg and Conron estimated 1,274,500 LGBT foreign-born adults in the United States, including 289,700 (22.7%) who were undocumented and 984,800 (77.3%) who were documented.[38] Moreover, they found that in the United States about 128,500 same-sex couples included at least one foreign-national partner/spouse. Approximately 94,400 of these couples were binational, meaning one partner/spouse was a native-born US citizen and the other was either a naturalized citizen or a noncitizen.

As LGBTQ2S+ identities and families are vulnerable to legal intervention and separation from the state, institutions, and/or nonqueer people, it is vital to protect the legalization of same-sex marriage and abolish Western binary gender norms (i.e., male/female) to provide a route to avoid and prevent adoption discrimination based on sexual/gender orientation.

ABOLISHING THE WESTERN SEX/GENDER BINARY

Origins of Gender

Indigenous people were colonized not only to take or control their land and natural resources but also their bodies and culture. Colonizers' insistence on adherence to Western gender roles began to change the way Indigenous people expressed their roles. Before colonization, traditional Indigenous women's roles were to collect food provisions and make household tools.[39] In contrast, young Indigenous girls who attended residential schools were taught domestic skills to enter occupations that affirmed their prescribed Westernized gender roles. Through colonization, Indigenous people devolved from matriarchal societies to patriarchal ones, which created a societal shift in gender dynamics, thus promoting a continuous cycle of violence and placing Indigenous women in more danger.[40]

As a system, the Western sex/gender binary is a classic prison system that further marginalizes females and trans and nonbinary (TNB) to do unpaid labor (e.g., reproductive labor, homemaking, and childcare), as cisgender men are the dominating class. A look at colonialism exposes discrimination toward Indigenous people and further discrimination toward nondichotomous gender-nonconforming people, who often face unique challenges related to their marginalized identities since colonization. The imposition of Western labels forced a semantic shift from their social roles to allegedly deviant and sexual behavior among those who did not conform to a dichotomous gender system.[41] Hence, transgender people are those whose gender identity, expression, and/or role does not conform to what is culturally associated with their sex assigned at birth.[42] Some transgender people hold Westernized binary genders (i.e., male/female). However, others have genders outside this binary, such as gender fluid or nonbinary (e.g., LGBTQ2S+).

Though the term *two-spirit* has been used since the 1990s,[43] the Indian Health Services (IHS) discuss how, traditionally, Indigenous two-spirit people were male, female, and intersex people who combined the activities of both men and women with traits unique to their status.[44] Two-spirit and muxes—Mexican Indigenous people who identify as a cultural third gender identity and spirituality—may act within a binary sex norm but express themselves in ways associated with their opposite gender or a cultural third gender with varying roles across North America. Additionally, they share common characteristics, such as specialized work roles, gender variation, spiritual sanction, and same-sex relations.[45] When navigating spaces regarding LGBTQ2S+ and Indigenous communities, it is imperative to acknowledge and understand the impact of colonization through historical trauma and oppression.[46]

When studying the history of gender through the lens of colonization, it is important to recognize that binary gender is a societal construct based on westernized notions of gendered behavior.[47] Regarding the concept of *coloniality of gender*, decolonial feminist Maria Lugones views gender as central to the conceptualization of the coloniality of power, as race was to Peruvian sociologist Anibal Quijano, who theorized the central decolonial concept, *the coloniality of power*, and hence as something to be equally understood as a *colonial* construct.[48] While Lugones's *coloniality of gender* is included in many of the Modernity/Coloniality Group's publications and given public lip service, few decolonial theorists incorporate the concept into their central tenets.[49]

Though adherence to binary gender has sociological, cultural, medical, legal, historical, and religious influences, its abolition must eliminate labels that have further stigmatized and discriminated against a person. However, to abolish Western notions of binary gender norms and roles, it is necessary to abolish cultural binary notions of sex, another social construct that groups genotypic and phenotypic characteristics (i.e., chromosomes and genitalia) into only two categories: male or female.[50] Binary male/female concepts do not adequately capture the evolution and diversity in society. Additionally, binary notions of sex and gender are rooted in violence and *gendercide* (e.g., third gender, genocide, femicide, or androcide). The compulsion to categorize bodies in binary terms implies that people identifying with other genders are invisible.

Hence, limited notions of gender variance only perpetuate the colonization of bodies. Still, the criminalization of gender diversity (e.g., banning gender-affirming care, binary bathroom bills, LGBTQ2S+ censorship, etc.) traps TNB people within their bodies and criminal processing systems.

Within Bodies and Systems

Western society perpetuates gendered material divisions through institutions and economic incentives. Eliminating these structures through policy action is necessary to abolish binary categorizations of gender through simple, prompt, low-cost, transparent procedures that also maintain the privacy of applicants' nonbinary gender by eliminating burdensome requirements on applicants (e.g., submitting psychological evaluations and other medical records).[51] Nevertheless, abolishing ICE and binary categorizations of sex and gender is complex and cannot be achieved with policy action alone due to the complex nature of sex and gender relationships deeply rooted in our bodies and mediated by societal ideas and beliefs. A path toward *postgenderism*—which challenges a social constructionist account of gender and sexuality and proposes the transcending of gender via social and political means[52]—can be found in modern fertility technology, universal health care, and acceptance of the LGBTQ2S+ communities. It is important to abolish the criminalization of sexuality and gender expression beyond the binary.[53] It is important, nevertheless, to note that postgenderists advocate for gender traits to become choices, rather than aiming for the elimination of all gender traits or universal androgyny.[54]

First, universal health care and accepting the LGBTQ2S+ communities are crucial, as LGBTQ2S+ people, especially transgender people, must often provide medical documents for name and gender changes. Legal scholar Lisa Mottet examines the literature and analyzes the 1977 Model State Vital Statistics Act (MVSA) developed by the U.S. Department of Health and Human Services, which guided states on the most efficient laws and procedures related to maintaining accurate birth, death, and other vital records at the state, local, and territorial level.[55] As a result, there is no current federal law, and states have varying policies. The 1977 MVSA acknowledged that vital records should be corrected for people who change their gender.[56] Unfortunately, states require evidence and documentation that applicants are privileged enough to go through a "surgical procedure" or have medical documentation but are highly encouraged to go through the process after applicants change their sex and provide a court order to that effect. Scholars and experts in transgender law and medicine reject the idea that gender recognition should come only after surgery.[57] This notion has also been significantly enshrined in law and policy. Despite opposition, some states have allowed a third gender marker on identification documents. Experiencing these unique obstacles, the United States has taken steps for passport applicants to self-select their gender without requiring medical documentation, even if their selected gender differs from their other citizenship or identity documents. Though universal health care would not eliminate gender and sex disparities, it would offer some relief regarding proper documentation on all state and federal records.

When LGBTQ2S+ people may be forced to flee their homes and seek refuge status, they typically fear persecution based on their sexual orientation, gender identity/expression, or sexual characteristics.[58] In addition to experiencing displacement from their physical homes, LGBTQ2S+ refugees, asylum seekers, and migrants experience discrimination, persecution, and violence, some of which occur daily.

Adopting the "X" gender marker option in official documents is increasing in some countries, but its usage is still relatively low. TNB people worry about safety while traveling with an unspecified marker. Given that most countries' visa applications and many airline systems offer predominantly binary options for identifying sex/gender, the "X" leads to discrepancies between documents, which can trigger security responses. Although border management systems and agencies have taken steps to train their personnel, much work is needed. The "X" remains unknown to many international and national border control agents and passport screeners. Not all security technologies and computer systems have been updated to include third-gender options.[59]

Including a third gender/sex in passports significantly impacts TNB travelers and migrants when crossing borders. Although it may seem a minor bureaucratic matter to those whose gender presentation aligns with their documentation, TNB populations regularly experience harassment and disenfranchisement while traveling internationally, including being questioned or detained because of documentation that does not meet the expectations of border control authorities and security technologies. This treatment is often due to discrepancies between physical appearance (e.g., gender expression, dress, behavior) and the sex/gender marker in identity documents. Updating documentation to align with their gender can be administratively and medically challenging, leading to inconsistencies across documents and possibly detainment due to alleged identity document falsification. Further, full body scans and pat-downs can humiliate or harass TNB people. Thus, a wealth gap and lack of documentation might hinder the process for undocumented citizens and noncitizens.[60]

Though the argument can be made that it would be easier if undocumented noncitizens migrated with current legal documentation, it is essential to note that immigration control has long been a key technology for producing a heteronormative US nation and citizenry.[61] Hence, such privilege is not possible for everyone, as LGBTQ2S+ migrants may not have the resources to go through the immigration process, even if their case is expedited. As with colonization, immigration controls took shape in the context of westward expansion; ongoing dispossession of Native communities through the Dawes Act of 1887; efforts to recruit recently freed Black people into state-sanctioned forms of marriage and subordinated labor that upheld White sexual, gender, and property relationships and logics; and a growing overseas empire.[62] According to Eithne Luibhéid and Karma R. Chávez, nation-state and federal-level immigration policies and practices became key instruments for producing and policing changing forms of nationalist heteronormativity in the 1880s.[63] A call to abolish ICE and the Western gender and sexual binary means decolonizing ourselves. Decolonizing oneself requires recognizing and acknowledging the effects of colonization on a personal level. It entails confronting and dismantling the internalized colonial systems, ideologies, and power structures that shape our identities and relationships. By engaging in this process, people can strive to reclaim their agency, challenge oppressive norms, and hold physical spaces to listen to the experiences of undocumented and queer migrants.

Regarding the LGBTQ2S+ communities, it is crucial to understand the historical and social context of terms, with a keen awareness that some terms (e.g., queer) have been used in the past to denigrate members of the LGBTQ2S+ communities and that the term continues to be rejected by many.[64] Similarly, understanding the intersectionality of race and the

LGBTQ2S+ communities, particularly evident in events like the Stonewall riots and symbols like the black and brown stripes on the rainbow flag, is vital. Studying the relationships between race, migration/immigration, and queerness helps us recognize that White queer people share a queer experience but benefit from White supremacy and are not above wielding that power when it comes to safe spaces and voting for anti-immigration policies. Ending the use of immigration policy to criminalize people of color, exploit workers, and perpetuate the deadly wealth gap within the legal process of the immigration process could be possible.

Secondly, it is essential to create space and be accepting of LGBTQ2S+ communities. However, with the rise of anti-LGBTQ2S+ policies, we continue to see state legislatures advancing bills targeting the LGBTQ2S+ communities by criminalizing TNB health care (e.g., restricting/banning access to gender-affirming care) to prohibiting TNB youth from athletics and academic institutions (e.g., restricting/banning LGBTQ2S+ topics and books), to name a few examples. Instead of creating space and being accepting of the LGBTQ2S+ communities, insincere rhetoric and ineligible policy reflect a polarized bipartisan consensus, where immigrant labor is feted, but their humanity is denied.

Lastly, by abolishing ICE and reforming the immigration system, we face the problem of institutional and societal adherence to Western notions of the sex/gender binary. That is a problem of categorization, which leads to criminalization that can be addressed by redesigning the system under abolitionist and decolonization principles. This is important, as detention facilities' administrative segregation disproportionately targets trans people and is enforced as solitary confinement.[65] For instance, trans people are housed away from the general population for seventy-two hours while the committee's assessment is completed.[66] Housing accommodations during this period may include placement in a medical unit, protective custody, or, as a last resort, administrative segregation.[67] However, scholars warn about the risks associated with solitary confinement.[68] Even though there are several standards of care and guidelines produced by TNB people in detention facilities, various reports have shown that ICE has not or has inappropriately implemented these guidelines; hence, ICE is to be abolished.[69]

Moreover, regardless of whether they can remain in the United States, transgender immigrants and asylum seekers are often detained until immigration courts decide their cases.[70] As a result, LGBTQ2S+ asylum seekers, particularly TNB people, face exacerbated risks of violence, policing, and containment at the hands of state and nonstate entities.

For example, in detention, lesbian, gay, bisexual, transgender, queer/questioning, and intersex (LGBTQI) migrants often get placed in solitary confinement and are at increased risk of sexual assault and physical violence at the hands of detention officials and other detainees and experience a higher risk of illness and medical neglect.[71]

LGBTQ2S+ people, especially transgender people, face discrimination and violence within prisons and detention facilities.[72] Historically, through the establishment of statutes and laws (e.g., the Lavender Scare; the Immigration and Nationality Act of 1965, explicitly preventing "sexual deviates" from entering the country; the Defense of Marriage Act), the stigma among gender identification beyond cisheterosexuality has persisted. By supporting the LGBTQ2S+ communities and their rights, allies are critical in combating harassment and discrimination. Additionally, with the help of nongovernmental agencies and local agencies intervening to prevent intergovernmental service agreements from housing detained immigrants or blocking funding for new jails, an independent immigration system can be created without the systemic abuses housed within the judicial and criminal processing systems.

DISCUSSION

With immigration action stalled, examining and questioning the current system's structure is crucial.[73] Rather than proposing theoretical changes, humanely implementing culturally fair changes dictates the nation's immigration laws. Nevertheless, dehumanizing rhetoric is used to justify xenophobic policies and influence public attitudes toward immigration. Language has been weaponized to attack entire communities and rationalize the cruel treatment of immigrants, asylum seekers, refugees, and migrants. The immigration system faces many issues due to Congress's failure to update immigration laws to reflect national needs. However, DHS also fails to address immigration problems systematically. Instead, attempts to rectify them within each department must be discussed as a system—a structure of society. Providing culturally informed practices and expenditures that shift from the ERO's detention practices to partnering with effective governmental agencies and establishing humane removal methods is needed.

Having legal gender recognition, which involves changing a person's sex/gender marker and name on official identity documents, is critical to abolish binary gender norms in a society that misgenders people in life and death. Demonizing and criminalizing LGBTQ2S+ identities insults their memory and disrespects their life. *Deadnaming*—referring to them by their former name—and *misgendering*—referring to them by a gender identity they do not identify as—can cause emotional distress to TGNC people and their loved ones. Missing/murdered TGNC people often go unreported when news outlets rely on police reports that misidentify trans people.

Moreover, society disregards conceptual considerations that may be indifferent to or do not directly impact them. However, abolition goes beyond dismantling a system of oppression, colonization, and genocide. By utilizing resources that protect fundamental human rights, particularly for marginalized populations who flee their homes in search of freedom, we can reimagine and transform these problems. The goal is to create sustainable solutions that reduce violence and deaths caused by oppressive government agencies and any manifestation of violence.

Hence, the fundamental aim is to decolonize and abolish binary sex/gender norms and sexuality. Decolonizing and abolishing binary sex/gender norms can be achieved by raising awareness of queer migration, which recognizes that institutional adherence to binary gender categorizations imprisons people in their bodies. Inhumane immigration systems often impose binary categorizations of sex/gender upon queer migrants, further reinforcing the need for abolition. By our abolishing ICE and challenging binary notions of gender, queer migrants can survive and be seen without judgment or prejudice, rather than being documented as statistics.

NOTES

1. Mittelstadt et al., "Through the Prism of National Security: Major Immigration Policy and Program Changes in the Decade since 9/11."
2. U.S. Immigration and Customs Enforcement, "History of ICE."
3. U.S. Immigration and Customs Enforcement, "Mission."
4. U.S. Immigration and Customs Enforcement.
5. Chang, Jarenwattananon, and Sirianni, "Biden Hasn't Changed ICE's Budget, but He Has Changed the Agency's Approach."
6. U.S. Immigration and Customs Enforcement, "Mission."
7. Buch, "ICE Criminal Investigators Ask to Be Distanced from Detentions, Deportations in Letter to Kirstjen Nielsen."
8. U.S. Immigration and Customs Enforcement, "Mission."
9. Grassini et al., "Characteristics of Deaths among Individuals in US Immigration and Customs Enforcement Detention Facilities, 2011–2018"; Terp et al., "Deaths in Immigration and Customs Enforcement (ICE) Detention: FY2018–2020."

10. Santos, "It's Children against Federal Lawyers in Immigration Court"; Kopan and Chavez, "There Are 2,300 Children Separated from Their Parents. What Will Happen to Them?"; "Children in Cages Are Not New."

11. Luibhéid and Chávez, *Queer and Trans Migrations: Dynamics of Illegalization, Detention, and Deportation.*

12. Pluralism Project, *The Right to Be Different.*

13. Pluralism Project.

14. Healey and O'Brien, "Assimilation and Pluralism: From Immigrants to White Ethnics."

15. Healey and O'Brien.

16. American Immigration Council, *Sanctuary Policies: An Overview.*

17. Healey and O'Brien, "Assimilation and Pluralism: From Immigrants to White Ethnics."

18. Luibhéid and Chávez, *Queer and Trans Migrations: Dynamics of Illegalization, Detention, and Deportation.*

19. Corradini et al., *Operation Streamline: No Evidence That Criminal Prosecution Deters Migration.*

20. Luibhéid and Chávez, *Queer and Trans Migrations: Dynamics of Illegalization, Detention, and Deportation.*

21. Mittelstadt et al., "Through the Prism of National Security: Major Immigration Policy and Program Changes in the Decade since 9/11."

22. Grassini et al., "Characteristics of Deaths among Individuals in US Immigration and Customs Enforcement Detention Facilities, 2011–2018"; Terp et al., "Deaths in Immigration and Customs Enforcement (ICE) Detention: FY2018–2020."

23. Gerena, "Clinical Implications for LGBT Asylum Seekers in US Detention Centers."

24. Freire, *Pedagogy of the Oppressed.*

25. Bach, "U.S. Sues Texas after Gov. Greg Abbott Declines to Remove Floating Border Barrier."

26. Hing, "Institutional Racism, ICE Raids, and Immigration Reform."

27. Bach, "U.S. Sues Texas after Gov. Greg Abbott Declines to Remove Floating Border Barrier."

28. Clarke et al., "Texas Troopers Told to Push Back Migrants into Rio Grande and Ordered Not to Give Water amid Soaring Temperatures, Report Says."

29. Aliens and Nationality, 8 U.S.C. et seq (1952).

30. Luibhéid and Chávez, *Queer and Trans Migrations: Dynamics of Illegalization, Detention, and Deportation.*

31. Luibhéid and Chávez.

32. *Economic Times*, "The Cost of Immigration to United States."

33. Nef, "The Aesthetics of Survival."

34. Goldberg and Conron, *LGBT Adult Immigrants in the United States.*

35. Gates, *LGBT Adult Immigrants in the United States*; Goldberg and Conron, *LGBT Adult Immigrants in the United States.*

36. Goldberg and Conron, *LGBT Adult Immigrants in the United States.*

37. Goldberg and Conron.

38. Goldberg and Conron.

39. McCallum, *Indigenous Women, Work, and History: 1940–1980.*

40. Gilbert, "Intimate Partner Violence in a Native American Community: An Exploratory Study."

41. Mongibello, "From 'Berdache' to 'Two-Spirit': Naming Indigenous Women-Men in Canada."

42. American Psychological Association, *Publication Manual of the American Psychological Association.*

43. Gilbert and Armenta Rojas, "Indigenous Victimization and the Colonized Rainbow."

44. Indian Health Services, "Two Spirit: Health Resources."

45. Garnets and Kimmel, *Psychological Perspectives on Lesbian, Gay, and Bisexual Experiences*; Indian Health Services, "Two Spirit: Health Resources."

46. Gilbert and Armenta Rojas, "Indigenous Victimization and the Colonized Rainbow."

47. Hegarty, Ansara, and Barker, "Nonbinary Gender Identities."

48. Mendoza, "Coloniality of Gender and Power: From Postcoloniality to Decoloniality."

49. Mendoza.

50. Decoster and Cannoot, "The Abolition of Sex/Gender Registration in the Age of Gender Self-Determination: An Interdisciplinary, Queer, Feminist and Human Rights Analysis."

51. Elias and Colvin, "A Third Option: Understanding and Assessing Non-Binary Gender Policies in the United States."

52. Dvorsky and Hughes, "Postgenderism: Beyond the Gender Binary."

53. Mottet, "Modernizing State Vital Statistics Statutes and Policies to Ensure Accurate Gender Markers on Birth Certificates: A Good Government Approach to Recognizing the Lives of Transgender People."

54. Dvorsky and Hughes, "Postgenderism: Beyond the Gender Binary."

55. Mottet, "Modernizing State Vital Statistics Statutes and Policies to Ensure Accurate Gender Markers on Birth Certificates: A Good Government Approach to Recognizing the Lives of Transgender People."

56. Mottet.

57. Mottet.

58. United Nations High Commissioner for Refugees, "LGBTIQ+ Persons."

59. Transportation Security Administration, "Transgender/Non Binary/Gender Nonconforming Passengers."

60. Elias and Colvin, "A Third Option: Understanding and Assessing Non-Binary Gender Policies in the United States."

61. Luibhéid and Chávez, *Queer and Trans Migrations: Dynamics of Illegalization, Detention, and Deportation.*

62. Luibhéid and Chávez.

63. Luibhéid and Chávez.

64. Lenning and Brightman, "Taking Stock of Queer Victimology."

65. Luibhéid and Chávez, *Queer and Trans Migrations: Dynamics of Illegalization, Detention, and Deportation*; Minero et al., "Latinx Trans Immigrants' Survival of Torture in U.S. Detention: A Qualitative Investigation of the Psychological Impact of Abuse and Mistreatment."

66. Human Rights Watch, "'Do You See How Much I'm Suffering Here?' Abuse against Transgender Women in US Immigration Detention."

67. Human Rights Watch.

68. Reiter, 23/7: *Pelican Bay Prison and the Rise of Long-Term Solitary Confinement*.

69. Minero et al., "Latinx Trans Immigrants' Survival of Torture in U.S. Detention: A Qualitative Investigation of the Psychological Impact of Abuse and Mistreatment."

70. Human Rights Watch, "'Do You See How Much I'm Suffering Here?' Abuse against Transgender Women in US Immigration Detention."

71. Gerena, "Clinical Implications for LGBT Asylum Seekers in US Detention Centers"; Minero et al., "Latinx Trans Immigrants' Survival of Torture in U.S. Detention: A Qualitative Investigation of the Psychological Impact of Abuse and Mistreatment"; Center for American Progress, "Release: LGBT Immigrants in Detention Centers at Severe Risk of Sexual Abuse."

72. Brown and McDuffie, "Health Care Policies Addressing Transgender Inmates in Prison Systems in the United States."

73. Weissert and Gomez Licon, "Immigration Reform Stalled Decade after Gang of 8's Big Push."

CHAPTER 10

A Conversation on the Criminalization of Queer People, Abolition Feminism, and Resisting Carceral Harms around Child Sexual Abuse

JENANI DEVI
MONICA RAMSY
ALISON REBA

Despite historic mobilizations calling for abolition of the prison-industrial complex (PIC) and its associated systems, addressing carceral responses around child sexual abuse (CSA) remains a "limit point" for widespread abolitionist action. Even with billions of dollars allocated for the policing and incarceration of "child sex offenders," the PIC ultimately exacerbates the marginalizations CSA survivors—especially QTBIPOC CSA survivors—face. On the one hand, mainstream conservative networks amplify fringe right-wing theories of the LGBTQ+ "superpredator" and invoke adultist rhetoric in the push for "parents' rights"; on the other hand, liberals and progressives push for "diversion" and "soft-on-crime" policies that help maintain the legitimacy of the larger system while failing to address the root factors of CSA. Considering today's resurgence of the 1960s–1970s frenzy against CSA, this bipartisan hesitation to resource community-led prevention praxis is troubling. The current landscape demands an abolitionist theory of change that acknowledges CSA's underlying individual, social, economic, and political conditions and centers prevention and healing, not disposability and punishment, as the path forward.

This conversation is between jenani devi, Monica Ramsy, and Alison Reba, three queer abolition feminists in their late twenties/early thirties who are working to increase the capacities of communities to engage in noncarceral CSA prevention.

HISTORY AND FRAMING

It's helpful to first ground this discussion with an overview of two major components of the CSA landscape: *(1) the legal histories that have created today's carceral CSA infrastructure*, and *(2) the statistics that outline the scope of the problem today.*

US lawmaking around CSA largely traces back to the 1970s—the flagship legislation on CSA, the Child Abuse Prevention and Treatment Act (CAPTA), was enacted in 1974.[1] Two political propaganda campaigns that reached their height in the 1970s and 1980s fueled the passage of CAPTA. The first campaign, largely led by politicians and mainstream media, called for an expanded carceral state by cultivating a widespread "sex panic" that "predators" lived among American communities.[2] Notably, the rhetoric used to create these "predator" images often relied on harmful stereotypes about Black, Brown, and LGBTQ+ individuals. As part of the second campaign, carceral advocates used the increasing awareness of child abuse as a public health problem—exemplified by the widespread attention given to Dr. Henry Kempe's work on "battered-child syndrome"—to create an expanded carceral state designed to "protect children."[3] CAPTA codified two prevailing vehicles of carceral CSA policy in the United States: sexual offender registries and mandated reporting policies.[4]

CSA legislation like CAPTA does not exist in a vacuum; rather, it exists as part of a larger "carceral feminist" legal universe that also includes legislation such as the Violence Against Women Act (VAWA). CAPTA expands carceral infrastructures established through VAWA by conditioning financial support on states' commitment to assess, investigate, and prosecute child abuse and neglect cases.[5] The federal establishment of CAPTA created a ripple effect; by 1976, all states had reporting laws requiring professionals to report sexual abuse.[6] Since its inception, CAPTA has been amended several times, most recently by the Victims of Child Abuse Act Reauthorization Act of 2018.[7]

Current statistics on CSA provide insights into the ongoing legacy of these carceral feminist laws. CSA is estimated to affect one in four girls and one in thirteen boys within the United States.[8] When looking at trans youth, research indicates that about one in five trans youth will experience sexual abuse, with trans kids being twice as likely to experience CSA as their cisgender peers.[9] Despite these already high figures, it is widely accepted that existing statistics grossly undercount the actual rates of CSA, as nearly 50 percent of people who have experienced CSA do not report the abuse.[10] A number of barriers contribute to these low disclosure rates, including trauma responses, fears of not being believed/being punished/being blamed, cultural barriers, a lack of understanding of what constitutes abuse, and limits to young people's confidentiality due to their minor status.[11]

Current statistics also help us make sense of how sensationalist narratives fail to capture the root causes of CSA. One such narrative suggests that child sexual abuse is solely perpetrated by the highly politicized figure of the "pedophile predator"—shadowy, more-animal-than-human adults that exist en masse in "bad" communities and lurk in "good" communities to prey on children. The reality is far from the propaganda. For example, research on criminalized child sex abuse shows that in 70.1 percent of cases involving girls who have been sexually abused and in 76.7 percent of cases involving boys who have been sexually abused, the abuser was another minor.[12] Furthermore, in only 9 percent of child sexual abuse cases is the harm-doer a total stranger; in 91 percent of cases, the individual who causes harm exists within the community of the young person.[13]

Federal dollar spending also fails to reflect or address what the statistics tell us about CSA. The United States spends $5.4 billion criminalizing and incarcerating 145,000 adults under CSA-related statues, and this does not even include maintaining the sex offender registry, surveillance, or policing.[14] *Essentially, then, $5.4 billion is allocated for the incarceration of adults when only 25 percent of reported CSA cases involve an adult harm-doer.* Even though cases between juveniles account for 75 percent of all reported CSA cases, we do not see three times this $5.4 billion funding being allocated to these sex offenses. For prevention, the United States allocates *$2 million* at the federal level to be dispersed for prevention research.[15] Even though the primary way to obtain funding for CSA prevention has been through upholding carceral regimes, the numbers reveal the inefficacy of these regimes—for every 1,000 sexual assaults, 975 cases do not lead to a conviction.[16]

In this sense, looking at CSA's legal history and current statistical landscape paints a grim picture, one in which nearly forty years of legislation has not only failed to meaningfully curb gender-based violence—let alone child sexual abuse—but has also expanded the reach of the carceral state in the name of feminist goals. By focusing particular attention on expanded investigation and reporting, CAPTA and VAWA have played a major role in providing the legal basis for our nationwide family policing and sex offense systems.[17] Rather than uprooting the structural causes of interpersonal violence, these laws address gender-based violence using "social death" mechanisms (i.e., sexual offense registries, incarceration, predictive policing, and civil commitment) that individualize blame and incentivize punishment over rehabilitation. These approaches have also systematically prevented communities from accessing the tools to prevent these forms of violence, making communities reliant on disposal in the hope that violence toward one will end the violence of another.

THE CONVERSATION

Section 1: Child Sexual Abuse, the Carceral State, Adultism, and "Parents' Rights"

jenani: It feels to me that when we talk about carceral CSA paradigms today, one important place to start is the current "parents' rights" movement. We know that the parents' rights movement has a long history here in the United States—I'm thinking, as one example, about the 1950s/1960s parents' rights movement to oppose desegregation in schools.[18]

    Today's parents' rights movement focuses deeply on schools as a cultural and political battleground *precisely because* it is in schools that parents have some of the weakest control over their children's indoctrination. Over the past two decades, we've seen big shifts in curriculum standards toward the inclusion of differing viewpoints—a necessity in line with best practices around a child's development and critical thinking. With schools being a source of exposure to information that would potentially counter a parent's preferences around hegemonic values, this site is a perfect entrance point toward generating the false consciousness among working class America.

Monica: I really like this framing, jenani, because it points to what I think is at the heart of the moral panic that gives these movements so much power—the notion and fear that children would be able to use, for example, information they learn from LGBTQ+ and BIPOC affirming curricula to assert their own identities, values, and power since now they have the language and frameworks to do so. It is in the context of this moral panic that we see how the parents' rights movement and other carceral movements weaponize CSA.

jenani: Yes, totally. We've seen for decades the false premise that exposure to LGBTQ+ identity will automatically create "unsafe environments" for children. The current resurgence of this rhetoric is responding to an era in US legal history that has seen some of the most progressive, decriminalizing amendments to federal and statewide statutory codes about LGBTQ+ people. This rhetoric takes what we've seen historically a step forward by insinuating, and in some contexts, directly correlating, exposure to these identities as child abuse. This rollback, being pushed in working class communities through vehicles such as the parents' rights movement, is contributing to an age-old playbook we've seen used over and over again by conservatives—appeal to the masses through moral panics, identify an "other" to blame, and encourage the working class to organize for solutions that may seem effective even though, when applied, they work against their interests.

Alison: Yes, and we're seeing this strategy grow and grow—in the past few years, a record number of anti-LGBTQ+ bills have been introduced. In 2023 alone, 508 anti-LGBTQ+ bills were filed and 84 of these bills were passed into law, continuing this notion that by criminalizing queer existence, we will "be keeping our children safer from child abuse," and ultimately child sexual abuse.[19] What's important to note here is that the focus by the parents' rights movement has not been the legislation itself, per se. Once these bills are filed, they quickly lose steam within their respective legislatures, and the bill filers know this may happen. The real intentions of these movement spaces is to gain enough exposure to make this kind of rhetoric commonplace so that more people feel emboldened, which is critical to the conservative party platform. This is evident by the rise in hate crimes toward queer folks—LGBTQ+ hate crimes hit their highest totals in five years, increasing by more than 10 percent since 2021. The most significant increase was 40 percent—in reported antitransgender incidents.[20]

jenani, you mentioned the way that a lot of these policies being pushed forward and spoken about in the public sphere are also inciting this immense moral panic around queer people. For me, I'm sitting with this layer around adultism and adult supremacy, which is already so pervasive in these institutions that are creating policies all developed and shaped by adults who are doing this "in service of children and young people" or to "save the children." When in reality these policies are in service of systems of power and domination that continue to give more power and agency to adults. It leads young people into or back into really violent systems that then offer the state even more power. Because adults don't actually see young people as real and active members of the community until they can be used.

What does it really mean to support youth power and intergenerational approaches as it relates to CSA? And what is the actual role of adults in that process and journey? This looks like seeing young people as policymakers, for example. Policymakers with the ability to set the framing around this issue and determine the systems of support needed to transform the conditions that lead to CSA taking place. Adults can be accomplices in that process in allocating the resources necessary to make those visions young people offer possible and using the positions of power they have in these institutions to do that.

jenani: I don't know if you guys saw these photos, but earlier this year Sarah Huckabee Sanders, the current Arkansas governor and former Trump White House press secretary, passed a bill banning instruction on critical race theory in schools, and preventing K–5 teachers from discussing gender identity or sexual orientation in classrooms, in the name of protecting children. She released this photo of the bill signing on her Facebook page, and there's another taken by the press, and these kids in these photos look miserable.[21] The only folks who are happy about these pieces of legislation being signed are the adults, who are most likely staffers or folks who directly worked on the bills. First question—who is in charge of PR in Arkansas that these photos were allowed to go out? On the other hand, these photos being the ones going out really says a lot about where we're at on the Right. What are the true parameters of childhood? We have to protect our kids from being queer so they can be kids, but our kids should have babies no matter the circumstance of their pregnancy. We have to protect our children from getting certain books at the library, but we can have our kids working in warehouses. Which of these things are visions that young people actually align with? There are all these specific things that young people *can* do and there are specific things that they *can't*, and adults are the deciders of that. This is what adultism is.

Monica: Honestly, these are such powerful images. They actually give such a good visual of these dynamics we're describing—the way that the adults are both looming over and smiling behind the kids, it looks predatory but with this Disney-fied veneer. I think it's also interesting to compare and contrast these images alongside how folks are reacting to young people who are doing climate justice work, for example. I'm thinking in particular here about the "Greta effect"—how Greta Thunberg has been lauded by every mainstream institution under the sun, even to the point of being nominated for a Nobel Peace Prize. It's like, when do the lives, voices, and well-being of young people matter? It totally speaks to that selective sort of invocation.

Alison: (cackling laughter) Not a Disney-fied veneer, Monica! But it's so true. And so (deep sigh) unbelievably frustrating. Monica, even you using the term *predatory* to describe these images when we're talking about policies that are created against "superpredators," and who are the real predators in this situation? Also, the way that the children in these photos—and children and young people more widely—are consistently used as props. It really points to this notion of only seeing children and young people as active members of a community when it's connected to supporting capitalism and all these systems of oppression, but not when it actually comes down to supporting their autonomy and self-determination.

Section 2: Barriers to the Proliferation of Community-Forward Child Sexual Abuse Prevention

jenani: I'm so sick and tired of this rhetoric that has been normalized to like, just openly hate queer and trans people. It's scary. Especially getting to see and experience so many strides for LGBTQ+ rights in this lifetime, seeing these protections roll back today under the guise of protecting against child abuse and child sexual abuse is disgusting. How are people believing, rallying behind, and justifying it?! It makes my heart even sadder that mainstream CSA organizations won't fight harder against this crusade.

Mainstream antiviolence advocates tend not to think beyond the PIC to address gender-based violence, since they are so firmly entrenched in their histories of carceral feminism. There's definitely more progress now within that movement space, but still a large reluctance to completely diverge from the courts because of how much of their funding is tied to their connections to these systems. On the other hand, there is so much evangelical money in work to end sexual violence against children, namely around child sex trafficking. Particularly with this Christian Nationalist–tint of the modern Republican party, we're seeing even more silence in the name of "being bipartisan." As a result, these sectors progress efforts that are incredibly anti–sex work and anti-porn, despite little-to-no evidence that by criminalizing these things, you end sexual violence.

Monica: For sure. On that point, it feels important to highlight how the rhetoric of the "perfect, innocent victim" forms both the general foundation for carceral feminism and also its specific interfaces with carceral CSA work. It's not a coincidence that the person who's been credited with coming up with the term *carceral feminism* came up with that term after doing ethnographic work around anti–sex trafficking advocacy.[22] That's actually where that term originally came from. In both the carceral feminist space focused on sex trafficking and the carceral feminist space focused on CSA, the logic of the "perfect, innocent victim" renders certain people—namely, white cis women and children—legible to the State as "worth saving" while excluding marginalized others from accessing whatever limited resources the State might have to offer.

jenani: Absolutely. We know these rhetorics do not reflect the realities of many survivor stories; there are complex realities at play here that often pit survivors against each other for who is the "victim." For example, there are a wide variety of circumstances where prosecutors will charge adult survivors of trafficking as codefendants just because they've interacted with a young survivor of trafficking. These circumstances are often around harm reduction, which can range from teaching a young person how to navigate survival street work to the trafficker utilizing coercive control. As a result, there are a number of adult sex trafficking survivors who are on the sex offender registry because they were charged as codefendants. There have been multiple legislative and nonprofit efforts (e.g., the work of the Freedom Network) for these victims to be candidates for expungement and record restriction; however, in most of these cases, the survivor needs to be charged, convicted, and serve time before they are eligible for these services.

The legal framework that creates survivor defense cases foreshadows what is coming from these harsher CSA laws—these laws will inevitably target and criminalize LGBTQ+ people and make it harder for these folks to fight against the use of the PIC as a tactic of abuse. Despite none of these harsher punishments decreasing the prevalence of these forms of violence, we continue to see these policies being pushed.

Monica: I think what you're naming, jenani, raises some really generative points. One place my brain is going is that it's really ironic, right? Because when we talk in movement spaces about "deservingness" narratives, and how respectability politics unfolds in terms of whose pain matters and whose stories matter, we always think of children and young people as like, one of the typologies of the "good victim," right? Because for many children, there is an imputation of innocence. Obviously, this is not universally true, we know that adultification is very prevalent in perceptions and treatment of Black children and also other BIPOC young folk. But holding that tension of how a lot of this rhetoric that is criminalizing CSA is invoking this idea of the child as the perfect victim, the child as this innocent figure, while also failing to provide meaningful support for those same children. It's a really powerful reminder that we don't win, that no one wins, ultimately, when we play the deservingness narrative game, right? Even in this situation, right? It's a reminder that we cannot use respectability politics to build more just and liberatory futures.

jenani: Totally, I love how you framed this point. I feel like particularly right now we're seeing "perfect, innocent victim" rhetoric used to justify criminalizing queer people.

Monica: This point you're making about queer criminalization specifically, jenani, and the moral panic that you mentioned earlier, Alison, has me thinking about how the current criminalization of CSA connects to an underlying panic about threats to nuclear family making, right? There's this idea that the nuclear family is this bastion and sanctuary for heteronormative (read: white supremacist, all the other "-ist") values. And the perception is that this bastion is under attack. It's under attack by the false perception that more queer people are engaging in legally sanctioned family making. It's under attack by the false perception that trans people have greater culturally accepted and legally protected opportunities to exist more fully. It's under attack by progressive communities that are trying to reimagine what it means to build kinship networks. Using the "harm to innocent children" prop as the pretext for creating all these criminalization schemas is, I think, expressive of these anxieties on some levels. And of this idea that our children are at risk of the "predatory homosexual" or the "predatory, indoctrinating woke left" or what have you.

One way we see this phantom phenomenon take flesh is in the disproportionate numbers of queer people on US sex registries.[23] Of course, the irony there, right, is that it is actually (hetero)normative nuclear family structures and values that dictate "power over" understandings of children—that understand children as the property and extensions of their family units rather than as fully realized, agentic people. It is these values and structures that dictate that children—and especially children socialized as girls—are meant to smile and be amenable to all kinds of physical contact from community members. These types of "power over" dynamics that are so deeply embedded in the nuclear family infrastructure are some of the things that most allow CSA to continue to flourish unchecked and unaddressed. Right. It feels like an important piece to name, how this is connected to fears around the nuclear family being destabilized, even as it is this same nuclear family that props up values that maintain CSA.

jenani: Totally, totally. Your point on the nuclear family really showcases the ulterior motive of these efforts on the Right—using fear to categorize individuals who support and validate falling outside this hegemonic expectation of the nuclear family as "child abusers." I'm not at all surprised that state governments feel sanctioned to create law in this way. The origin of this whole country is to uphold a specific vision of humanity and society and not necessarily to promote safety.

Now that we've hashed out the strategies we've seen used by the Right, let's talk a little more about the liberal/progressive Left. One big push right now from the liberal/progressive Left is around creating diversion programs (i.e., restorative justice in courts, pretrial programs, etc.). While these programs have a benevolent or "softer" face in comparison to traditional incarceration, they still expand the reach of the carceral state. Diversion programs still rely heavily on surveillance and coercion, which the harm-doer (and often, their intimate partner) finances. However, these programs are already a nonstarter when it comes to CSA prevention and intervention because they tend not to be offered to people who commit sexual offenses. This highlights how the carceral paradigm will only support alternative options as long as they ultimately support the status quo. In that vein, diversion programming does not provide those it attempts to rehabilitate the opportunity to address the root causes that led to the incident or exacerbated its outcome. How then are these programs truly rehabilitative?

I remember when I myself had to attend the required "values class" for a diversion program. There were about fifteen other people in this all-day class with me. The first thing the person leading the course asked was "How many of y'all are here because you got caught shoplifting at the Walmart?" *Every single person in the class raised their hand.* Then the teacher lectured us for the entire remainder of the day that we need to set goals and "not take shortcuts." To this day it's chilling to me, that all our experiences that led us to this place were diluted down to "don't take shortcuts." It could never be capitalism and class and surviving the vehicles that necessitate the act of shoplifting—only personal fault. And that's the real danger of a lot of these diversion programs. If we surgically remove all the levels of oppression and insecurity that we know statistically lead to crime and violence, not only do we never end violence itself, but we further lock folks into all the emotions and circumstances that keep them from asking for help or accessing the resources to survive in this world.

Monica: I really resonate with everything you shared, jenani, and I appreciate you sharing from your own experiences. This conversation reminds me of a case I supported while in law school, *Sigma Beta Xi v. County of Riverside.*[24] The case was about this diversion program in Riverside, a hugely BIPOC county in Southern California, that had been created through a partnership between juvenile probation and Riverside schools. Under this program, if a kid had, for example, a couple tardies or something else that itself would not rise to the level of criminalization, the school could call these "probation" officers to meet with that student and coerce them into signing up for this program under the pretext that it would "keep them on track." But the program had a lot of strict conditions, and if students didn't fully comply with all of them, the program became a streamlined mechanism to criminalize the young person and send them away. And so, what the program was actually doing was expanding the net of surveillance and shunting more of these students into the school-to-prison pipeline under the guise of being a soft alternative to incarceration.

I tell this story because it is the story of diversion that I see time and time again. It's not only about the eligibility requirements; it's not only about the ways in which these "soft" programs often skirt the very few procedural and legal protections that people have in the more formalized legal processes. It's also a sanitization piece. We know these programs don't work, we know that they actively cause harm—but even aside from all that, they are harmful in the sense that they make our systems seem more palatable to those who are not paying close attention or who seek to justify their complacency. They make it seem like "yes, we know it was bad that we were throwing kids away, but that was then and this is now, now we have this softer program, so we don't have anything to worry about. And if kids still get locked up, well, then those were the ones who lost their second chance from that softer approach." That's often what I think about in terms of diversion.

jenani: Diversion will never exist on the left in a way that doesn't, like, validate the need for the PIC. I think what abolition is really beautiful for is that it also gives people permission to think outside the frame and the structures we currently have to address gender-based violence and really ask ourselves deeply, what do we need to do to increase the capacities of communities to be able to address this fight? Because really, it's in the hands of community members where true prevention can actually exist, right? There are always several escalation factors to any incident of violence. Those are all real and genuine opportunities to intervene without necessitating a legal response.

Alison: Yeah, diversion programs rely on that personal blame game versus acknowledging the role of systems of oppression doing what they're intended to do. That's where I feel like so many conversations get caught up around prisons and policing. And if we bring CSA into the conversation around abolition or just sexual violence more widely, I think people continue to be absorbed by individual blame without connecting things back to the root causes that sit inside these larger systems, and this impacts the creativity involved in addressing that kind of violence.

Then we look at the radical Left, where there are experimentations with transformative justice and cultural shifts toward a noncarceral understanding of violence. And even here some of that same conditioning around what acts of violence are "irredeemable" pops up that limit our imaginative capacity. I feel like a lot of folks are here for transformative justice until we talk about CSA. And I think we just gotta be really honest about that. Because that conditioning, in turn, also restricts our ability to create solutions that don't replicate the forms of punishment being enacted by the State.

For people I love and care about who are survivors of CSA, it's all intimate interpersonal relationships with folks who were or are still present in their lives in some way. People didn't call the police because what were the police gonna do? And at the same time, how do we sit with folks in the community who've enacted this kind of violence and actually address what people have done so that it doesn't happen again? This isn't part of the national conversation, but it is a conversation in movement space. Also, sometimes it feels a little like we're all about transformative justice and have prevention/intervention responses in theory, but when it's really time to be inside that work, all those principles go out the window and the response we're socially conditioned to have takes over.

Monica: Because we don't practice.

Alison: Yep. And practicing can be really, really hard and scary. I say scary because when we practice, we're also touching so many parts of ourselves—our values and belief systems (i.e., societal, those ingrained in us from childhood, the ones we've developed for ourselves throughout our life); our personal experiences; the histories of our families, communities, and ancestral/cultural lineages—and this can completely upend things for us individually and collectively. That's deep work. It's meant to be. That's part of why transformative justice is *transformative*. It's culture-shifting work.

So when we say transformative justice is a *practice*, there can be a lot of blocks to the practicing. It's one thing to resonate with the theory of something and be inside of conversations conceptualizing praxis, and it can be a whole 'nother world to actually do the things we've been talking about. Because we get confronted with ourselves and the things within us that are being challenged, and in turn, called to change to do this work. So when it's time to be in praxis and actively engaged with the things we say we believe, how do we sit with that contention we feel and allow it to be a driver for more creative solutions and possibilities rather than a deterrent?

Monica: One hundred percent, that's totally true to my experiences as well. I think that a big piece of it is, again, that we're not embedding these values in a lot of our movement spaces on a daily basis. I feel that there's a lot of, like you've said, like, theorizing. Which I do believe is absolutely important—to draw from Assata Shakur, we need to be diligent and vigilant students of these movements, structures, and histories, right? Not dissing that. *And also*, there seems to be a missing connection between "here's our values and analysis" and "this is how we're embedding this analysis in our daily culture and practice, this is how we're working these muscles so that when a crisis emerges, we actually have practiced in advance multiple times," right?

And I think that a big part of this issue stems from how gender and gendered labor and gendered work shows up in social movements. Care work, community work, relationship building—all these things have historically been gendered as feminine and as a result get sidelined or devalued in favor of work that is also hugely important but more masculine in its posture—the much more public facing work around abolition, or the work focused on the destruction of systems. It feels like the piece that people are most stuck around is the sort of life building institutions work that Ruthie Gilmore talks about, in terms of actually bringing these values into their daily practices.[25] I think that's something that needs to be unpacked and continues to be something that I find really concerning.

jenani: I really resonate with what you bring up around this predominant push around participating in thought leadership and not participating in incorporating these theories and values into day-to-day practices. Hot takes are an easier way to feel like you did something, huh? It's much harder to incorporate transformative practices into the day-to-day when we're so incentivized to channel tactics of disposability, rage, and spectacle. Let's be real—it's not the State alone that's ripping communities apart. It's our communities' continued internalization that experiences of violence should always be framed in the abuser/victim dichotomy and that justice comes from solidifying who carries which label. That is how we're ripping our own communities apart—through our internalization, and therefore legitimization, of the PIC. I would really like to encourage praxis that challenges individuals to start at the reality that violence is a lose-lose situation for everyone involved, always.

Child sexual abuse is one of the most prevalent and underrecorded forms of gender-based violence in our communities. Criminal-legal methodologies to address gender-based violence promote a specific narrative of CSA that relies on sensationalized cases—which are also the cases that are so extreme a prosecutor can obtain a guilty conviction. Our cultural understandings of CSA are equated to these more extreme, conviction-obtaining instances of violence and do not accurately communicate the escalatory and cyclical nature of CSA. This minimization starkly limits our ability to prevent CSA within communities, since we are not addressing the intergenerational, interpersonal, and systemic factors that allow CSA to occur. I think there is genuine power that can be built with people of a variety of backgrounds around this issue because people want their kids to be safe. People are desperate to see something, anything, happen to make the world feel safer for their kids, especially when they're feeling so unsafe in this world as it is. They'll grab onto and move anything that will help—even if the strategies are at the expense of their benefit. It's one of the most glaring modern examples of collective false consciousness. For us on the Left, what this shows is that we need to better prioritize finding common ground with different elements of our larger "Left"—because the base is clearly there—and shift power based on the understanding that safer communities do not mean more cops and prisons.

Sadly, I don't think we will ever achieve those numbers if we continue to be so rigid. My praxis and relationship building has led me to center harm reduction abolition. In centering praxis and harm reduction in abolitionist efforts, we refuse to center theory that enforces a dichotomy between the desire to overthrow oppressive systems and the belief that it is critical to engage in harm reduction with and for those who are currently affected by these systems. These types of prison abolitions encourage intersectionality and power building, while also making sure we're not building a coalition of only the folks who have the privilege to have these views without retaliation or harm. Part of me feels this struggle on the Left to hold both is a replication of what we see on the Right—a lack of critical thinking combined with those willing to capitalize on it. Regurgitation of theory is not an emblem of the ability to think critically, and acting as a one-stop shop for theory is not critical analysis. At its worst, this negative feedback loop has directly set back and been detrimental to our movement's larger goals. We have to call bullshit on those who wear our skin but contribute to these forms of fractures—it's a relic of COINTELPRO, it's not generative, and whether people like to own it or not, it's a distraction.

Section 3: Praxis, Intergenerational Action, and Child Sexual Abuse Prevention

Alison: There's a chapter in the book *Trust Kids! Stories on Youth Autonomy and Confronting Adult Supremacy* that explores more specifically, what does it mean to create systems with children and young people where they actually exist at the center?[26] I think this intersects with multiple conversations we're having around CSA prevention. Because what currently dominates national conversation, especially around CSA, is all the things that are created by adults "in service of" young people that not only inherently give adults more power but they're actually not working. Emphasis on the last part. It's just not giving. I'm curious what y'all think about that?

jenani: I really resonate with that framing, because I do feel that the biggest cultural shifts over the past few decades in the United States have been championed by young people. While shock-value rhetoric seems to be a quick way to immediate change, it's culture-shift work that is creating the society where long-term change can be sustainable. I mean, just think about where the Green New Deal started and how far it has gone since being pushed by the Sunrise Movement! That was young people. Think of the impact of March for Our Lives! That was young people.

Alison: When you talk about laws that have been passed by young people and even some of the culture shifts that have been created in turn, jenani, it makes me think about . . . what does it actually look like to have children at the center of the creation of our world? And that idea gets me really excited. Because I'm also thinking about all the ways children especially have not been socialized in the same way that adults have been to accept the world as it is now.

In my experience as an adult, I've felt really deeply challenged around my own capacity to dream and vision beyond the world as it is. All these systems of oppression make it really hard, and I've really questioned . . . do I even have the capacity to imagine and dream under capitalism, under white supremacy, under all these things? Children have a different ability to imagine and conceptualize the world from a space of what could be. Adults really diminish and undermine their thinking by using age as the ultimate marker of wisdom.

jenani: Another thing I'm thinking about in terms of developing praxis is the role culture plays in this conversation—because praxis never can happen in a vacuum. You can't build successful structures without a cultural environment that supports said structures. What's beautiful about the younger generations right now is so many folks' deliberate refusal to accept the world as it has been taught to us, to refuse replicating those systems and dynamics that will continue to lead to the erosion of our planet and all the species that inhabit it. There is real potential to make huge cultural shifts that support the true prevention of child sexual abuse. The question is how.

Alison: There's something in the rhetoric around CSA that mirrors a lot around how prisons are conceptualized in media and culture—this idea that they're filled with scary, violent rapists and murderers who have done the most horrible things you could possibly conceptualize. When people think of CSA, those same images come to mind. What pervades the media and national conversation is experiences with CSA between children and adults, and like you noted, jenani, that's only around 25 percent of cases. That statistic is so powerful. Because it points to this conversation we really need to be having around the 70–75 percent of cases of CSA that are between minors.

So, what does CSA prevention look like from a place where children and young people are actively engaged in bodily autonomy, consent, and boundaries in order to not replicate power and control dynamics? Even talking with friends about early experiences with sex as young people, where those first experiences were as children with other children playing out scenarios, pretending to be adults and exploring their bodies together. So, I think we do a huge disservice to children and young people when we treat them as if they don't have a body through which they deserve to explore and experience pleasure, joy, and connection. And how do we begin having those conversations very, very early on, long before people are in sex ed classes in high school? What does it look like to teach bodily autonomy and talk about consent and boundaries with children?

Monica: Alison, I love what you're saying—have you seen on TikTok that little singy-song that a lot of children are learning about boundaries and consent?[27] It's meant to be a song that kids can sing to say, you know, "I don't want to be touched right now or in this way. I'm not trying to hurt your feelings, but these are my boundaries." I remember feeling very emotional the first time I saw these videos because I, like so many, never grew up feeling that I could say no to hugs from aunties, or ask people to stop touching my hair, or that saying no is an acceptable thing in general. It also made me emotional to see that these tools are starting to mainstream and normalize the idea that young people do have autonomy over their bodies. I'm also thinking of some of the programs across the world teaching the basic concepts of consent to kids as young as four and five. It all speaks to what you're describing, Alison.

jenani: I love that question. It was really important to me when I started doing dating violence prevention education to take fifteen minutes at the end of the class to just ask, is there any other information I could provide today that would be helpful for you to know? Mostly because I wished I had that. I would get a lot of questions and then update my curriculum. When I first started at the program, the curriculum was incredibly cut-and-dried and based off national standards. The curriculum I got at the end of my time with this program was pretty different. Young people were more curious about the nitty gritty: What really is a healthy relationship? How do you know if someone likes you? When should you mind your own business? If something wasn't physical violence, then was it still unhealthy? I also feel like the connection I was able to have with young people toward the end of teaching versus the beginning was largely different. I really do feel that at the end of the day, the final curriculum just related more and was more legitimate to these teens because it actually answered their dating questions, instead of basically fearmongering and presenting relationship violence as black-and-white.

Sharing this information means nothing if there aren't active efforts by those in that person's life to showcase what healthy boundaries and consent look like. These curricula are just more information during a period of life where all you're doing is getting information on what the world is and how you are "supposed to be" within those frames. If adults take on being more active role models of these healthy behaviors, then we actively reinforce them for our kids and resist normalizing the escalation period of the cycle of violence. This is people's first experiences of love, y'all. Or even a step back, this is their first experience of dating. Nobody wants to think someone who loves them can hurt them. Everyone hopes the people who love them will change for them. Everyone can justify someone who loves them treating them badly because that person is a victim of something else. The current carceral curricula and statutes don't afford these realities, and it's leading to violence continuing, not reducing. Adults can have a real impact here as allies.

Alison: I'm also thinking about how neither sex-ed nor dating violence prevention curricula for youth teach young people what mandated reporting is, yet they encourage young people to talk to a "trusted adult" if something is wrong. And more likely than not, this "trusted person" is code for a mandated reporter. It's like, we'll give you all this information, and we'll tell you who to go to, but we're not going to tell you what's going to happen when you go have that conversation.

jenani: Mandated reporting as a practice does not create a culture that supports young people in learning about consent, bodily autonomy, and boundaries. When I was in elementary school, I told a trusted adult what was going on in my household and it led to the school contacting my state's Department of Family and Children's Services. My home was already used to having the government in our household, but this was the first time I remember as a kid being so scared that I was going to be alone. I had gotten through all these years with them and realized that I might not have them.

I don't hate the adult I told in the slightest—she was an incredible figure in my life during really hard years, and she was the first person to offer resources for my family as we were thrust into the family policing environment. She checked in on me all the way to when she passed away. I feel emotional even remembering her because she really did protect me, you know. It was just a bad situation where nobody "won." And it really made me think—now that I reflect on it as an adult—that this experience really made me stop asking people for help for a really long time, you know? Now I'm redeveloping this relationship, but I grew up with my family saying to never say shit to anyone. And it creates this sense of desperation as a kid, you know, living this public face versus a private face. A lot of child survivors experience this and spend their whole lives unlearning it. Mandated reporting is honestly the most sinister way to take advantage of this desperation to be seen.

Alison: That's something really significant to speak to, that sense of desperation.

So, what does it really mean when young people asking for support get to determine, themselves, what support looks like? This circles back to earlier parts of our conversation on youth autonomy and self-determination. I'm really curious about what that looks like in terms of organizing, what's out there and who is and has been doing this kind of work, where young people are addressing interpersonal violence, and I think that's part of what we're exploring with the Wayfinding Project.[28] From me doing initial research and being in conversation with folks, it seems like there are youth development programs that do work around some of the things we talked about, like consent, dating practices, sex education, and bodily autonomy. And then there's abolitionist youth organizing happening across the country to close prisons and jails, for example. I wonder what the intersections are between these and where the entry points are for conversations around ending sexual violence among young people. These intersections may be surfacing in ways that are not as explicit as "this is the organizing campaign we're running right now."

jenani: I hear you on that. I think community organizing hubs are a great site for sex and dating education. It'd be great to have a self-guided curriculum out there for sex-ed and healthy relationships, like a "do it with a group" or "move at your own pace" resource that young people identified with and felt motivated to do. That itself would be such a radical form of prevention, because roughly three out of four cases of reported CSA involve two young people. I wonder where campaigns could go if youth organizing sites took more of an initiative to develop an ethos around these topics.

In a more macro sense, no matter what our campaigns target, if we're replicating power and control within our interpersonal relationships, then what new world are we truly creating? Every organizer needs information on healthy relationships and bodily autonomy because those are two things that we require in order to even have a chance at tackling oppression without replicating its vehicles—no matter what the issue or platform. I think it's easy for Leftists/Liberals to point at those on the Right when seeking examples of how propaganda and words can be and are used to assert power and control over others and act like the surprised Pikachu meme when asked if these dynamics are present in their spaces. We all know they are, and we all know it's what's keeping us as a movement from moving forward. In order to bring forward change, any sort of change, isn't tackling bodily autonomy and healthy relationships within our containers and communities truly step one over proliferating the reach of purity politics? Who— working class, marginalized, or oppressed—would want to join something offering the potential of new when, in reality, it's just a lot of the same old thing?

I genuinely feel lucky to be able to build with folks like you two—

Alison/Monica: (interrupting) Awwwww . . .

jenani: (laughs) Um, excuse me . . . I wasn't finished talking . . .

Alison: Okay, Scorpio. (laughter)

jenani: I genuinely feel lucky to be able to build with folks like you two who are really looking at expanding the reach of the people that we can build power with in this space, which means moving toward an intersectional vision. Because ultimately, that's what we need to win.

NOTES

1. Child Welfare Information Gateway, *About CAPTA: A Legislative History.*
2. Lancaster, *Sex Panic and the Punitive State.*
3. Kempe, "The Battered-Child Syndrome."

4. Anderson, "Child Sexual Abuse Prevention Policy: An Analysis of Erin's Law"; Plummer, "The History of Child Sexual Abuse Prevention: A Practitioner's Perspective."

5. National Association of Mandated Reporters, "A History of CAPTA Legislation"; Myers, "A Short History of Child Protection in America."

6. Myers, "A Short History of Child Protection in America."

7. Child Welfare Information Gateway, *About CAPTA: A Legislative History.*

8. Centers for Disease Control and Prevention, *Preventing Youth Violence.*

9. Thoma et al., "Disparities in Childhood Abuse between Transgender and Cisgender Adolescents."

10. Collin-Vézina, Daigneault, and Hébert, "Lessons Learned from Child Sexual Abuse Research: Prevalence, Outcomes, and Preventive Strategies."

11. National Child Traumatic Stress Network, *Why Don't They Tell? Teens and Sexual Assault Disclosure.*

12. Gewirtz-Meydan and Finkelhor, "Sexual Abuse and Assault in a Large National Sample of Children and Adolescents."

13. Centers for Disease Control and Prevention, *Preventing Youth Violence.*

14. Letourneau and Malone, "America Has Been Going about Stopping Child Sex Abuse the Wrong Way."

15. Letourneau and Malone.

16. RAINN, "The Criminal Justice System: Statistics."

17. Myers, "A Short History of Child Protection in America."

18. Anderson, "Child Sexual Abuse Prevention Policy: An Analysis of Erin's Law."

19. Alfonseca, "Record Number of Anti-LGBTQ Legislation Filed in 2023."

20. U.S. Department of Justice, "2022 FBI Hate Crimes Statistics."

21. DeMillo, "Arkansas Gov. Sanders Signs Bill Creating School Vouchers"; Sarah Huckabee Sanders, "Arkansas Made History Today, Setting the Education Model for the Nation. The Failed Status Quo Is Dead, and Hope Is Alive for Every Kid in Our State!," Facebook, March 8, 2023, https://www.facebook.com/photo.php?fbid=751976452953830.

22. Bernstein, "The Sexual Politics of the 'New Abolitionism.'"

23. Wahl and Pittman, "Injustice: How the Sex Offender Registry Destroys LGBTQ Rights."

24. ACLU Southern California, "ACLU Files Lawsuit against Oppressive 'YAT' Youth Program in Riverside."

25. Gilmore, *Abolition Geography.*

26. bergman, *Trust Kids!: Stories on Youth Autonomy and Confronting Adult Supremacy.*

27. Peanut, (@learnwithcharz #kids #cute #da), "The Boundary song is adorable," Video, n.d., https://www.tiktok.com/@peanut/video/7187444017376824582?_r=1&_t=8g6QMWjT2iI.

28. Just Beginnings Collaborative, "Wayfinding Project," https://justbeginnings.org/wayfinding/.

PART THREE

Branches of Progress

Reaching for Queer Justice in Criminology

CHAPTER 11

Critiquing Criminology

*Toward an Abolitionist-Centered Pedagogy
and Discipline*

CANDICE CRUTCHFIELD, THE OHIO STATE UNIVERSITY

"Well, I definitely want to be a cop, but if that doesn't work out, I could keep people in line as a corrections officer," proudly remarked a colleague from the back of the classroom, no more than twenty years old. It was the first day of CRIM430: The American Correctional System, an elective satisfying requirements toward a bachelor's degree in criminology. As the course title alludes, the class was designed to "examine the correctional system from sentencing to release," and it attracted the attention of over fifty enrolled students at my alma mater, Penn State University. "I'd like to be a prosecutor, send the bad guys to prison," remarked another student, responding to the instructor's prompt to introduce oneself and state the kind of job they'd like to obtain after graduation. I hadn't raised my hand to participate in the icebreaker, instead, making note of the number of students hoping to pursue careers in law enforcement. "A cop, but a good one," "sheriff," "a federal agent," and "a prison warden" disproportionately filled the room in comparison to people interested in public defense, social work, research careers, and community organizing—all of whom could be counted on one hand.

As a then upper-level student, I'd spent the greater portion of my undergraduate career learning the basics of criminological thought, engaging with foundational theories, and understanding largely social constructions of both crime and justice. With the exception of some critical scholars and instruction, I'd come to realize that the majority of my courses had prepared me and other students to view criminology as a discipline that centered on reform. As advocates and activists beyond academic walls called for justice and safety in the wake of police brutality, enhanced criminalization, and the ever-fluctuating incarceration rates across the nation's prisons and jails, traditional criminology study remained largely stagnant, following theoretical traditions of labeling people as "good" or "bad," centering largely social constructions of what constitutes a crime, and encouraging short-term reforms. I began to understand the traditional discipline of criminology as a central tenet of the criminal legal system, often reaffirming the social structures that have and continue to perpetuate harm. It was no wonder a large portion of my colleagues went on to pursue careers in law enforcement. Criminology wasn't broken, but was instead doing exactly what it has been doing for decades. From my view, criminology has operated and continues to operate as a discipline expanding the very systems it claims to challenge.

ENGAGING (OR DISENGAGING?) CRIMINOLOGY

Since its earliest conception, the criminological landscape has experienced many transformations and contradictions. As a field of study, criminology has commonly produced two schools of thought, both of which hold differing perspectives on the role and function of the criminal legal system. To some, criminology is a critical tool for analyzing and reducing the reach of the carceral system, often employing reformist strategies and finding the ever-fluctuating incarceration rates troublesome but necessary. Others see criminology as an institution directly upholding pillars of the carceral state, arguing that reformist analyses and the discipline's deep-seated connection to the state are simply a mark of criminology's complicity in expanding power and supporting harmful structures.[1]

As scholars Schept and Brown note in their piece on the future direction of criminology, the second thought is not merely a radical form of thinking or a conspiratory ideal, but instead extends a long tradition of critical examinations into the prison industrial complex and the ways in which criminology has operated as a complicit entity.[2] Within this subset of critical scholars, advocates, and scholar-activists emerges a guiding ideology interested in understanding the ways the discipline not only supports but upholds the larger prison industrial complex (PIC). Rather than centering criminological study on traditional theoretical frames of who is law-abiding or lawbreaking, this subset of criminologists has sought to study law and justice by framing it within examinations of anti-Black racism, the criminalization of poverty, and social constructions of deviant behavior.[3] This approach, commonly referred to by some as critical criminology, recognizes the impact of social structures, inequality, and power dynamics.[4] It also draws upon the voices of Black, disabled, queer, trans, nonbinary, and other socially vulnerable groups to uplift its ideals. Importantly, these alternative approaches to studying crime, law, and justice have historically coincided with times of social movements and increased collective action, often relying on the scholarship and efforts of those closest to issues of policing, courts, and incarceration.[5] From the prisoners' rights movement of the mid-1970s to the present calls for defunding police and the abolition of the carceral state, the field of criminology remains a critical figure within the "prison nation," and as such, scholars have a present opportunity to move the discipline forward.

In this chapter, I grapple with myriad questions, some of which remain unanswered: How might criminology fully embrace abolition? Is criminology even capable of such an action? How do Black women and Black queer and trans perspectives inform ongoing calls for PIC abolition? Despite advocacy and a budding awareness of noncarceral alternatives, transformative justice, and accountability measures, structures of retribution dominate the criminological landscape. *I suggest the discipline draw specifically from elements of Black women's, queer, and trans abolitionist perspectives.* Often at the forefront of movement work and collective advocacy, and present in historical moments surrounding the carceral crisis, criminology can and must draw upon these perspectives to challenge traditional frames.

CRITICAL EXAMINATIONS OF AND WITHIN THE DISCIPLINE

The discipline of criminology, through its historical focus on crime control and punitive measures, has often perpetuated and reinforced the very ideology and structures that abolitionists seek to dismantle within the carceral system. This phenomenon can be seen unfolding in the discipline through classroom pedagogy, politically motivated collaborations, and the dissemination of flawed ideologies through well-respected publication outlets. As such, criminology has been reluctant to incorporate more critical viewpoints and interdisciplinary perspectives that critique the carceral state, thereby hindering comprehensive understanding and transformation within the field. Despite societal and academic attempts to normalize systems of punishment, critical scholars have constantly looked to the margins, exploring and interrogating the "sacred and founding myths of the discipline."[6] Given traditional criminology's prominence within the legal system, the academy, and political culture, perhaps criminology's most promising step forward is found within the interdisciplinary fields of critical carceral studies and contemporary critical criminology.

Critical criminologists, that is, scholars critical of the punishment system, aren't a new phenomenon; rather, they have a long-standing history of being marginalized and sidelined within the field. Despite taking root in the 1960s during a period in which scholars questioned dominant narratives of criminology, the field has drawn from a variety of disciplines (sociology, geography, African American studies, women's gender, and sexuality studies) but has often failed to follow suit in drawing connections to abolition. For instance, critical criminology openly recognizes the prison as a perpetrator of violence, harm, and inequality, particularly among marginalized communities, including but not limited to Black women, women of color, queer, trans, and non-binary people.[7] Scholars in the field of critical carceral studies frequently articulate concerns regarding carceral rhetoric, advocate for divestment from punitive systems, and delve deeper into the mechanisms through which the PIC operates within individuals' daily lives. As such, their work directly intersects with abolitionist principles.

Abolitionist Visions and Critical Carceral Studies

Critical carceral studies scholars engage with abolitionist frameworks to analyze and understand how the prison system perpetuates inequality, racial disparities, and systemic oppression. Both critical criminologists and PIC abolitionists recognize the punishment system as deeply intertwined with structures of power, anti-Black racism, and social control. Critical scholars, particularly those grounded in Black feminism, race, gender, and sexuality, have engaged in rigorous research, analysis, and activism, uncovering the multiple ways the carceral state targets and harms marginalized communities. As Davis has made clear, the state has often turned to systems of punishment to "solve" largely social problems.[8] Both critical criminologists and abolitionists examine systemic factors that contribute to racial disparities in rates of arrest, sentencing, and incarceration rates. By examining the sociological and political forces that shape the PIC, abolitionists and scholars expose and challenge mechanisms through which oppression is perpetuated within and beyond the system.

Another point of convergence between critical criminology and abolitionism is through the critique and rejection of carceral rhetoric, the language and discourse that commonly surrounds ideas, practices, and policies within the criminal legal system. Both abolitionists and critical scholars acknowledge the dangers of carceral rhetoric, highlighting the traditional emphasis on punishment and retribution, and stigmatizing individuals who've had involvement in the legal system. Rather than ignoring the predominantly social and economic factors that contribute to incarceration and system involvement, critical scholars and abolitionists aim to shift the focus away from desires for punishment and control. Ultimately, they argue that such rhetoric contributes to the further dehumanization and stigmatization of individuals who make contact with the criminal legal system, again, expanding social inequalities and further marginalization. Abolitionists emphasize the need to challenge and dismantle the stereotypes, language, and narratives that justify punishment and instead advocate for alternative approaches that center on restoration and addressing the root causes of crime and other harms. By challenging carceral rhetoric, both abolitionists and critical scholars implore a shift in public discourse and move toward affirming solutions.

PIC abolitionists and critical carceral studies also view the PIC as an entrenched system that permeates various aspects of everyday life. From rapidly expanding surveillance technologies and new constructions of power to increased criminalization, scholars must examine how the PIC functions beyond the prison. Abolitionists and critical carceral studies argue that the PIC extends beyond physical prisons and encompasses a "web" of interconnected institutions, policies, and practices, all of which perpetuate social control and inequality.[9] The web engages with individuals and society in a number of ways, often without inherent realization. The carceral system makes itself known through the continued criminalization of marginalized communities, including but not limited to Black and other people of color, LGBTQ+ individuals, and those experiencing poverty and homelessness. Scholars analyze how the PIC intersects with education, employment, housing, and health care, ultimately revealing how individual experiences and opportunities are shaped by its presence. By examining the everyday manifestations of the PIC, abolitionists and critical scholars aim to challenge its normalization and advocate for alternatives that prioritize community well-being, social justice, and the ultimate dismantling of systems of oppression.

Critical carceral studies and critical criminologists have not operated in a silo. Their scholarship is often produced and informed by those closest to issues surrounding the carceral state. Of those close connections, Black women, queer, and trans abolitionists have often served as community leaders and disrupters of violence, promoting alternatives to reliance on legal systems and creating solidarity frameworks to care for those most frequently targeted by the state. Thus, Black women, queer, and trans abolitionists hold critical insight from which the criminology discipline must draw. Despite their leadership and advocacy work, these voices remain marginalized within criminology and only recently have increased within the subfield of critical criminology. These perspectives, when incorporated into the broader criminological landscape, can push the discipline closer to transformation.

BLACK WOMEN, QUEER, AND TRANS ABOLITIONIST PERSPECTIVES

Black women, queer, and trans people have played significant roles in shaping abolitionist frameworks as well as critical criminological perspectives. Their identities and experiences have long been topics of analysis through social movements and collective advocacy. These histories, however, have often witnessed the erasure and further marginalization of certain identities and, as such, are not without limitations. This is particularly evident in the context of Black women–centered approaches and early Black feminisms, where the experiences and narratives of queer and trans people have been historically overlooked and often excluded. Similarly, within queer and trans spaces, early theoretical frames often exhibited race-neutral perspectives, leading to the neglect of intersecting oppressions faced by Black queer and trans people. While both Black feminist and queer and trans studies have been crucial in framing abolitionist ideals and challenging oppressive systems, early framings of both have largely neglected the unique experiences of queer Black people. I argue it is both Black women and Black queer and trans abolitionist perspectives, taken together, that fill the gaps left by both traditional Black feminist and early queer theorists.

Black women have long been at the forefront of fights against systemic oppression and violence, often using their voices, experiences, and advocacy to challenge oppressive systems, including the PIC. As such, the connection between Black feminism, Black Feminist Thought, and abolition is deeply intertwined in a shared commitment to challenging intersecting systems and envisioning just societies. Black feminism first emerged as a response to the limitations of mainstream feminist movements, most of which failed to acknowledge the unique experiences and struggles of Black women. Black Feminist Thought, as articulated by scholar Patricia Hill Collins, further developed these ideas, providing scholars with a framework to analyze intersections of race, gender, class, and other social categories.[10] As such, Black Feminist Thought centers the voices and perspectives of Black women who were and are often relegated to the sidelines. These interdisciplinary fields of knowledge have played important roles in informing abolitionist goals and extending existing frameworks to recognize how the criminal legal system disproportionately targets and harms Black women.[11] In the late twentieth century, the concepts of both Black feminism and abolition gained momentum, as scholars and Black feminists Angela Davis, Audre Lorde, bell hooks, and others highlighted the various ways the PIC perpetrated systemic violence and oppression, particularly against Black women and Black communities. Ultimately, their perspectives have challenged mainstream understandings of crime and punishment as they've articulated visions of a society that has moved beyond incarceration.

Similarly, queer and trans activists have fought against the constant criminalization of their identities and individual experiences. Queer and trans abolitionist perspectives emerged during the 1960s and 1970s as scholars and activists viewed the prison as a site of violence and discrimination, and a perpetrator of harm against LGBTQ+ individuals. The Stonewall Inn uprising in 1969 is often hailed as a pivotal movement in LGBTQ+ history and greatly informed the queer and trans abolitionist movement.[12] Led by Black and Latinx trans women Marsha P. Johnson and Sylvia Rivera, the uprising ultimately operated as a catalyst for transformative movements led by queer people. In the years following the Stonewall uprising, queer and trans scholars and advocates began to challenge not only the criminalization of queer identities, but also systems of incarceration, policing, and punishment—all of which disproportionately target and further marginalize queer and trans people. As such, the fight for LGBTQ+ rights became deeply intertwined with broader struggles for equity and justice, including the fight against racial discrimination and the far reach of the prison industrial complex.

The Black trans lives matter movement stands as a powerful and critical continuation of early LGBTQ+ abolitionist advocacy. By focusing on the experiences of Black trans people, advocates have directed needed attention toward the marginalization, violence, and discrimination faced by Black trans people within and beyond the prison system. The movement highlights the need for policy change and acknowledges the inherent goals of seeking the safety, dignity, and rights of trans folks. Building upon the foundation laid by early LGBTQ+ advocates and abolitionists, current work also includes organized advocacy surrounding incarcerated trans populations and a desire to challenge the systems that have long perpetuated dehumanization, criminalization, exploitation, and harm. Through grassroots advocacy, legal organizing, and coalition building, the movement strives for a world where Black and other trans lives are not only protected but also celebrated.

Considered collectively, Black women and Black queer and trans people have contributed to shaping abolitionist spaces by centering the experiences and struggles of the most socially marginalized communities. Their intersectional analyses, scholarly contributions, and ongoing advocacy have challenged the narrow focus of critical criminology and have also expanded abolitionist discourse to be both inclusive and comprehensive. From the Black women–founded Combahee River Collective to queer-led organizations like Black & Pink, Black women, queer, and trans perspectives must be at the forefront of the ongoing fight to dismantle carceral systems. By incorporating an understanding of the interconnectedness of race, gender, sexuality, and other axes of oppression, these perspectives broaden the scope of abolitionist movements within and beyond critical carceral studies and contribute to a transformative vision of justice, safety, and community. Below, I draw upon abolitionist visions that incorporate both Black women and Black queer and trans perspectives in response to two critical areas in which abolitionists and criminologists must engage.

Perspectives on Crime, Law, and Its Enforcers

Criminalization serves as the framework for mass incarceration, perpetuating a cycle of systemic inequality and social control. It's within the framework of criminalization that marginalized communities, particularly Black women and LGBTQ+ individuals, are disproportionately targeted and subjected to coercive forces of the criminal legal system. As the Prison Policy Initiative indicates, LGBTQ+ people are overrepresented at every stage of the criminal legal system.[13] More specifically, LGB people are much more likely to be arrested than their straight counterparts.[14] According to the National LGBTQ Task Force,

Black LGBTQ+ people are disproportionately targeted by policing practices, with many facing heightened levels of discrimination, violence, and surveillance, often intersecting both racism and homophobia/transphobia. Similarly, Black women are disproportionately impacted by the criminal legal system, having increased encounters with police through racial profiling and biased practices. Historically, Black women have faced significant challenges when seeking justice through the legal system. As reported by the African American Policy Forum, Black women are more likely to be wrongfully convicted and are often subject to harsh sentences, as compared to their non-Black counterparts.

In response to this overt criminalization, and increased risk of contact with police, Black women, queer, and trans abolitionists have long critiqued traditional understandings of crime and the role of law enforcement within the punishment system. As such, abolitionists view crime as a social construct, often referring to its commission as "fluid not static."[15] Black women, queer, and trans abolitionists reject the notion that increased policing leads to safety. They also challenge the pervasive narrative that portrays overpolicing as a necessary response to crime, placing emphasis on how it often perpetuates systemic racism and reinforces a cycle of criminalization. Black women abolitionists have highlighted overpolicing as an infection to Black communities, bringing with it constant surveillance, harassment, and further exacerbating inequalities.

Black women abolitionists and Black, queer, and trans abolitionists share a commitment to dismantling oppressive structures, including socially constructed definitions of crime, law, and policing. Additionally, they advocate for divestment from law enforcement and the reinvestment of resources and finances toward community initiatives, particularly those addressing the causes of crime, including but not limited to poverty, education, health care, and social services. Their perspectives ultimately offer a comprehensive critique of the criminal legal system and encourage a shift away from punishment and toward restoration. As is argued throughout this chapter, by centering the voices and experiences of those most impacted by these vicious systems, we are presented with critical insight into the potential of abolitionist approaches and visions.

Perspectives on Prisons and Punishment

Black women, queer, and trans abolitionists have sought to "queer the carceral," placing emphasis and focus on the ways in which the prison and the overall carceral system operate through a gendered, sexualized, and racialized lens.[16] As such, queerness, race, and what is deemed "deviant" are inherently intertwined, significantly impacting the lives of Black women and Black LGBTQ+ individuals. While the incarcerated women's population has dramatically increased since the 1980s, Black women and other women of color remain disproportionately impacted by systems of punishment. Black women account for approximately 7.8 percent of the general population but make up 29 percent of incarcerated women.[17] While there is considerably little information available regarding trans people and their distinct experiences within the carceral system, the National Center for Transgender Equality reports that Black trans people have considerably more police contact and, according to the Prison Policy Initiative, have the highest percentage of lifetime rates of incarceration.[18] While incarcerated in prisons, jails, immigration detention facilities, and probation systems, Black women, queer, and trans people often experience increased emotional and physical damage through categorization, surveillance, and further criminalization.[19] Given the troubling statistics and individual narratives of those harmed by the present systems of punishment, critical criminologists must turn to these same individuals for solutions.

Borrowing from the words of Black feminist and abolitionist Angela Davis, "prisons do not disappear social problems, they disappear human beings."[20] Black women, queer, and trans abolitionists have a critical and nuanced perspective on prisons and punishment. They acknowledge such systems perpetuate harm and cycles of violence, and disproportionately target socially marginalized groups. Rather than viewing prisons and systems of incarceration as effective means of addressing harm, they recognize the inherent flaws and seek alternatives, like supportive, community-based initiatives that restore individuals and groups. For Black women abolitionists, there is a deep understanding of the historical and ongoing target that the criminal legal system places on their communities. Black women have had a front-row seat to the devastating toll of mass incarceration, ultimately resulting in the separation of loved ones, loss of economic opportunities, and increased trauma. Black women and Black, queer, and trans abolitionists also bring a unique perspective. They ultimately recognize that LGBTQ+ individuals, particularly Black trans people, face higher rates of criminalization, harassment, and violence within systems of punishment. As abolitionists, they challenge the notion that prisons have the capacity to provide safety and justice for the queer community.

Collectively, Black women, queer, and trans abolitionists pursue transformative approaches to justice, moving society beyond punishment incarceration. Instead of ideals aligned with traditional criminology, they emphasize the need to address root causes of harm, highlighting systemic inequalities, poverty, homelessness, trauma, and other social conditions that produce hyperincarceration and criminalization. They prioritize community-based alternatives that center on healing, restoration, and accountability. By uplifting and centering the voices of those most impacted by the carceral system, Black women, queer, and trans abolitionists work toward building a more compassionate and equitable future that adequately addresses harms brought by the prison industrial complex, while uplifting the humanity and dignity of all.

CHALLENGING AND MOVING THE DISCIPLINE FORWARD

Ultimately, the integration of critical criminology along with the inclusion of perspectives of Black women and Black, queer, and trans abolitionists can—and if embraced, will—profoundly transform the criminological landscape. As such, critical criminology plays a crucial role in transforming the discipline by challenging and disrupting conventional understandings of crime, punishment, and carcerality, as well as centering the experiences of those most socially marginalized. By centering the narratives, experiences, and insights of the often overlooked, critical criminology and abolitionist perspectives bring forth a more nuanced understanding of the intersecting systems of oppression that perpetuate traditional understandings of mass incarceration and uphold the carceral state.

Earlier in this chapter, I critiqued traditional criminology's functions, particularly surrounding its use within the criminal legal system and in teachings in the academy, and its prominence within political culture. While connections within the legal system and political culture are important, I place particular emphasis on criminology's function in the classroom, especially as the discipline continues to teach and mold individuals who leave educational systems in pursuit of jobs in, including but not limited to, law enforcement, policy, and research. Given this, incorporating the perspectives of Black women, queer, and trans abolitionists within critical criminology and critical carceral studies is an essential step in ensuring a comprehensive understanding of systems of punishment.

In the classroom, integrating critical criminology and Black abolitionist frameworks can provide students with a more comprehensive understanding of the punishment system and its social contexts. If we're to draw inspiration from the late bell hooks, we understand that the classroom remains a "radical space to transform the academy."[21] Incorporating a more concentrated effort to understand perspectives from Black women, queer, and trans abolitionists encourages a shift away from traditional, punitive approaches to crime and justice. Instead, it emphasizes the importance of restorative justice practice, community accountability, and addressing root causes of incarceration, rather than focusing on retribution and deterrence. A transformative pedagogy that centers on abolitionism also encourages students to examine the social, economic, and political factors that may contribute to the prison nation and explore effective strategies for responding to or even preventing harm.

Furthermore, transforming—or at least challenging—the discipline of criminology through a critical and abolitionist approach necessitates a change in pedagogy. It ultimately requires educators to adopt or uplift abolitionist ideals that challenge traditionally punitive paradigms. Instead, instruction should embrace transformation and promote classroom environments where students are not only prompted but encouraged to ask questions and challenge the status quo. In doing so, we invite imagination back into the classroom, allowing students and professors alike to envision alternative approaches to justice and actively work toward dismantling oppressive systems.

In conclusion, the importance of critical criminology, particularly that which centers and uplifts Black women and Black, queer, and trans abolitionist perspectives, lies in its potential to fully expose and participate in dismantling oppressive structures within the carceral system. By critically examining and challenging assumptions, ideologies, and structures that underpin the prison nation, these abolitionist ideologies help create space for alternative visions of transformation, resistance, justice, and change. Perhaps the question regarding criminology's ability to embrace abolition is not yet answered; however, small steps can help shift perspectives. By embracing the insights and perspectives of those closest to systems of oppression, shifting research initiatives, and uplifting differing perspectives within and beyond the classroom, the discipline of criminology (or at least those within it) can move toward a just and equitable understanding of abolition.

NOTES

1. Cohen, *Against Criminology*; Murakawa, *The First Civil Right: How Liberals Built Prison America*.

2. Brown and Schept, "New Abolition, Criminology and a Critical Carceral Studies."

3. Coyle and Schept, "Penal Abolition and the State: Colonial, Racial and Gender Violences"; Woodall, "We Are All Criminals."

4. Alexander, *The New Jim Crow: Mass Incarceration in the Age of Colorblindness*; Davis, *Are Prisons Obsolete?*; Kilgore, *Understanding Mass Incarceration: A People's Guide to the Key Civil Rights Struggle of Our Time*.

5. Berger and Losier, *Rethinking the American Prison Movement*; Greene, "Gender Bound: Making, Managing, and Navigating Prison Gender Boundaries, 1941–2018."

6. Thorneycroft and Asquith, "Cripping Criminology"; Carlen and França, *Alternative Criminologies*.

7. Martensen and Richie, "Prison Abolition."

8. Davis, *Are Prisons Obsolete?*

9. Gottschalk, "Democracy and the Carceral State in America."

10. Collins, *Black Feminist Thought: Knowledge, Consciousness, and the Politics of Empowerment*.

11. Bailey, "Misogynoir Transformed."

12. Walker et al., "Why Don't We Center Abolition in Queer Criminology?"

13. Jones, "Visualizing the Unequal Treatment of LGBTQ People in the Criminal Justice System."

14. Jones.

15. Richie and Martensen, "Resisting Carcerality, Embracing Abolition: Implications for Feminist Social Work Practice."

16. Vitulli, "Queering the Carceral."

17. Budd and Monazzam, *Incarcerated Women and Girls*.

18. Jones, "Visualizing the Unequal Treatment of LGBTQ People in the Criminal Justice System."

19. Walker et al., "Why Don't We Center Abolition in Queer Criminology?"

20. Davis, "Masked Racism: Reflections on the Prison Industrial Complex."

21. hooks, *Teaching to Transgress: Education as the Practice of Freedom*.

CHAPTER 12

From Prison to Police Abolition

Challenging Queer Criminology's
Investments in the Police

EMMA K. RUSSELL, LA TROBE UNIVERSITY

In February 2012, the middle of summer in so-called Australia, I was organizing at the interstice of two grassroots collectives—Queering the Air and the Abolition Collective—to intervene in the normalization of "carceral pride" encapsulated by the growing Victoria Police contingent at the annual Pride March in Melbourne.[1] We created a double-sided A5 flyer printed on hot-pink paper, titled "NO PRIDE IN A POLICE STATE," to hand out to marchers and spectators, which argued that LGBT partnerships with police "legitimise, strengthen and expand the reach of existing police practices" that "target poor and racialized communities" (figure 2).[2] At the time, Victoria Police had been subject to sustained criticism in the media for racial profiling of African-Australian youth, and we wanted to develop an analysis of racialized policing and anti-trans/queer violence as interlinked, rather than discrete, phenomena.[3] By asserting that "police racism is a queer issue," we wanted to highlight that LGBTIQ+ partnerships with police weren't the only way to secure queer and trans safety, and indeed were risky and exclusionary. Alternative solidarities and alliances were (and are) possible. My own perspective on the police was shaped by my experiences of gendered-sexualized police violence during arrests as a student activist and witnessing police brutality and misinformation campaigns wielded against friends during and after protests. I was also aware of how my racialization (as white) and class ascendancy (as a student at a prestigious university) buffered me from the pervasive surveillance recounted by others without access to that same racial-class mobility.

This was a largely symbolic action, unlike many instances of queer disruption to pride events that preceded us—and that would follow us.[4] Indeed, "No Police in Pride" protest actions calling for the decentering of police are now a staple at Melbourne's Pride March, spurred by the persistence of the Victoria Police contingent, accompanied by many of its carceral collaborators: the Sheriff's Office, Corrections, and private detention companies, such as Serco. There are likewise numerous international examples of similar modes of queer/trans disruption of carceral inclusion.[5] Alongside other forms of lobbying, queer protesters have successfully compelled organizers to ban uniformed police presence at Pride events, such as in Auckland, New York, San Francisco, Vancouver, and London.[6]

While our action at Melbourne Pride March in 2012 was limited in its capacity to force a confrontation or "carceral reckoning" within this space, the organizing process allowed us to collectively develop a queer critique of police power that wasn't new but was specific to our local time, context, and perspective.[7] For me, it spurred a series of questions about queer complicity in racial state violence that I was driven to explore through my next few years of study as a PhD student.

A few months later, in July 2012, I attended a critical criminology conference at the University of Tasmania. I presented a conceptual paper based on the early ideas I was exploring for my PhD project. The paper was called "Police Relations with LGBTQ Communities: Challenging the Narrative of 'Progress.'" I sought to critique the seeming "embrace" of policing and punishment by LGBTIQ organizations, exemplified by the growing visibility of not only police "pride" at LGBTIQ events, but also LGBTIQ campaigns for inclusion in police anti-hate crime strategies, community liaison initiatives, and traditional "crime-stoppers" approaches to public safety.[8] After delivering this paper, I was privately approached by a senior gay male academic in my field, who insisted upon the irrelevance of my critique. From my recollection, his perspective was essentially that progress in policing had, in fact, been achieved, such that a critique of queer investments in police reform was redundant, because police were now on "our" side. In his eyes, it seemed, mounting this argument positioned me as an "unhappy queer"—the cultural figure that feminist theorist Sara Ahmed describes as being cast as immature, ungrateful, and paranoid upon refusing the

NO PRIDE IN A POLICE STATE

POLICE IN THIS PARADE DON'T MAKE US SAFE

The recent enthusiasm some LGBTI groups have shown for collaborating and aiding policing operations is disturbing considering the police's historical and ongoing targeting of people who are queer, trans, Indigenous, racialised, dis/abled, poor, and/or homeless. It was only in 1981 that homosexuality was decriminalised in Victoria. Yet today the PR unit in the Victoria Police convey a narrative of 'progress' that moves from the active persecution of queers under anti-sodomy laws only 30 years ago to the establishment of the *Gay and Lesbian Liaison Officer'* ('GLLO') unit over the past decade and the *'Prejudice Motivated Crime'* (PMC) strategy released last year. These developments have come about, in part, through vocal queer criticism of longstanding police homophobia and discrimination. Some prominent LGBTI groups have received these initiatives as welcome reforms, disregarding the ways that queer and trans people continue to criminalised. To work towards safety for all queers and trans folk we need to tackle transphobia and homophobia at their roots.

TRANSPHOBIA AND HOMOPHOBIA ISN'T JUST ABOUT INDIVIDUALS

LGBTI groups working collaboratively with the police focus on homophobic and transphobic violence and oppression in terms of individual behaviours and ignorance. Instead, we see transphobia and homophobia as structural issues. Queer and trans folks are more vulnerable to employment and housing discrimination than our straight peers, and almost a quarter of homeless youth are queer or trans. Dominant belief systems promote the ideas that queer and trans folks are worth less, are dangerous just by existing, that our identities are a lie, or that we need to be pressured or punished into acting straight. These ideas are widespread, often legally sanctioned and form part of the status quo. Approaches focusing on GLLOs and individual crimes won't get to the roots of queer and trans oppression.

POLICE RACISM IS A QUEER ISSUE

The ongoing effects of colonialism displace and impoverish Aboriginal communities, making Aboriginal people vulnerable to racist street policing. As public spaces are increasingly privatised, people who lack wealth are over-policed and excluded. Recent reports show that African young people in Melbourne experience disproportionate police surveillance, harassment and violence on a daily basis. Police often use ethnic descriptors of perpetrators to target racialised communities and sections of the queer media perpetuate racist sentiments and stereotypes by describing the perceived ethnicity of perpetrators. This further fuels the myth that communities of colour are more homophobic than white communities. Queer and trans people are present in many different communities. Many queer and trans people are also poor, or Aboriginal, or migrants, or dis/abled. **We must move beyond single-issue politics.** Different forms

FIGURE 2. "No Pride in a Police State" flyer, created by Queering the Air 3CR Community Radio and the Abolition Collective, 2012. Photo by the author.

of oppression - whether based on race, class, ability, gender or sexuality - cannot be neatly divided up or separated out. Our queerness and gender non-conformity aren't isolated from other aspects of our lives. Our presence in every community is our strength and that's been our rallying cry for decades.

"STILL, AREN'T GLLOS BETTER THAN NOTHING?!"

Police GLLOs and the PMC strategy co-opt the fear and rage queer and trans people experience as targets of both state-administered and interpersonal violence. LGBTI collaborations with the police legitimise, strengthen and expand the reach of existing policing practices that focus on individual punishment and target poor and racialised communities. We can't let police initiatives couched in progressive rhetoric deflect our attention away from police brutality and a rapidly expanding criminal punishment system. Not in our name. We will not be complicit. As police collaboration remains at the top of many LGBTI agendas, the routine police harassment confronting queer Indigenous people, queers of colour, poor queers, and their communities, is silenced and ignored by mainstream gay organising. **Collaborating with police excludes too many queers.** If our goal is to create safer lives for all queer people then we need to tackle homophobia, transphobia, racism, sexism and ableism in all their forms.

WE SUPPORT STRATEGIES THAT WEAKEN OPPRESSIVE INSTITUTIONS, NOT STRENGTHEN THEM

Today's Pride March is an international tradition that commemorates the Stonewall riots, an historical event catalysed by queers and transwomen of colour defending themselves against a transphobic, homophobic and racist bar raid by police. In order to honour this legacy, we're organising against state violence and multiple forms of oppression, continuing radical queer histories that span across borders. **Instead of directing our energies towards creating alliances with the police we should build alternative solidarities that resist and refuse oppressive relations.** By focusing on grassroots organising with other progressive community-based groups we can create social change from the ground up rather than relying on a "trickle down" effect. We can imagine more creative ways to open up discussions in our communities around intertwined issues of homophobia, transphobia, racism, poverty, sexism, ableism and how to address these on all levels. We can campaign for increased access to services and support for those most marginalised in queer communities - such as housing, healthcare, education and welfare. These approaches encourage more holistic and long-term visions of community safety for all queers and our allies. *None of Us or All of Us.*

Contact: abolitioncollective@gmail.com
*This pamphlet was created by **Queering the Air**, a new queer radio show on 3CR Radio 855am 3pm every Sunday, and **The Abolition Collective**, committed to creating safer communities without prisons or policing.*

promises of inclusion extended by the state.[9] The evidence cited for progress, in this incident, was his recent experience reporting homophobic harassment to receptive and friendly cops.

Putting aside the power dynamics in this exchange, the lack of reflexivity displayed by this academic was striking. As numerous critical scholars have pointed out, liberal rights–based advances in movements for lesbian and gay rights—often conceived narrowly through frames of recognition and inclusion in powerful institutions of governance, rather than liberation from them—can give the misleading impression that the problem of coercive state intervention has been solved for white, upwardly mobile, cisgendered lesbians and gay men.[10] However, the notion that the "violence work" of policing is no longer a queer/trans issue belies the escalation of aggressive drug policing in some jurisdictions and the persistent criminalization of homelessness and sex work.[11] It also relies on a myopic view of queer/trans communities that attempts to bracket out the issues of racism, poverty, and disability that intersect us with numerous overpoliced groups.[12] When approached intersectionally and structurally, the relationship between queer/trans communities and the police continues to be fraught, violent, and, of course, profoundly unequal.

Rather than narrate anti-trans/queer violence as a discrete event perpetrated by individual "homophobic" actors, Eric Stanley argues that we should understand it as a structuring force that is foundational to the democratic state. As they elaborate, "Thinking violence as individual acts versus epistemic force works to support the normative and normalizing structuring of public pain. This is to say, privatizing anti-trans/queer violence is a function through which the social and its trauma are whitewashed, heterosexualized, and made to appear gender-normative. . . . Through a reproduction of the teleological narrative of progress, it also reproduces the idea that anti-trans/queer violence is an aberration of democracy—belonging only to a shadowed past, and increasingly anachronistic."[13]

Stanley's point that anti-queer/trans violence is structuring, not aberrational, is important to reframe debates about police as perpetrator or protector for queer communities. They write, "Rather than imagining the law as the mechanism through which relief from [anti-trans/queer violence] might be offered, it is one of its methodologies of proliferation."[14] Thinking of policing as violence work moves us beyond a framework of liberal reform that pursues equal rights in a carceral state. Instead, this presents the possibilities of refusal and abolition.

I ground this chapter in these personal stories to prompt deeper reflection on the questions that these moments raised for me and that are central to queer criminology: How do we meaningfully connect scholarship and activism? What are the conceptual preconditions for queer scholars to confront our investments in police power? How do we challenge criminological collusion with the police and instead build an abolitionist ethic and praxis in scholarship? To explore these questions, I canvas the amplification of police abolition praxis over the past decade and consider how it builds upon prison abolitionist theory. How are abolitionist movements resisting and theorizing the police power? I contend that a deeper analysis of the coloniality of the police power in queer/trans justice movements will enhance our capacity to elucidate the violence work of policing, which will aid in contesting criminological complicities in recuperating a police project in crisis. I further argue that the notion that abolition is simply about targeting a singular institution in isolation should be replaced by a more expansive confrontation with the social power relations that reproduce carcerality. Together, these ideas enhance the toolkit for scholars and activists navigating the treacherous terrain of policing in unequal societies.

THE AMPLIFICATION OF POLICE ABOLITION THEORY

Historical lineages of abolition theory are varied across different geographical and cultural contexts. Within the academic discipline of criminology, the idea that the prison is beyond reform has been debated since at least the 1970s.[15] At the more liberal end of this spectrum, critical criminologists have challenged the prison as a counterproductive response to harm and argued instead for more restorative approaches to justice. More radical lineages of abolitionist thought have advanced understandings of the prison not as a response to crime, per se, but as a mode of containment for the "surplus populations" produced by racial capitalism.[16] These varying conceptualizations of prison abolition have informed the emergence of a paradigm of police abolition, which presents many of the same tensions.

While there has been a rich tradition of critical police studies,[17] abolitionist scholarship on policing has rapidly expanded in the past decade, alongside increasing calls for an end to policing emerging from transnational movements for Black lives in the wake of sustained patterns of lethal racial violence perpetrated by police.[18] This gives rise to the question, what changes when police, rather than prisons, become the target of abolitionist praxis? Meghan McDowell and Luis Fernandez describe a praxis of police abolition that revolves around the push to "disband, disempower and disarm" law enforcement institutions.[19] They posit that eliminating the institution of policing is the overall goal, then disarmament and disempowerment are the interconnected tactics used to achieve this goal.[20] As abolitionist demands for an end to police become more central, the new generation of abolitionists needs to take an uncompromising position that can resist co-option and incorporation,[21] lest campaigns to defund the police lead to compromises that amount to what Schenwar and Law call "non-alternative alternatives," or carceral net-widening and recuperation.[22]

In practice and theory, abolitionism necessitates vigilant engagement with the problem of reform. As the tensions between more liberal and radical iterations of social change manifest in debates over injustice in policing, prison abolitionist theory brings a framework to distinguish between and parse out reforms that weaken the system (nonreformist reforms) and those that risk recuperating and expanding it (reformist reforms).[23] The danger of the latter is that reform and abolition come to be seen as reconcilable, which results in "humanising police and cages while defusing and domesticating abolition's political potential."[24] As Zhandarka Kurti and Michelle Brown affirm, "while abolitionists have not completely disregarded reform or incremental changes, they absolutely refuse them as end goals."[25]

In practice, abolitionist campaigns tend to be leveled against specific institutional "objects"—especially the prison, and now, the police. However, theorizing on abolition tends to be broader and more nuanced. In her seminal text *Is Prison Obsolete?*, Angela Davis challenges the idea that the prison could be replaced or superseded by a singular institution without transforming the social and economic conditions that give rise to the prison. Instead of trying "to imagine one single alternative . . . we might envision an array of alternatives that will require radical transformations of many aspects of our society," she writes.[26] As Stefano Harney and Fred Moten define abolition, it is "not so much the abolition of prisons but the abolition of a society that could have prisons, that could have slavery, that could have the wage, and therefore not abolition as the elimination of anything but abolition as the founding of a new society."[27] In this reading, the task is to dismantle not just the institutions of prisons and police, but the very social conditions for mass criminalization, which returns us to the importance of a structural critique of policing. Rather than attempting to repair the worst excesses of police power through a series of reforms and safeguards without fundamental and transformative social change, an abolitionist position relies on a particular analysis of the role of police in colonialism and racial capitalism that has been stridently advanced by racial justice movements in distinct local and regional contexts.[28] Linking these transregional analyses is the idea that racial violence is "a constitutive, rather than aberrant, element of policing."[29] This gives rise to further questions for scholars of critical and queer criminology: How does history shape the present? How does policing reproduce queer injustice? If violence is constitutive of policing, how might queer/trans safety, justice, and liberation be pursued?

RECKONING WITH THE COLONIALITY OF THE POLICE POWER

To develop a structural analysis of the police and advance an abolitionist ethic in queer justice work, it is essential to draw the links between coloniality and the policing (and production) of sexuality and gender categories. This foremost requires reckoning with the central role that institutions of policing have played in the attempted genocide and dispossession of Indigenous peoples as part of settler colonial projects of land acquisition in various white settler colonial contexts, including Australia, New Zealand, Canada, and the United States.[30] These genealogies of "white settler violence," Canadian critical race scholar Sherene Razack argues, "flow through institutions such as policing," and policing is a site where people "can enact racial hierarchy on behalf of the colonial state."[31] In Australia, police-perpetrated massacres and displacements have formed part of a larger mobile strategy of producing "safety" for settlers through establishing and expanding "white space."[32] Historicizing policing as a tool of racial and colonial dominance enables deeper appreciation of policing as "violence work," challenging the idea that police brutality is somehow excessive or aberrational to the system, rather than intrinsic to it.[33]

Police both instantiate and enforce racial, gender, sexual, and class boundaries.[34] Through various forms of surveillance, spatial containment, and violent intervention, police practices have disciplined sexual and gender expression and marked queerness as variously excessive and threatening, "unthinkable and unknowable,"[35] and perpetually "out-of-place."[36] As many critical policing scholars have elucidated, policing is not merely a repressive apparatus of power, but a productive one.[37]

Policing is actively involved in reconstituting public space as hetero-sexual space and reinforcing the heteronormative social order.[38] In *Queer Histories and the Politics of Policing*, I argue that "a historicised critique of policing solely based on its gender and sexual disciplinary techniques and effects would result in a myopic view" of the institu-tion's relationship to dominant structures of racial and class power.[39] For instance, conventional stories about the criminalization of sodomy in Australia and the United States have been challenged by queer schol-ars highlighting the reality of uneven enforcement and the embedded-ness of these laws in anti-Blackness.[40] A more thoroughly intersectional and coalitional queer justice project requires critiques that "encompass broader recognition of the violence of policing that is continually visited upon First Nations people and others marginalised by their race, class, disability, gender, sexuality, or any combination of these."[41]

Studying police history further reveals the duplicitous role of seem-ingly progressive reforms in consolidating and expanding state power. For instance, historians Leigh Boucher and Robert Reynolds point out that decriminalization of homosexuality in Australia has been partial and inconsistent.[42] While sodomy was slowly removed from crime leg-islation in the late 1970s and early 1980s, various other queer practices were recriminalized, or remained outside the scope of redemption, such as expungement legislation excluding cases of public sex, or age of con-sent laws only being equalized in Queensland in 2016.[43] This reminds us that queer/trans justice cannot be conceptualized on a historical arc of progress and that moral boundaries are redrawn by law and its enforcement even in times of seemingly progressive reform.

The importance of this critical work persists for queer studies as the scope and scale of police power continues to expand. In my local con-text, Victoria Police has received more than three thousand new officers since 2016, as part of an AUD$2 billion investment—reportedly "the biggest in the history of the force."[44] Against this backdrop of sustained carceral buildup and the slow violence of police militarization, State Premier Daniel Andrews often "relies on the gay community to appear progressive."[45] However, there are flashpoints that, as Gunnai/Kurnai, Gunditjmara, Wiradjuri, and Yorta Yorta writer Nayuka Gorrie argues, shock "white queers to recognize what the relationship [with police] really is and how quickly the supposed contract between queer com-munities and police can be broken."[46] In May 2019, there was the 2 a.m. raid by Victoria Police's Critical Incident Response Team on the residence attached to Melbourne's iconic queer bookstore Hares &

Hyenas, which resulted in a fleeing Nik Dimopoulos having a broken arm zip-locked behind his back.[47] In March 2023, there was the "pushing, shoving, encircling and pepper-spraying" of pro-trans protesters by Victoria Police, "while a group of neo-Nazis were allowed to assemble behind police lines and perform a lengthy succession of Nazi salutes on the steps of Parliament House."[48] These instances of assault are rare only insofar as they succeed in capturing wider media attention and index only the most visible forms of anti-trans/queer state violence.

Lest we fall into the trap of exceptionalizing this violence, scholars engaging in queer criminology need to push the field's ambit beyond "legible, pre-established, singularising axes of sex/gender identity ('LGBTQI')."[49] As queer cultural studies scholar Kane Race argues, the critical eye of queer criminology should be trained squarely on those "structurally routinised" forms of violence and degradation: "drug policing, border patrol, structural racism, and endemic, uneven carceralism."[50] This returns us to the importance of engaging with not only intersectionality, but the politics of disposability to ensure that no one is left behind in queer/trans justice scholarship.[51] This involves reflecting on questions such as, "Who counts as an endangered party worthy of sympathy and protection, and who/what is constituted as abominably endangering?"[52] Part of developing an alternative and abolitionist framework for resisting the impulse to liberal reforms that rely on minoritarian identity categories and reinforce moral hierarchies might be what Stanley sets out in *Atmospheres of Violence* as the trans/queer ungovernable. That is, a collectivization of practices that "refutes the state" and sidesteps "classical recognition by way of provoking an encounter with unintelligibility."[53] This might be conceptualized as a kind of trans/queer appropriation of the "unintelligibility" with which our sexualities and genders have often been cast by the law and provoke a more radical embrace of abolitionism by queer scholars.[54]

CONCLUSION

In *Practising Everyday Abolition*, queer socio-legal scholar and organizer S Lamble argues that we cannot treat "abolition as a singular or revolutionary 'event' but as an ongoing process and practice." What Lamble describes as "everyday abolition" encompasses the "double work" of reducing the power of the criminal legal system and building our capacity for "alternative systems of preventing, addressing and responding to harm." It thereby involves connecting "efforts toward structural change with everyday cultures and practices" to challenge punitive logics (and the equation of punishment with justice) wherever they manifest in our lives.[55]

While Lamble's notion of "everyday abolition" is elaborated mostly in terms of activist communities and the various spaces that we/they work and live within (schools, etc.), the idea of everyday abolition and building decarceral cultures is eminently relevant to our scholarship, especially for those of us entangled in the discipline of criminology, which is the knowledge-production arm of the carceral state.[56] Queer scholarship can refute the state logics that individualize violence through the way we frame our research aims and questions, and how we interpret data and texts. We can also be attuned to who our research is aligning with, and who our universities are partnering with, and collectively organize to push back against knowledge production that advances the capacity for carceral systems to profile "suspect" populations more effectively.[57]

In *The Horror of Police*, critical criminologist Travis Linnemann attends to the question, what are the police afraid of? He concludes that "police fear a change to the present state of affairs."[58] If the transformative possibilities of collective action and solidarity haunt the police, how do we build intersectional and coalitional forms of critique and struggle that will unsettle the police power? The proliferation of anti-racist queer/trans interventions at Pride events shows how highly visible political contestations can raise broader questions about the hierarchizing and exclusionary effects of enfolding of queerness into the police power. However, these are no more important than quieter forms of abolitionist solidarity, such as projects with currently and formerly incarcerated queer, trans, and gender-diverse people. These, and myriad others, are ways that we can experiment with forms of solidarity that refuse the logics of disposability that underpin policing and the settler carceral state.

NOTES

1. Russell, "Carceral Pride: The Fusion of Police Imagery with LGBTI Rights."

2. The flyer is published online by 3CR Community Radio and is available at https://www.3cr.org.au/files/NO%20PRIDE%20IN%20A%20POLICE%20STATE.pdf.

3. See Porter, Ironfield, and Hopkins, "Racial Profiling, Australian Criminology and the Creation of Statistical 'Facts': A Response to Shepherd and Spivak."

4. Russell, *Queer Histories and the Politics of Policing*.

5. Greey, "Queer Inclusion Precludes (Black) Queer Disruption: Media Analysis of the Black Lives Matter Toronto Sit-in during Toronto Pride 2016"; Lamusse, "Politics at Pride?"; Linnemann, *The Horror of Police*; Russell, "Carceral Pride: The Fusion of Police Imagery with LGBTI Rights."

6. Holmes, "Marching with Pride? Debates on Uniformed Police Participating in Vancouver's LGBTQ Pride Parade"; Walker et al., "Why Don't We Center Abolition in Queer Criminology?"

7. Kurti and Brown, "Carceral Reckoning and Twenty-First Century US Abolition Movements: Generational Struggles in the Fight against Prisons."

8. Russell, "Queer Penalities: The Criminal Justice Paradigm in Lesbian and Gay Anti-violence Politics."

9. Redd and Russell, "'It All Started Here, and It All Ends Here Too': Homosexual Criminalisation and the Queer Politics of Apology"; Ahmed, *The Promise of Happiness*.

10. Lamble, "Queer Necropolitics and the Expanding Carceral State: Interrogating Sexual Investments in Punishment"; Mikell, "Trans Black Women Deserve Better: Expanding Queer Criminology to Unpack Trans Misogynoir in the Field of Criminology."

11. Stardust et al., "'I Wouldn't Call the Cops If I Was Being Bashed to Death': Sex Work, Whore Stigma and the Criminal Legal System"; Seigel, "Violence Work: Policing and Power"; Race, "Public Orders: The Sex Crimes of Policing."

12. Hodge, *Colouring the Rainbow: Blak Queer and Trans Perspectives*; Mikell, "Trans Black Women Deserve Better: Expanding Queer Criminology to Unpack Trans Misogynoir in the Field of Criminology"; Thompson, "Policing in Europe: Disability Justice and Abolitionist Intersectional Care."

13. Stanley, *Atmospheres of Violence: Structuring Antagonism and the Trans/Queer Ungovernable*, 6.

14. Stanley, 5.

15. Kurti and Brown, "Carceral Reckoning and Twenty-First Century US Abolition Movements: Generational Struggles in the Fight against Prisons"; Mathiesen, *The Politics of Abolition*.

16. Gilmore, *Golden Gulag: Prisons, Surplus, Crisis, and Opposition in Globalizing California*.

17. Hall et al., *Policing the Crisis: Mugging, the State, and Law and Order*.

18. Cunneen, *Defund the Police: An International Insurrection*; McDowell and Fernandez, "'Disband, Disempower, and Disarm': Amplifying the Theory and Practice of Police Abolition"; Vitale, *The End of Policing*.

19. McDowell and Fernandez, "'Disband, Disempower, and Disarm': Amplifying the Theory and Practice of Police Abolition."

20. McDowell and Fernandez; see also Vitale, *The End of Policing*.

21. Carlton and Russell, *Resisting Carceral Violence: Women's Imprisonment and the Politics of Abolition*; McDowell and Fernandez, "'Disband, Disempower, and Disarm': Amplifying the Theory and Practice of Police Abolition"; Spade, *Normal Life: Administrative Violence, Critical Trans Politics, and the Limits of Law*.

22. Rodriguez, "Abolition as Praxis of Human Being: A Foreword"; Schenwar and Law, *Prison by Any Other Name: The Harmful Consequences of Popular Reforms.*

23. Gilmore, *Golden Gulag: Prisons, Surplus, Crisis, and Opposition in Globalizing California*; Mathiesen, *The Politics of Abolition.*

24. Kurti and Brown, "Carceral Reckoning and Twenty-First Century US Abolition Movements: Generational Struggles in the Fight against Prisons," 5; Rodriguez, "Abolition as Praxis of Human Being: A Foreword".

25. Kurti and Brown, "Carceral Reckoning and Twenty-First Century US Abolition Movements: Generational Struggles in the Fight against Prisons," 4.

26. Davis, *Are Prisons Obsolete?*, 108.

27. Harney and Moten, *The Undercommons: Fugitive Planning and Black Study*, 42.

28. Cunneen, *Defund the Police: An International Insurrection*; Maynard, *Policing Black Lives: State Violence in Canada from Slavery to the Present*; Porter, "The Criminal Foundations of Australian Policing"; Vitale, *The End of Policing.*

29. McDowell and Fernandez, "'Disband, Disempower, and Disarm': Amplifying the Theory and Practice of Police Abolition," 379.

30. Cunneen and Tauri, "Indigenous Peoples, Criminology, and Criminal Justice"; Maynard, *Policing Black Lives: State Violence in Canada from Slavery to the Present*; Porter, "The Criminal Foundations of Australian Policing"; Seigel, "Violence Work: Policing and Power."

31. Razack, "Settler Colonialism, Policing and Racial Terror: The Police Shooting of Loreal Tsingine," 1.

32. McQuire, "National Accounts: Black and White Witness"; Nettelbeck and Ryan, "Salutary Lessons: Native Police and the 'Civilising' Role of Legalised Violence in Colonial Australia."

33. See Vitale, *The End of Policing*; Seigel, "Violence Work: Policing and Power."

34. Russell, *Queer Histories and the Politics of Policing.*

35. Lamble, "Unknowable Bodies, Unthinkable Sexualities: Lesbian and Transgender Legal Invisibility in the Toronto Women's Bathhouse Raid."

36. Berlant and Warner, "Sex in Public"; Boon-Kuo, Meiners, and Simpson, "Queer Interruptions: Policing Belonging in a Carceral State."

37. Ponton, "Clothed in Blue Flesh: Police Brutality and the Disciplining of Race, Gender, and the 'Human'"; Russell, "'Seeing Like a Cop': Police Perception in Spaces of Gender and Racial Criminalization"; Sentas, *Traces of Terror: Counter-Terrorism Law, Policing, and Race.*

38. Berlant and Warner, "Sex in Public."

39. Russell, *Queer Histories and the Politics of Policing*, 20.

40. Mogul, Ritchie, and Whitlock, *Queer (In)Justice: The Criminalization of LGBT People in the United States*; Riggs, *Priscilla, (White) Queen of the Desert: Queer Rights/Race Privilege.*

41. Russell, *Queer Histories and the Politics of Policing*, 30.

42. Boucher and Reynolds, "Decriminalisation, Apology and Expungement: Sexual Citizenship and the Problem of Public Sex in Victoria."

43. Redd and Russell, "'It All Started Here, and It All Ends Here Too': Homosexual Criminalisation and the Queer Politics of Apology."

44. Ore, "No Proof a 2,700 Boost in Victorian Police Numbers Has Improved Safety, Audit Finds."

45. Gorie, as cited in Holas, "Police Raid at Hares & Hyenas Building"; Redd and Russell, "'It All Started Here, and It All Ends Here Too': Homosexual Criminalisation and the Queer Politics of Apology."

46. Cited in Holas, "Police Raid at Hares & Hyenas Building."

47. Russell and Ison, "Why the Violence of Policing Is a Queer Issue."

48. Race, "Public Orders: The Sex Crimes of Policing," 4.

49. Race, 5.

50. Race, 5.

51. Dillon, *Fugitive Life: The Queer Politics of the Prison State*; Lamble, "Practising Everyday Abolition"; Lean, "Why I Am an Abolitionist."

52. Race, "Public Orders: The Sex Crimes of Policing," 4.

53. Stanley, *Atmospheres of Violence: Structuring Antagonism and the Trans/Queer Ungovernable*, 123.

54. Lamble, "Unknowable Bodies, Unthinkable Sexualities: Lesbian and Transgender Legal Invisibility in the Toronto Women's Bathhouse Raid."

55. Lamble, "Practising Everyday Abolition."

56. Saleh-Hanna, "A Call for Wild Seed Justice."

57. Porter, Ironfield, and Hopkins, "Racial Profiling, Australian Criminology and the Creation of Statistical 'Facts': A Response to Shepherd and Spivak."

58. Linnemann, *The Horror of Police*, 193.

CHAPTER 13

"Queer" Means Centering Criminalized Survivors

Lessons from Abolition Feminism

ASH STEPHENS, UNIVERSITY OF ILLINOIS AT CHICAGO
JANE HERETH, UNIVERSITY OF WISCONSIN—MILWAUKEE

INTRODUCTION

As scholars engaged in research and teaching related to the experiences of LGBTQ+ individuals within the criminal punishment system and LGBTQ+ survivors of victimization, we are hopeful about the possibilities of queer criminology to offer analysis of how hetero/cisnormativity shape systems and institutions that perpetuate harm against LGBTQ+ people. And as organizers who use abolition feminist frameworks to inform our support work with survivors of victimization who have been criminalized for defending themselves, we are concerned about frameworks that do not include an explicit abolitionist stance. Numerous scholars and organizers offer critiques of mainstream feminist criminology and feminist anti-violence organizing for contributing to the expansion of the carceral state in their efforts to bring awareness to, respond to, and prevent violence against women. As Richie writes in her book *Arrested Justice*, feminist organizers "won the mainstream but lost the movement."[1] This chapter asks this question: What can queer criminology learn from abolition feminist analysis that centers survivors of interpersonal violence? After reviewing the state of research documenting the prevalence of interpersonal violence against LGBTQ+ individuals, we provide an overview of abolitionist feminism. Finally, we offer suggestions for how queer criminologists might incorporate abolitionist feminism into our work to document, examine, and address interpersonal violence against LGBTQ+ individuals.

QUEERING CRIMINOLOGY

As early as the 1990s, critical criminologists began examining cultural expectations of heterosexuality.[2] Addressing these forms of social construction that ultimately categorized gays and lesbians as "deviants," these critical criminologists argued that the criminalization of gays and lesbians looked like applying explicit expectations and scripts to uphold heterosexuality. And more contemporarily, heteronormativity is applied to gays and lesbians for the purpose of criminalizing queer people. For some, these examinations were some of the earliest disciplinary conversations that led to the subfield of queer criminology studies.

Yet into the mid-2010s, as the field of queer criminology began to take root, scholars contributed even more research about the experiences of queer people within and outside of the criminal punishment system. At the same time, there was still a sense that LGBTQ+ people were absent from criminological theory and research practice in the field of mainstream criminology. Consequently, "the journal *Critical Criminology* dedicated a special edition to Queer/ing Criminology."[3] In this special edition, criminology scholars' writings were intended to provide more research representation of LGBTQ+ people's experiences with the criminal punishment system, as well as contributing additional theoretical lenses to discuss what queerness and queer theory have to offer criminology.[4]

Around the same time, criminologists Dana Peterson and Vanessa Panfil edited the *Handbook of LGBT Communities, Crime, and Justice*, which built a patchwork of queer criminological research.[5] Of the chapters in that volume, Matthew Ball's work titled "What's Queer about Queer Criminology?" is particularly applicable to this chapter's arguments that "queer" means centering criminalized survivors.[6] Drawing heavily from queer theory, Ball argues that queer criminology as a subfield of study should consider queer beyond identity categories and instead grapple with how it engages with queer research and theorizing, beyond the mainstream.

Similar to feminist criminologists' resistance to the "add gender and stir" approach, which simply extends theories and frameworks for considering the experiences of men within the criminal punishment system to women, without considering distinct impacts of sexism, patriarchy, and gender-based violence,[7] many queer criminology scholars insist that we critically examine the intersection of heteropatriarchy, anti-LGBTQ+ violence, and the criminal punishment system. Ball argues that queer criminology as a subfield of study should "always sit at an oblique angle to the rest of criminological discourse, remaining in the margins in order for its critical potential to have any impact."[8] Ball suggests that the adoption of a queer critique opens space to imagine new ways of thinking and being and supports resistance to assimilation and settling for the status quo. Therefore, a queer critique helps us challenge the carceral state by encouraging and requiring that an analysis of power, in all its forms, be at the center of our queer criminological work so that we recognize the many areas that participate in the buildup of the carceral state through the continuation of structural oppression. In doing so, a queer critique encourages us to imagine alternatives to and transformation of these power relations, toward anti-carceral ends.

Significantly, this chapter embraces Ball's charge to consider queer beyond identity categories and "remain at the margins" by centering LGBTQ+ people's experiences as survivors of violence. Drawing from abolition feminism, we offer suggestions for how queer criminologists might resist assimilation to the mainstream by applying a critical lens to our scholarship and organizing efforts to document, examine, and address interpersonal violence against LGBTQ+ individuals in ways that do not continue to prop up the criminal punishment system.

PREVALENCE OF INTERPERSONAL VIOLENCE AGAINST LGBTQ+ INDIVIDUALS

LGBTQ+ individuals experience high rates of forms of interpersonal violence, including child abuse,[9] school bullying,[10] intimate partner violence (IPV),[11] sexual assault,[12] and bias-related victimization.[13] However, prevalence varies within the LGBTQ+ community; for example, this research indicates that transgender people and LGBTQ+ Black, Indigenous, and People of Color (BIPOC) experience particularly high rates.

LGBTQ+ survivors of victimization experience multiple barriers to accessing help, including legal services.[14] According to a study of LGBTQ+ individuals conducted by Lambda Legal, 62 percent of LGBTQ+ respondents who experienced physical assault, 41 percent of respondents who experienced IPV, and 39 percent of respondents who experienced sexual assault felt that the police did not fully address their complaints.[15] Worse, LGBTQ+ individuals experience further victimization by the police when seeking assistance, including verbal, physical, and sexual assault.[16]

Members of LGBTQ+ communities have a long history of experiencing victimization and harassment by the police.[17] Police harassment and violence was codified through laws criminalizing LGBTQ+ identities, like those prohibiting "homosexual" sex or wearing clothing of the "opposite" gender,[18] and continues today through legislation prohibiting accessing gender-affirming care, using public facilities, or performing in drag.[19] While little data exists on the subject, anecdotal evidence indicates that, lacking safety and support from the legal system, LGBTQ+ survivors may defend themselves and then be criminalized for doing so.[20]

REMEDIES AND THEIR COLLATERAL CONSEQUENCES

In response to these high rates of victimization and failures of the carceral state to respond, some community members, advocates, and scholars call for state and local police departments to adopt a range of policies and practices to improve the relationship between LGBTQ+ communities and the police. These policies and practices include non-discrimination policies, sensitivity and diversity trainings, civilian review boards, and harsher punishments for individuals who perpetrate victimization against LGBTQ+ people.[21] However, others question the efficacy of relying on carceral solutions to prevent and respond to violence against LGBTQ+ individuals.[22] For example, criminologist Doug Meyer calls out mainstream gay rights movements for supporting hate crime laws, arguing that they are part of the neoliberal "tough on crime" strategy that disproportionately impacts low-income communities of color.[23] While one could argue that responding to the high level of victimization against LGBTQ+ individuals is critical and that these laws may to some extent serve as an acknowledgment of and draw attention to the high prevalence of violence against LGBTQ+ individuals, the reality is that hate crime laws increase surveillance and visibility of LGBTQ+ individuals, particularly LGBTQ+ individuals of color. Meyer states, "A progressive, queer critique of hate crime laws contends, in contrast to the conservative position, that violence and discrimination directed against marginalized groups remains pervasive and widespread—built into how our society operates—while also declaring, in contrast to the mainstream liberal position, that hate crime laws do more to reinforce existing power imbalances than to challenge them. The laws, quite simply, do not protect LGBT people from violence."[24]

Hate crime laws also center the experiences of White gay men; in order for a crime to be classified as a hate crime, a clear case needs to be made that anti-LGBTQ+ bias motivated the crime, yet research indicates that White gay men are more likely to classify experiences as homophobic, while LGBTQ+ BIPOC individuals are less certain if experiences are motivated by anti-LGBTQ+ bias, sexism, racism, or a combination.[25] Criminologists Carrie Buist and Codie Stone describe the ways in which transgender victims face particular bias and discrimination when attempting to frame their experiences as hate crimes.[26] They describe the deployment of "trans panic defenses" in high-profile cases involving the murders of transgender people, in which defendants attempt to claim that their acts of violence were motivated by transgender victims concealing and then disclosing their identities. Hate crime laws do very little to protect LGBTQ+ individuals who defend themselves against bias-motivated violence and are then criminalized for doing so, as in the case of CeCe McDonald, who faced a manslaughter conviction after defending herself from an assailant who shouted racist and transphobic slurs at her and her friends before physically attacking them.[27] As legal scholar Jean Strout points out, for all these reasons several organizations that serve transgender and/or LGBTQ+ BIPOC communities voiced concerns about hate crime legislation.[28] Hate crime laws also focus on a specific form of violence—public victimization, often perpetrated by strangers—while doing little to address intimate partner violence or child abuse, which are much more pervasive forms of victimization against LGBTQ+ individuals.[29] Furthermore, abolitionist legal scholar Dean Spade argues that these laws are predicated on the conceptualization of violence against LGBTQ+ individuals as an individual problem, while doing little to address the structures that perpetuate or perpetrate violence, including police harassment.[30] The current rise of anti-LGBTQ+ legislation poses a much greater threat to the safety and well-being of LGBTQ+ individuals than street violence.

Organizers and scholars also question the efficacy of policies aimed at responding to bullying and other forms of anti-LGBTQ+ violence in schools.[31] Over the past few decades, schools have increasingly adopted harsh policies to respond to violence and other rule infractions, including zero-tolerance policies that result in mandatory suspensions or expulsions for students accused of fighting.[32] The term *school-to-prison pipeline* describes the interplay between harsh disciplinary policies, school pushout, increasing police presence in schools, and juvenile justice system involvement that disproportionately impacts students of color.[33] While LGBTQ+ students report high rates of verbal and physical harassment in schools, LGBTQ+ students, particularly LGBTQ+ students of color, are at heightened risk of being swept into the school-to-prison pipeline.[34] Due to anti-LGBTQ+ bias and unsafe school climates, LGBTQ+ youth are often punished more harshly than their peers for infractions and do not receive necessary support or assistance from teachers or school staff when they report bullying.[35]

A common pathway for LGBTQ+ youth into the school-to-prison pipeline begins with LGBTQ+ students experiencing bullying, schools failing to respond, students being left with no other option than to defend themselves, and then those students being punished more harshly than the peers responsible for the bullying.[36] As abolitionist writer, organizer, and educator Erica Meiners argues, "our 'remedies' have collateral damages."[37] Meanwhile, recent legislative attempts to prohibit content related to LGBTQ+ history or communities will only serve to foster hostile school climates for LGBTQ+ youth and increase bullying. Groups working to interrupt the school-to-prison pipeline argue that harsh disciplinary practices and police presence in schools be replaced with restorative justice practices that offer opportunities for students who are responsible for bullying to take accountability for their actions and repair harms.[38]

Our reliance on neoliberal and carceral solutions to hate crimes and school bullying has led to this moment in which our communities have become hypervisible and highly surveilled within society and particularly within the criminal legal system. Furthermore, the laws criminalizing drag performances, accessing gender-affirming care, or including content on LGBTQ+ individuals in schools will rely on the criminal legal system and family policing systems as enforcement, putting more LGBTQ+ individuals and our allies at risk for violence by police and other criminal legal system actors. While LGBTQ+ people are experiencing high rates of victimization, we must carefully consider the collateral damages likely to be caused by remedies like hate crime legislation and school zero-tolerance policies. These questions parallel those raised by feminist scholars who question the proposition that criminalizing victimization perpetration effectively deters victimization.[39] Next, we examine the work of anti-carceral and abolitionist feminist scholars and organizers, who offer a roadmap queer criminologists and organizers can follow in our work.

CARCERAL FEMINISM

Numerous feminist scholars, writers, and activists have used the term *carceral feminism* to critique the reliance of many researchers, anti-violence practitioners, nonprofit organizations, and others on the criminal legal system. Abolitionist author Victoria Law notes that "carceral feminism describes an approach that sees increased policing, prosecution, and imprisonment as the primary solution to violence against women."[40] With analytical roots in intersections among feminist anti-violence work and abolitionist movements, carceral feminism has largely come to be understood as dependence on the criminal legal system to address issues of gender-based violence. Carceral feminism as a term was coined by feminist sociologist Elizabeth Bernstein in a 2007 article where she discusses the social and political motivations and consequences of conservative and religious so-called anti-trafficking groups' lobbying for the elimination of sex work (although Bernstein uses the term *prostitution*).[41] Bernstein describes the efforts of these groups to frame any kind of consensual exchange of sex for money as human trafficking, which not only criminalizes clients who pay for sex, but also people who trade or who are perceived to trade sex for money. Bernstein notes that through this "advocacy," anti-trafficking groups are expanding the reach of the criminal punishment system under the guise of saviorism. In addition, Bernstein more explicitly notes the ways in which this advocacy contributes to the disproportionate criminalization and incarceration of BIPOC and poor people. Bernstein classifies this turn to law-and-order politics as "a drift from the welfare state to the carceral state as the enforcement apparatus for feminist goals."[42] Likewise, carceral feminist proposals for addressing issues of gender-based violence, particularly domestic and sexual violence, share the same feminist goals of enforcement. These proposals have looked like advocating for mandatory arrest policies and harsher sentencing, including the new proposals by some domestic violence advocates to close the "boyfriend loophole" by ultimately expanding criminalization efforts. Unofficially, these are the types of legal and policy proposals that are thought of as doing the work of "carceral feminism."

Informed by Bernstein and other abolition feminist scholarship, we argue that "carceral feminism" brings to light the seemingly contradictory links between feminism(s) and the criminal punishment system. It is assumed that all feminists care about all the gendered and racialized dimensions of inequity and inequality in our social and political world. However, critiques of carceral feminism allow us to point out the ways in which "feminist" interventions to address gender-based violence that rely on continued investments in capture, detainment, criminalization, incarceration, deportation, and the like actually perpetuate racialized, gendered, and classed value onto some women (i.e., cisgender middle-class White women), while devaluing and dehumanizing marginalized people (i.e., BIPOC, trans, disabled, and immigrants). In other words, carceral feminism offers more examples of the collateral consequences of "remedies."

When we discuss feminist anti-violence policies and organizations in this context, we are most certainly referring to those LGBTQ+ policies and organizations that use the rhetoric of inclusion and gender and sexual freedom, while simultaneously advocating for more police, more jails/prisons, more detention centers, and more enforcement. Related to earlier discussions in this chapter, more explicitly LGBTQ+ related responses to harm and violence, like hate crime legislation and bullying policies, also fall within these kinds of carceral feminist frames. Both hate crime legislation and bullying policies rely on what Bernstein named as law-and-order politics for feminist goals. And while harm and violence tragically happen to LGBTQ+ people, the "remedies" of hate crime enhancements and zero tolerance for bullying policies extend the life of the criminal punishment system instead of providing redress, healing, or transformative justice. Thus, we encourage queer criminologists and all critical criminology scholars concerned with issues of gendered and racialized justice to consider what abolitionist feminism offers to our understandings of structural and interpersonal harm, as well as our propositions to address it.

EMERGENCE OF ABOLITIONIST FEMINISM

How does carceral feminism differ from abolition feminism? Or, how is understanding carceral feminism central to the development of abolition feminism? The concept of abolition feminism predates the label, as feminist organizers, particularly organizers of color, warned us about the danger of relying on the carceral state to respond to gender-based violence long before the term became more widely adopted. As an alternative to carceral feminism, abolition feminists advocate for strategies to address structural harm that do not rely on the carceral state. As Ruth Wilson Gilmore asserts, "abolition means not just the closing of prisons but the presence, instead, of vital systems of support that many communities lack. Instead of asking how, in a future without prisons, we will deal with so-called violent people, abolitionists ask how we resolve inequalities and get people the resources they need."[43] Abolition feminism brings an intersectional feminist analysis grounded in understandings of racialization and racial capitalism, state-sanctioned violence, and gender and sexuality to understanding the complex inequalities that people face, as well as the systems and resources that they need.[44]

In what will likely be recognized as the authoritative abolitionist feminist text, longtime abolition feminist authors Angela Y. Davis, Gina Dent, Erica Meiners, and Beth E. Richie authored a genealogical text titled *Abolition. Feminism. Now.*[45] In *Abolition. Feminism. Now.*, the authors resist a hegemonic definition of abolition feminism, noting that developing an absolute definition would hinder the abolitionist work of revision, editing, and collective world-making that is required for an expansive definition of abolition that itself is fluid, unsettled, and ever changing.[46] Instead, the authors document the work of abolitionists, feminists, and abolition feminists around the world over the past decades. In several interviews, some of the authors describe this method of writing about and not completely defining abolition feminism as something like a mosaic or a tapestry that weaves together a genealogy of abolition feminist projects, organizations, campaigns, and locations.[47]

At the same time, the authors do invite various contours of what informed the text *Abolition. Feminism. Now.*, which offers a definitional starting point. In an interview with *Harper's Bazaar*, Angela Davis notes that part of the motivation for the text was to encourage all readers to think about abolition and feminism together.[48] Just as abolition requires us to think about the structural and root causes of harm and violence, Davis notes "that in the same way we have to learn how to think in structural terms about racism, we also have to think in structural terms about gender violence."[49] Abolition feminist perspectives offer that kind of interrogation of the structural and root causes of racism and gender-based violence simultaneously.

INCORPORATING ABOLITIONIST FEMINISM INTO QUEER CRIMINOLOGY

As an early and still burgeoning subfield of study, queer criminology has really laid the groundwork within the larger fields of criminal justice and criminology (CJC) studies for expanding on the links between gender fluidity and punishment. At the same time, queer criminology and queer criminologists have struggled to develop a cohesive framework for what guides an analysis of structural harm, violence, and power. A discussion of whether it is important for scholars to all agree on the future direction of queer criminological scholarship is beyond the scope of this chapter. Instead, and along with a growing group of abolitionist queer criminology scholars, we encourage other queer criminologists to apply an abolition feminist lens to resist the overreliance on policing and punishment to address violence.[50] When we center the experiences of LGBTQ+ survivors of victimization, it is clear to see that the criminal punishment system does not prevent victimization or provide healing. Instead, carceral "remedies" only serve to further perpetuate racism and hetero/cisnormativity.

Applying an abolitionist feminist lens to victimization against LGBTQ+ individuals means applying a both/and analysis. It allows us to both acknowledge the reality that LGBTQ+ people, particularly LGBTQ+ BIPOC individuals, are at increased likelihood of experiencing victimization and support examination of the root causes of that victimization. It means conceptualizing victimization against LGBTQ+ individuals as both an individual and a structural problem. It means working to meet the needs of individual LGBTQ+ survivors of victimization and addressing policies and legislation that are creating more violence and harm among our communities. It makes space to consider how to prevent interpersonal victimization, while also considering and working to avoid collateral consequences that could include further extending the life of the carceral state. On the ground, much of this work is happening within grassroots, volunteer-led projects and collectives (see transformharm.org for examples and resources). We hope that queer criminologists and organizers will take to heart the lessons learned from the mainstreaming of efforts to address gendered violence and avoid a similar fate. Instead, we encourage future research, theorizing, and advocacy that centers the actual needs and experiences of LGBTQ+ survivors in our dreams and efforts to build abolitionist futures.

NOTES

1. Richie, *Arrested Justice: Black Women, Male Violence, and the Build Up of a Prison Nation*, 65.

2. Ferrell and Sanders, *Cultural Criminology*.

3. Buist and Lenning, *Queer Criminology*.

4. Ball, Buist, and Woods, "Introduction to the Special Issue on Queer/Ing Criminology: New Directions and Frameworks."

5. Panfil and Peterson, *Handbook of LGBT Communities, Crime, and Justice*.

6. Ball, "What's Queer about Queer Criminology?"

7. Covington and Bloom, "Gendered Justice: Women in the Criminal Justice System"; Daly and Chesney-Lind, "Feminism and Criminology."

8. Ball, "What's Queer about Queer Criminology?," 552.

9. Friedman et al., "A Meta-Analysis of Disparities in Childhood Sexual Abuse, Parental Physical Abuse, and Peer Victimization among Sexual Minority and Sexual Nonminority Individuals"; Irvine and Canfield, "The Overrepresentation of Lesbian, Gay, Bisexual, Questioning, Gender Nonconforming and Transgender Youth within the Child Welfare to Juvenile Justice Crossover Population."

10. Friedman et al., "A Meta-Analysis of Disparities in Childhood Sexual Abuse, Parental Physical Abuse, and Peer Victimization among Sexual Minority and Sexual Nonminority Individuals"; Kosciw, Clark, and Menard, *The 2021 National School Climate Survey: The Experiences of LGBTQ+ Youth in Our Nation's Schools*; Mitchum and Moodie-Mills, *Beyond Bullying: How Hostile School Climate Perpetuates to School-to-Prison Pipeline for LGBT Youth*; Snapp et al., "Messy, Butch, and Queer: LGBTQ Youth and the School-to-Prison Pipeline."

11. Peitzmeier et al., "Intimate Partner Violence in Transgender Populations: Systematic Review and Meta-Analysis of Prevalence and Correlates"; Reuter et al., "Intimate Partner Violence Victimization in LGBT Young Adults: Demographic Differences and Associations with Health Behaviors."

12. Coulter et al., "Prevalence of Past-Year Sexual Assault Victimization among Undergraduate Students: Exploring Differences by and Intersections of Gender Identity, Sexual Identity, and Race/Ethnicity"; Friedman et al., "A Meta-Analysis of Disparities in Childhood Sexual Abuse, Parental Physical Abuse, and Peer Victimization among Sexual Minority and Sexual Nonminority Individuals"; Messinger and Koon-Magnin, "Sexual Violence in LGBTQ Communities."

13. James et al., *The Report of the 2015 U.S. Transgender Survey*.

14. Guadalupe-Diaz and Jasinski, "'I Wasn't a Priority, I Wasn't a Victim': Challenges in Help Seeking for Transgender Survivors of Intimate Partner Violence"; Hereth, "'Where Is the Safe Haven?': Transgender Women's Experiences of Victimization and Help-Seeking across the Life Course"; Hirschel and McCormack, "Same-Sex Couples and the Police: A 10-Year Study of Arrest and Dual Arrest Rates in Responding to Incidents of Intimate Partner Violence"; Lambda Legal, "Protected and Served?: Executive Summary."

15. Lambda Legal, "Protected and Served?: Executive Summary."

16. Guadalupe-Diaz and Jasinski, "'I Wasn't a Priority, I Wasn't a Victim': Challenges in Help Seeking for Transgender Survivors of Intimate Partner Violence"; Hereth, "'Where Is the Safe Haven?': Transgender Women's Experiences of Victimization and Help-Seeking across the Life Course"; James et al., *The Report of the 2015 U.S. Transgender Survey*; Lambda Legal, "Protected and Served?: Executive Summary"; Wolff and Cokely, "'To Protect and to Serve?': An Exploration of Police Conduct in Relation to the Gay, Lesbian, Bisexual, and Transgender Community."

17. Mogul, Ritchie, and Whitlock, *Queer (In)Justice: The Criminalization of LGBT People in the United States*; Ritchie, *Invisible No More: Police Violence against Black Women and Women of Color*.

18. Buist and Stone, "Transgender Victims and Offenders: Failures of the United States Criminal Justice System and the Necessity of Queer Criminol-

ogy"; Mogul, Ritchie, and Whitlock, *Queer (In)Justice: The Criminalization of LGBT People in the United States*; Ritchie, *Invisible No More: Police Violence against Black Women and Women of Color.*

19. Squirrell and Davey, "A Year of Hate: Understanding Threats and Harassment Targeting Drag Shows and the LGBTQ+ Community."

20. Johnson, "Cisgender Privilege, Intersectionality, and the Criminalization of CeCe McDonald: Why Intercultural Communication Needs Transgender Studies"; Stanley and Smith, *Captive Genders: Trans Embodiment and the Prison Industrial Complex.*

21. Mallory, Hasenbush, and Sears, *Discrimination and Harassment by Law Enforcement Officers in the LGBT Community.*

22. Meyer, "Resisting Hate Crime Discourse: Queer and Intersectional Challenges to Neoliberal Hate Crime Laws"; Spade, *Normal Life: Administrative Violence, Critical Trans Politics, and the Limits of Law.*

23. Meyer, "Resisting Hate Crime Discourse: Queer and Intersectional Challenges to Neoliberal Hate Crime Laws."

24. Meyer, 119.

25. Meyer, 119.

26. Buist and Stone, "Transgender Victims and Offenders: Failures of the United States Criminal Justice System and the Necessity of Queer Criminology."

27. Buist and Stone.

28. Strout, "The Massachusetts Transgender Equal Rights Bill: Formal Legal Equality in a Transphobic System."

29. Meyer, "Resisting Hate Crime Discourse: Queer and Intersectional Challenges to Neoliberal Hate Crime Laws."

30. Spade, *Normal Life: Administrative Violence, Critical Trans Politics, and the Limits of Law.*

31. Meiners, "Ending the School-to-Prison Pipeline/Building Abolition Futures"; Snapp et al., "Messy, Butch, and Queer: LGBTQ Youth and the School-to-Prison Pipeline."

32. Heitzeg, "Education or Incarceration: Zero Tolerance Policies and the School to Prison Pipeline."

33. Heitzeg, "Education or Incarceration: Zero Tolerance Policies and the School to Prison Pipeline"; Wald and Losen, "Defining and Redirecting a School-to-Prison Pipeline."

34. Himmelstein and Bruckner, "Criminal-Justice and School Sanctions against Nonheterosexual Youth: A National Longitudinal Study"; Snapp et al., "Messy, Butch, and Queer: LGBTQ Youth and the School-to-Prison Pipeline"; Kosciw, Clark, and Menard, *The 2021 National School Climate Survey: The Experiences of LGBTQ+ Youth in Our Nation's Schools.*

35. Kosciw, Clark, and Menard, *The 2021 National School Climate Survey: The Experiences of LGBTQ+ Youth in Our Nation's Schools*; Snapp et al., "Messy, Butch, and Queer: LGBTQ Youth and the School-to-Prison Pipeline"; Himmelstein and Bruckner, "Criminal-Justice and School Sanctions against Nonheterosexual Youth: A National Longitudinal Study."

36. Snapp et al., "Messy, Butch, and Queer: LGBTQ Youth and the School-to-Prison Pipeline."

37. Meiners, "Ending the School-to-Prison Pipeline/Building Abolition Futures," 561.

38. Meiners, 561.

39. Goodmark, *Decriminalizing Domestic Violence: A Balanced Policy Approach to Intimate Partner Violence*; Richie, *Arrested Justice: Black Women, Male Violence, and the Build Up of a Prison Nation*.

40. Law, "Against Carceral Feminism."

41. Bernstein, "The Sexual Politics of the 'New Abolitionism.'"

42. Bernstein, 143.

43. Kushner, "Is Prison Necessary? Ruth Wilson Gilmore Might Change Your Mind."

44. Davis, *Are Prisons Obsolete?*; Gilmore, *Golden Gulag: Prisons, Surplus, Crisis, and Opposition in Globalizing California*; Richie, *Arrested Justice: Black Women, Male Violence, and the Build Up of a Prison Nation*; Stanley and Smith, *Captive Genders: Trans Embodiment and the Prison Industrial Complex*.

45. Davis et al., *Abolition. Feminism. Now.*

46. Davis et al.

47. Davis et al.

48. Phifer, "For Angela Davis and Gina Dent, Abolition Is the Only Way."

49. Phifer.

50. Walker et al., "Why Don't We Center Abolition in Queer Criminology?"

CHAPTER 14

Toward a Pedagogy of Possibility

On Abolitionist Teaching

IHSAN AL-ZOUABI, RUTGERS UNIVERSITY NEWARK

The classroom remains the most radical space of possibility
in the academy.

—bell hooks

The killing of George Floyd by a police officer, followed by an unprecedented wave of national and international protests for civil rights, catapulted abolitionist discourse into the public sphere.[1] Many found themselves grappling with calls to defund the police and interrogate the legal frameworks and social mechanisms enabling the use of lethal force with a startling lack of robust mechanisms for holding actors of the state accountable for their actions.[2] Yet this engagement, in many respects, was often surface-level and overlooked the foundational role of settler colonial and imperial contexts underpinning contemporary policing and caging paradigms.[3]

These historical backdrops permeate nearly every social institution, insidiously shaping even our most intimate relationships with one another.[4] White supremacist logics touch the parts of our lives we think of as impenetrable to outside forces.[5] While exhaustively exploring how whiteness manifests is beyond this chapter's scope, it will delve into the reach of it within the boundaries of the classroom, guided by the works of Black, Brown, and Indigenous scholars. Their deconstruction of white supremacist narratives has carved out spaces for new realities within the classroom, and beyond, grounded in justice and equity.[6]

Before exploring abolitionist pedagogy, I offer this 1996 quote from Greg Jackson's "Authoritarian Leftists: Kill the Cop in Your Head" for reflection: "Because the white left refuses to combat and reject reactionary tendencies in their (your) own heads and amongst themselves (yourselves), and because they (you) refuse to see how white culture is rooted firmly in capitalism and imperialism . . . you in fact re-invent racist and authoritarian social relations as the final product of your so-called 'revolutionary theory'; what I call Left-wing white supremacy."[7]

This excerpt, presented without analysis or critique, aims to jolt us into scrutinizing our assumptions about what is considered proper teaching and by whose standards. It underscores the unavoidable truth that our classrooms, often hailed as bastions of objectivity, are not exempt from settler colonial influences.[8]

What is abolitionist pedagogy? Bettina Love articulates abolitionist pedagogy as a vibrant practice opposing the "educational survival complex"—a system problematizing marginalized students, subjecting them to punitive practices prioritizing policing over nurturing.[9] This approach urges educators to stand with their communities, fostering immediate changes while "freedom dreaming"—envisioning a future free from oppressive structures.[10] Ultimately, it centers on dismantling systems that recreate subjugation within classrooms.

In her groundbreaking work *Teaching to Transgress*, bell hooks advocates for engaged, liberatory pedagogy recognizing classrooms as sites for healing from oppression's wounds and achieving self-actualization.[11] hooks emphasizes the transgressive power of centering marginalized voices, fostering critical consciousness, and linking education to practicing freedom.

Building on this vision, abolitionist pedagogy demands complete transformation toward schools nurturing students' full humanity.[12] Central themes across the abundant literature include the following:

1. Anti-oppressive education challenging racism, colonialism, and other oppressive social structures[13]
2. Community-centric, collaborative learning connecting to local/global issues[14]
3. Restorative justice focusing on healing over punishment[15]
4. Critical pedagogy fostering questioning of norms for social change[16]
5. Inclusive curriculum representing diverse voices and holistic needs[17]
6. Student-centered approaches valuing agency and individuality[18]

7. Ecological and wellness-oriented practices[19]
8. Creativity and arts-based learning[20]
9. Ties to social movements and collective liberation[21]

I have found teaching to be sacred, liberatory work. I have been deeply honored to work with students from various walks of life. When I began approaching teaching through an abolitionist lens—a modality that honored and centered my students' lived experiences and the knowledge they brought into the classroom—I was able to learn more and become a significantly more effective instructor. By recognizing the inherent value and wisdom each student possesses, I have been able to create a learning environment that is both empowering and transformative. This shift in perspective has not only enriched my students' learning experiences but has also profoundly impacted my own growth as an educator and as a human being.

I have found that teaching *must* be liberatory, transformative, and rooted in an equitable, just love for students.[22] This chapter explores how radical scholars are cultivating these possibilities, illuminating paths toward emancipatory futures where education is reclaimed as a practice of shared freedom and healing.

MANIFESTATIONS OF SETTLER COLONIAL LOGICS IN THE CLASSROOM

The white supremacist logics of settler colonialism are not static; they maintain their dominance through an ability to adapt and morph, ensuring their survival by any means necessary.[23] Historically, these logics centered explicitly on the elimination and exploitation of land, people, and resources, culminating in the justification of the violent dispossession and subjugation of Indigenous peoples.[24] However, in the modern era, settler colonial logics operate through more convoluted and subtle methods, often cloaked in the legal language of equity, civility, and progress.[25]

It is through these evolving ideologies that the colony, and by extension, the settler, is granted unlimited access to people, land, and resources that are subsequently deemed unworthy of the state's protection.[26] The logics of extraction and exploitation, which are central to settler colonialism, categorize certain groups, especially historically vulnerable ones, as less deserving of protection from a myriad of harms.[27] This calculated neglect is a form of state violence, perpetuating the oppression and marginalization of communities already bearing the brunt of systemic injustices.

Bettina Love's conceptualization of the "educational survival complex" provides a powerful lens for understanding how settler colonial logics manifest in contemporary educational settings.[28] This conceptualization represents a set of policies, practices, and ideologies that perpetuate the dehumanization and marginalization of students, particularly those from Black, Brown, and Indigenous communities.

The educational survival complex, at its core, treats marginalized students as problems to be fixed instead of recognizing their vibrant knowledge and potential. This perspective stems from the settler colonial mindset, which sees nondominant cultures as inferior and in need of assimilation.[29] By framing students as deficits, the educational survival complex denies their inherent worth and agency, reproducing the dehumanizing logics of colonialism.

This dehumanization is further reinforced through harsh disciplinary practices and policing in schools. Zero-tolerance policies, surveillance, and school resource officers disproportionately target Black and Brown students, subjecting them to punitive measures that reflect the carceral logics of the settler state.[30] Instead of nurturing relationships, these practices prioritize control and compliance, creating an environment of fear and alienation that hinders learning and growth.

Furthermore, the educational survival complex reduces students to mere data points and standardized test scores, disregarding their complexity and individuality. This emphasis on quantifying worth aligns with the settler colonial focus on productivity and efficiency, where value is determined by conformity to dominant standards.[31] By narrowly defining success, the educational system overlooks the diverse strengths, experiences, and ways of knowing that marginalized students bring to the classroom.

The survival complex also perpetuates narratives of resilience, grit, and individual effort, placing the burden of overcoming systemic barriers solely on students. This framing obscures the ongoing legacies of settler colonialism, racism, and oppression that contribute to educational inequities, instead attributing disparities to personal failings.[32] By prioritizing individual survival over collective uplifting and liberation, the educational system maintains the status quo and avoids addressing structural injustices.

Moreover, the curriculum and pedagogical practices within the educational survival complex often alienate and exclude marginalized students. Eurocentric knowledge dominates, Indigenous histories and perspectives are erased, and educational materials lack representation, creating a sense of disconnection and disengagement.[33] By failing to center the identities, experiences, and cultural wealth of marginalized communities, the educational system reinforces the settler colonial project of cultural assimilation and erasure.

The educational survival complex also upholds ideas of colorblindness, meritocracy, and neutrality, which mask and perpetuate racial inequities. By denying the significance of race and the ongoing impacts of systemic racism, the educational system fails to confront and dismantle the white supremacist foundations on which it is built.[34] This refusal to engage in anti-racist and social justice–oriented practices ensures that settler colonial logics remain deeply embedded in the structures and processes of schooling.

Ultimately, the educational survival complex is a manifestation of the settler colonial imperative to dominate and control marginalized populations. It reflects the historical legacies of forced assimilation, cultural genocide, and the suppression of Indigenous and Black knowledge systems.[35] By recognizing and acknowledging these oppressive logics within education, we can begin to envision and create liberatory alternatives that affirm the humanity and potential of all students.

Abolitionist teaching provides a powerful framework for dismantling the educational survival complex and envisioning a transformative approach to education rooted in love, justice, and liberation. By centering the voices, experiences, and cultural wealth of marginalized communities, abolitionist pedagogy aims to create classrooms that foster critical consciousness, healing from the traumas of oppression, and cultivating the agency necessary for collective liberation. It is through this radical reenvisioning of education that we can begin to disrupt the settler colonial logics that have long shaped the educational landscape and work toward a future where all students can thrive.

THE CLASSROOM AS A SITE OF RESISTANCE

Abolitionist teaching practices in the classroom must be firmly situated within the context of resisting and dismantling the ever-adapting colonial and white supremacist logics that shape our educational institutions.[36] Similarly to the ways that criminology, as a discipline, has been critiqued for its focus on the interpersonal violence of racialized communities at the expense of scrutinizing other forms of violence, traditional educational practices often perpetuate and reproduce those very systemic inequities.[37]

In the classroom, abolitionist teaching recognizes that students from race-class subjugated communities are disproportionately harmed by oppressive educational practices and policies, such as punitive and harsh disciplinary measures, Eurocentric and exclusionary curricula, and the varying manifestations of the school-to-prison pipeline.[38] These harms persist despite the capacity of educational institutions to create more equitable and just learning environments, reflecting the ongoing legacy of settler colonialism in education.[39]

Abolitionist teaching aims to collapse the artificial and deliberate distinction between students' lived experiences and the content and practices of the classroom. By interrogating the ways in which settler colonial logics shape educational priorities and blind spots, abolitionist educators seek to unravel the complex web of power relations that sustain the marginalization of certain communities within schools.[40] This critical examination is crucial for pushing educational practices toward a more holistic, intersectional, and justice-oriented approach that acknowledges the inextricable links between social, environmental, and educational justice.[41]

In practice, abolitionist teaching involves centering the voices, experiences, and knowledge systems of marginalized communities in the classroom.[42] This requires a critical examination of curricular materials, pedagogical strategies, and classroom dynamics to ensure that they are not perpetuating oppressive narratives or excluding certain perspectives. Abolitionist educators also prioritize building relationships of trust and care with their students, recognizing that healing and wholeness are essential for learning.[43]

Furthermore, abolitionist teaching practices encourage students to develop critical consciousness and engage in social action to address injustices within their schools and communities.[44] This involves creating opportunities for students to analyze and challenge oppressive systems, while also developing the skills and agency to imagine and create more just alternatives. By positioning students as cocreators of knowledge and agents of change, abolitionist educators aim to disrupt traditional power dynamics in the classroom and foster a more democratic and liberatory educational experience.[45]

Ultimately, abolitionist teaching practices in the classroom contribute to the growing body of work that challenges education's complicity in perpetuating systemic injustices.[46] By shedding light on the insidious adaptability of settler colonial logics and their impact on educational discourse and practice, abolitionist educators aim to disentangle schooling from its white supremacist underpinnings and work toward a more equitable and liberatory future for all students.[47] It is through this critical introspection and the centering of marginalized voices that education can begin to fulfill its transformative potential as a site of resistance and liberation.

My first encounter with the exclusionary dynamics of settler colonialism came in the wake of the September 11 attacks, which thrust my identity as a Muslim, Arab student into sharp relief. As a young Arab girl with a distinctly Arabic name, I was forced to navigate a complex terrain of marginalization. On the one side, I endured exclusion and bullying from peers—clear manifestations of the deep-seated mistrust and suspicion harbored toward the Muslim community during that time. These interactions starkly revealed how dominant settler colonial narratives often marginalize and demonize those considered "other" or outside the imagined national community.

On the other side, I was supported by a group of educators who understood the urgent need to protect and support all students, particularly those from targeted and vulnerable groups. These teachers went above and beyond to ensure not only my safety but also that of my hijab-wearing mother, offering transportation and initiating dialogues with other parents. Their efforts highlighted how educational spaces can act as powerful arenas for resisting the dehumanizing effects of settler colonialism.

ABOLITIONIST PEDAGOGY AS PRACTICE

Abolitionist pedagogy, at its core, represents a fundamental shift away from the oppressive and dehumanizing practices that have long characterized traditional educational spaces. It is a rejection of the punitive, hierarchical, and controlling measures that prioritize compliance over genuine learning and growth. Instead, abolitionist pedagogy embraces a vision of education rooted in inclusivity, community, and the pursuit of collective liberation.[48]

bell hooks, in her formative work *Teaching to Transgress: Education as the Practice of Freedom*, provides a powerful framework for understanding what this transformative approach to teaching looks like in practice.[49] hooks advocates for an engaged pedagogy that recognizes the classroom as a space for holistic growth, healing, and the development of critical consciousness.

At the heart of engaged pedagogy is a commitment to the well-being of students in their entirety. It moves beyond the narrow focus on academic achievement and cognitive development to encompass the emotional, social, and spiritual dimensions of learning. In this approach, teachers are not mere transmitters of knowledge but rather facilitators of a reciprocal and participatory learning process. They create a classroom environment that encourages students to bring their whole selves into the educational experience, fostering a sense of belonging and community.[50]

Putting these concepts in conversation with criminological theory, in *Causes of Delinquency*, Travis Hirschi argues that strong social bonds are essential for preventing delinquency and fostering positive youth development.[51] Hirschi's social control theory suggests that individuals with weak or fragmented social ties are more prone to delinquent behavior, while those with robust connections to family, school, and community are less likely to deviate from societal norms. This concept complements bell hooks's principles of engaged pedagogy, which stress the importance of cultivating a sense of belonging and community within educational settings.[52]

Hirschi's theory underscores the value of such a holistic educational approach, particularly through the concept of attachment—the emotional bonds linking individuals with significant figures in their lives, such as parents, teachers, and peers. He posits that strong attachments help individuals internalize societal norms and values, thereby decreasing the likelihood of delinquency. In educational terms, this suggests that students who feel connected to their school community are more likely to participate positively in learning activities and less likely to engage in disruptive behaviors.

Engaged pedagogy plays a critical role in nurturing these attachments by addressing students' emotional and social needs alongside their academic growth. This approach involves fostering meaningful interactions between students and teachers, promoting collaborative learning, and recognizing and celebrating diverse identities and experiences within the classroom.

Additionally, Hirschi highlights the importance of commitment to and involvement in conventional activities, such as education, in mitigating delinquency. He argues that individuals deeply invested in and actively engaged with conventional pursuits are less likely to engage in delinquency due to having more at stake. Engaged pedagogy enhances this investment by encouraging deep participation in the learning process. Methods such as student-centered learning, project-based assignments, and opportunities for student choice and autonomy help cultivate a profound sense of ownership and commitment among students.

This emphasis on wholeness and humanity is particularly crucial for students from marginalized backgrounds, who have long been subjected to the dehumanizing practices of the educational survival complex.[53] By centering the experiences, knowledge, and cultural wealth of these students, abolitionist pedagogy seeks to disrupt the deficit narratives and oppressive structures that have silenced and excluded them. It recognizes students as coconstructors of knowledge, valuing their insights, stories, and ways of being as integral to the learning process.

Abolitionist teaching also prioritizes the cultivation of critical consciousness and the development of students' agency to challenge and transform oppressive systems. It encourages students to interrogate the social, political, and economic forces that shape their lives and to envision alternative possibilities for a more just and equitable world. This involves engaging with issues of race, class, gender, and other forms of oppression, not as abstract concepts but as lived realities that impact students' experiences and opportunities.[54]

In practice, this means creating curricula and learning experiences that are relevant, culturally sustaining, and grounded in the histories, struggles, and aspirations of marginalized communities. It means incorporating diverse perspectives, voices, and ways of knowing that have been historically excluded from dominant educational narratives. It means embracing the arts, creativity, and imagination as powerful tools for self-expression, healing, and resistance.[55]

Furthermore, abolitionist pedagogy recognizes that the work of liberatory transformation extends beyond the classroom walls. It is deeply connected to the broader struggles for social justice and liberation in our communities and society at large. As such, abolitionist educators seek to build relationships and solidarity with grassroots movements, community organizations, and activists who are fighting against oppression in all its forms. They understand that the classroom is just one site of struggle in the larger project of building a more just and equitable world.[56]

Ultimately, abolitionist pedagogy is a radical reenvisioning of what education can and should be. It is a call to dismantle the oppressive structures and logics that have long defined our educational institutions and to create spaces where all students can thrive, heal, and develop the skills and consciousness necessary for collective liberation. It is a pedagogy rooted in love, justice, and the unwavering belief in the inherent dignity and potential of every human being.

As educators committed to this vision, we must continually reflect on our own practices, challenge our assumptions, and work to create classrooms that embody the values of abolitionist pedagogy. It is a journey that requires courage, humility, and a willingness to transgress the boundaries and norms that have long constrained our educational imaginations. But it is a journey that holds the promise of transforming not only our schools but also our society as a whole, one classroom at a time.

DISCUSSION: ENVISIONING A LIBERATORY FUTURE FOR EDUCATION

The exploration of abolitionist pedagogy and its manifestations in practice reveals a transformative approach to education that challenges the deeply entrenched logics of settler colonialism and white supremacy. By centering the experiences, knowledge, and humanity of race–class subjugated students,[57] abolitionist teaching offers a radical departure from the dehumanizing practices that have long characterized traditional educational spaces.[58]

The works of scholars such as Bettina Love and bell hooks provide a powerful theoretical and practical foundation for reimagining education as a site of liberation and healing. Their emphasis on engaged pedagogy, critical consciousness, and the cultivation of agency highlights the potential for classrooms to become spaces where students can not only learn but also grow, heal, and develop the tools necessary to challenge oppressive systems.[59]

However, the realization of this vision requires a fundamental shift in how we understand the purpose and practice of education. It necessitates a willingness to confront and dismantle the settler colonial logics that have shaped our educational institutions and to create new paradigms that center the experiences and aspirations of marginalized communities. This is not a simple or easy task, as it involves grappling with deep-seated patterns of power, privilege, and oppression that have long been normalized within our society.[60]

One of the key challenges in implementing abolitionist pedagogy is the resistance and backlash that it may face from those who benefit from the current system. The educational survival complex, with its emphasis on control, compliance, and the maintenance of the status quo, serves the interests of those in power and may be fiercely defended by those who seek to preserve their privilege.[61] As such, the work of abolitionist teaching is not only pedagogical but also deeply political, requiring educators to take a stand against injustice and to build alliances with communities and movements fighting for social change.

Another challenge is the need for ongoing self-reflection and growth among educators themselves. Abolitionist pedagogy demands that teachers interrogate their own biases, assumptions, and complicity in oppressive systems and continuously work to create more equitable and inclusive learning environments.[62] This requires a willingness to engage in difficult conversations, to listen to the perspectives and experiences of marginalized students, and to be open to feedback and critique. It also necessitates a commitment to ongoing professional development and the cultivation of a supportive community of practice among abolitionist educators.

Despite these challenges, the potential benefits of abolitionist pedagogy are immense. By creating educational spaces that affirm the humanity and potential of all students, abolitionist teaching has the power to transform not only individual lives but also entire communities and societies. It offers a vision of education as a liberatory practice, one that empowers students to become critical thinkers, compassionate leaders, and agents of social change.[63] In doing so, it lays the foundation for a more just and equitable world, one in which every individual has the opportunity to thrive and to contribute to the collective well-being of all.

CONCLUSION

The journey toward abolitionist pedagogy is one that requires courage, commitment, and a willingness to imagine possibilities beyond the boundaries of our current reality. The challenge rests in our capacity to confront the deep-seated inequities and injustices that have long shaped our educational landscape and to envision a future in which all students can flourish.

I am Syrian and Jordanian, from a family from Daraa, a place that has witnessed both immense devastation and remarkable resistance. My understanding of the world—of my own identity—is perpetually entangled with the fabric of the SWANA region, its history, struggles, and triumphs. However, it is Gaza that has become my barometer. The indomitable spirit of the Palestinian people in the face of unrelenting oppression and injustice has been a humbling and harrowing reminder of the urgency of our collective struggle for liberation.

As I finalize this chapter, I feel a compounding and profound sense of fury and grief as I learn of the Israeli government's latest attack on Rafah. The timing of this assault is not lost on me, and it would be disingenuous, even hypocritical, to conclude this work without acknowledging the ongoing violence and dispossession faced by Palestinians.

The struggle for justice and freedom in Palestine is inextricably linked to the fight against oppression everywhere. Though this chapter was undeniably focused on a Western pedagogical lens, Palestine remains a stark reminder that the systems of power and domination we seek to dismantle through abolitionist pedagogy are not confined to the classroom or even to national borders. They are global in their reach and impact, and they manifest in the bombs that rain down on Gaza, the checkpoints that restrict movement, and the walls that separate families and communities.

I am reminded of the words of the Palestinian poet Rafeef Ziadah: "We teach life, sir."[64] In the face of unimaginable violence and loss, Palestinians continue to resist, to create, to love, and to teach. They embody the very essence of the liberatory education we strive for—one that affirms life, honors our students and teachers, and refuses to be silenced in the face of injustice. As I reflect on the role of education in the struggle for social justice, I cannot help but think of the countless Palestinian educators who have dedicated their lives to teaching under the most unimaginable circumstances. They are a testament to the transformative power of education as a tool for resistance, healing, and liberation.

Love reminds us that "abolitionist teaching is not a teaching approach: it is a way of life, a way of seeing the world, and a way of taking action against injustice."[65] It is in this spirit of solidarity, liberation, and shared struggle that I humbly offer this work. May it contribute, in some small way, to the ongoing fight for justice, dignity, and freedom in our classrooms, in Palestine, and beyond. And may we all continue to courageously teach life, to resist, to love, and to dream of a world where liberation is not just a possibility, but a reality.

NOTES

Epigraph: hooks, *Teaching to Transgress: Education as the Practice of Freedom*, 12.

1. Buchanan, Bui, and Patel, "Black Lives Matter May Be the Largest Movement in U.S. History."

2. McDowell and Fernandez, "'Disband, Disempower, and Disarm': Amplifying the Theory and Practice of Police Abolition."

3. Vitale, *The End of Policing.*

4. Love, *We Want to Do More than Survive: Abolitionist Teaching and the Pursuit of Educational Freedom*; Tuck and Yang, "Decolonization Is Not a Metaphor."

5. Gillborn, "Education Policy as an Act of White Supremacy: Whiteness, Critical Race Theory and Education Reform."

6. Grande, *Red Pedagogy: Native American Social and Political Thought*; Paris and Alim, "What Are We Seeking to Sustain through Culturally Sustaining Pedagogy? A Loving Critique Forward."

7. Jackson, "Authoritarian Leftists: Kill the Cop in Your Head," para. 11.

8. Tuck and Yang, "Decolonization Is Not a Metaphor."

9. Love, *We Want to Do More than Survive: Abolitionist Teaching and the Pursuit of Educational Freedom*, 89.

10. Love, 101.

11. hooks, *Teaching to Transgress: Education as the Practice of Freedom*, 15.

12. Love, *We Want to Do More than Survive: Abolitionist Teaching and the Pursuit of Educational Freedom.*

13. Kumashiro, "Toward a Theory of Anti-oppressive Education."

14. Ginwright, *Hope and Healing in Urban Education: How Urban Activists and Teachers Are Reclaiming Matters of the Heart.*

15. Winn, *Justice on Both Sides: Transforming Education through Restorative Justice.*

16. Freire, *Pedagogy of the Oppressed.*

17. Ladson-Billings, "Toward a Theory of Culturally Relevant Pedagogy"; Paris and Alim, *Culturally Sustaining Pedagogies: Teaching and Learning for Justice in a Changing World.*

18. Ayers, Quinn, and Stovall, *Handbook of Social Justice in Education.*

19. Gruenewald, "The Best of Both Worlds: A Critical Pedagogy of Place."

20. Greene, *Releasing the Imagination: Essays on Education, the Arts, and Social Change.*

21. Davis, *Abolition Democracy: Beyond Empire, Prisons, and Torture.*

22. Darder, *Reinventing Paulo Freire: A Pedagogy of Love.*

23. Wolfe, "Settler Colonialism and the Elimination of the Native."

24. Tuck and Yang, "Decolonization Is Not a Metaphor."

25. Coulthard, *Red Skin, White Masks: Rejecting the Colonial Politics of Recognition.*

26. Moreton-Robinson, *The White Possessive: Property, Power, and Indigenous Sovereignty*; Tuck and Yang, "Decolonization Is Not a Metaphor."

27. Whyte, "Settler Colonialism, Ecology, and Environmental Injustice."

28. Love, *We Want to Do More than Survive: Abolitionist Teaching and the Pursuit of Educational Freedom.*

29. Tuck and Yang, "Decolonization Is Not a Metaphor."

30. Annamma, *The Pedagogy of Pathologization: Dis/Abled Girls of Color in the School-Prison Nexus.*

31. Grande, *Red Pedagogy: Native American Social and Political Thought.*

32. Duncan-Andrade, "Note to Educators: Hope Required When Growing Roses in Concrete."

33. Paris and Alim, *Culturally Sustaining Pedagogies: Teaching and Learning for Justice in a Changing World.*

34. Gillborn, "Heads I Win, Tails You Lose: Anti-Black Racism as Fluid, Relentless, Individual and Systemic."

35. Smith, *Decolonizing Methodologies: Research and Indigenous Peoples.*

36. Love, *We Want to Do More than Survive: Abolitionist Teaching and the Pursuit of Educational Freedom.*

37. Agozino, *Counter-Colonial Criminology: A Critique of Imperialist Reason.*

38. Winn, *Justice on Both Sides: Transforming Education through Restorative Justice.*

39. Paris and Alim, *Culturally Sustaining Pedagogies: Teaching and Learning for Justice in a Changing World.*

40. Smith, *Decolonizing Methodologies: Research and Indigenous Peoples.*

41. Gruenewald, "The Best of Both Worlds: A Critical Pedagogy of Place."

42. Paris and Alim, "What Are We Seeking to Sustain through Culturally Sustaining Pedagogy? A Loving Critique Forward."

43. Duncan-Andrade, "Note to Educators: Hope Required When Growing Roses in Concrete."

44. Camangian, "Teach Like Lives Depend on It: Agitate, Arouse, and Inspire."

45. Freire, *Pedagogy of the Oppressed.*

46. Davis, "Foreword: Transforming Anthropology."

47. Love, *We Want to Do More than Survive: Abolitionist Teaching and the Pursuit of Educational Freedom.*

48. Love.

49. hooks, *Teaching to Transgress: Education as the Practice of Freedom.*

50. hooks.

51. Hirschi, *Causes of Delinquency.*

52. hooks, *Teaching to Transgress: Education as the Practice of Freedom.*

53. Love, *We Want to Do More than Survive: Abolitionist Teaching and the Pursuit of Educational Freedom.*

54. Love.

55. hooks, *Teaching to Transgress: Education as the Practice of Freedom*; Love, *We Want to Do More than Survive: Abolitionist Teaching and the Pursuit of Educational Freedom.*

56. Love, *We Want to Do More than Survive: Abolitionist Teaching and the Pursuit of Educational Freedom.*

57. Soss and Weaver, "Police Are Our Government: Politics, Political Science, and the Policing of Race–Class Subjugated Communities."

58. Love, *We Want to Do More than Survive: Abolitionist Teaching and the Pursuit of Educational Freedom.*

59. hooks, *Teaching to Transgress: Education as the Practice of Freedom*; Love, *We Want to Do More than Survive: Abolitionist Teaching and the Pursuit of Educational Freedom.*

60. Tuck and Yang, "Decolonization Is Not a Metaphor."

61. Love, *We Want to Do More than Survive: Abolitionist Teaching and the Pursuit of Educational Freedom*.

62. hooks, *Teaching to Transgress: Education as the Practice of Freedom*.

63. Love, *We Want to Do More than Survive: Abolitionist Teaching and the Pursuit of Educational Freedom*.

64. Ziadah, "We Teach Life, Sir."

65. Love, *We Want to Do More than Survive: Abolitionist Teaching and the Pursuit of Educational Freedom*, 89.

Bibliography

13th. Kandoo Films, 2016.

Absolon, K. E. *Kaandossiwin: How We Come to Know: Indigenous Re-Search Methodologies*. 2nd ed. Fernwood, 2022.

Acker, J. "Gendering Organizational Theory." *Classics of Organizational Theory* 6 (1992): 450–59.

ACLU Southern California. "ACLU Files Lawsuit against Oppressive 'YAT' Youth Program in Riverside." Press release. July 2, 2018. https://www.aclusocal.org/en/press-releases/aclu-files-lawsuit-against-oppressive-yat-youth-program-riverside.

African American Pamphlet Collection. *To the Colored Men of Voting Age in the Southern States*. Press of E. A. Wright, 1900. https://www.loc.gov/item/92838850/.

Agozino, B. *Counter-Colonial Criminology: A Critique of Imperialist Reason*. Pluto Press, 2003.

Ahmed, S. *The Promise of Happiness*. Duke University Press, 2010.

Alexander, M. "The New Jim Crow." *Ohio State Journal of Criminal Law* 9, no. 7 (2011): 7–26.

———. *The New Jim Crow: Mass Incarceration in the Age of Colorblindness*. New Press, 2010.

Alfonseca, K. "Record Number of Anti-LGBTQ Legislation Filed in 2023." *ABC News*, December 28, 2023. https://abcnews.go.com/US/record-number-anti-lgbtq-legislation-filed-2023/story?id=105556010.

———. "Some Republicans Use False 'Pedophilia' Claims to Attack Democrats, LGBTQ People." *ABC News*, May 7, 2022. https://abcnews.go.com/US/republicans-false-pedophilia-claims-attack-democrats-lgbtq-people/story?id=84344687.

Alper, M., M.R. Durose, and J. Markman. *2018 Update on Prisoner Recidivism: A 9-Year Follow-up Period (2005–2014).* U.S. Department of Justice, Bureau of Justice Statistics, Special Report NCJ 250975, May 2018. https://www.bjs.gov/content/pub/pdf/18upr9yfup0514.pdf.

Alsharif, M., and E. Levenson. "Buffalo Police Officers Who Pushed 75-Year-Old during Black Lives Matter Protest Cleared of Wrongdoing." *CNN*, April 11, 2022. https://www.cnn.com/2022/04/11/us/buffalo-police-push-protest-arbitration/index.html.

American Civil Liberties Union. *Captive Labor: Exploitation of Incarcerated Workers.* June 15, 2022. https://www.aclu.org/report/captive-labor-exploitation-incarcerated-workers.

———. "Mapping Attacks on LGBTQ Rights in U.S. State Legislatures." September 15, 2023. https://www.aclu.org/legislative-attacks-on-lgbtq-rights.

American Immigration Council. *Sanctuary Policies: An Overview.* December 2020. https://www.americanimmigrationcouncil.org/sites/default/files/research/sanctuary_policies_an_overview.pdf.

American Psychological Association. *Publication Manual of the American Psychological Association.* 7th ed. American Psychological Association, 2020.

Anderson, C. *White Rage: The Unspoken Truth of Our Racial Divide.* Bloomsbury, 2016.

Anderson, D.A. "The Aggregate Cost of Crime in the United States." *Journal of Law and Economics* 64, no. 4 (2021): 857–85.

Anderson, G.D. "Child Sexual Abuse Prevention Policy: An Analysis of Erin's Law." *Social Work in Public Health* 29, no. 3 (2014): 196–206. https://doi.org/10.1080/19371918.2013.776321.

Anderson, L.A., M.O. Caughy, and M.T. Owen. "'The Talk' and Parenting While Black in America: Centering Race, Resistance, and Refuge." *Journal of Black Psychology* 48, no. 3–4 (2021): 475–506. https://doi.org/10.1177/00957984211034294.

Angelides, S. "The Homosexualization of Pedophilia." In *Homophobias: Lust and Loathing across Time and Space*, edited by D.A.B. Murray, 65–81. Duke University Press, 2009.

Annamma, S.A. *The Pedagogy of Pathologization: Dis/Abled Girls of Color in the School-Prison Nexus.* Routledge, 2018.

Anti-Defamation League. "What Is 'Grooming'? The Truth behind the Dangerous, Bigoted Lie Targeting the LGBTQ+ Community." September 16, 2022. https://www.adl.org/resources/blog/what-grooming-truth-behind-dangerous-bigoted-lie-targeting-lgbtq-community.

Anti-Defamation League and GLAAD. "Year in Review: Anti-LGBTQ+ Hate & Extremism Incidents." 2023. https://www.adl.org/resources/report/year-review-anti-lgbtq-hate-extremism-incidents-2022-2023.

Applebaum, K.L., J.A. Savageau, R.L. Trestman, J.L. Metzner, and J. Baillargeon. "A National Survey of Self-Injurious Behavior in American Prisons." *Psychiatric Services* 62, no. 3 (2011): 285–90.

Arnold, D., W. Dobbie, and C.S. Yang. "Racial Bias in Bail Decisions." *Quarterly Journal of Economics* 133, no. 4 (2018): 1885–1932. https://doi.org/10.1093/qje/qjy012.

Ayers, W., T. Quinn, and D. Stovall, eds. *Handbook of Social Justice in Education*. Routledge, 2010.

Bach, G. "Defining 'Sufficiently Serious' in Claims of Cruel and Unusual Punishment." *Drake Law Review* 62, no. 1 (2013): 1–40.

Bach, N. A. "U.S. Sues Texas after Gov. Greg Abbott Declines to Remove Floating Border Barrier." *Texas Tribune*, July 24, 2023. https://www.texastribune.org/2023/07/24/texas-border-rio-grande-floating-barrier-greg-abbott-lawsuit/.

Bagaric, M., D. Hunter, and J. Svilar. "Prison Abolition: From Naïve Idealism to Technological Pragmatism." *Journal of Criminal Law and Criminology* 111, no. 2 (2021): 351–406.

Bagno/Maariv, Y. "Israel Sees Record Number of Anti-LGBTQ+ Incidents in 2022—Report." *Jerusalem Post*, March 19, 2023. https://www.jpost.com/israel-news/article-734812.

Bailey, M. *Misogynoir Transformed*. New York University Press, 2021.

Bakunin, M. *Statism and Anarchy (Gosudarstvennost' i anarkhiia)*. Translated by Marshall S. Shatz. Cambridge University Press, 1990.

Balko, R. *Rise of the Warrior Cop: The Militarization of America's Police Forces*. Public Affairs, 2013.

Ball, M. "Queer Criminology as Activism." *Critical Criminology* 24, no. 4 (2016): 473–87. https://doi.org/10.1007/s10612-016-9329-4.

———. "Queering Penal Abolition." In *The Routledge International Handbook of Penal Abolition*, edited by Michael J. Coyle and David Scott, 179–89. Routledge, 2021.

———. "What's Queer about Queer Criminology?" In *Handbook of LGBT Communities, Crime, and Justice*, edited by D. Peterson and V. R. Panfil, 531–55. Springer, 2014.

Ball, M., C. L. Buist, and J. Blair Woods. "Introduction to the Special Issue on Queer/Ing Criminology: New Directions and Frameworks." *Critical Criminology* 22, no. 1 (March 2014): 1–4. https://doi.org/10.1007/s10612-013-9231-2.

Bandes, S. A. "Victims, Closure, and the Sociology of Emotion." *Law and Contemporary Problems* 72, no. 2 (2009): 1–26.

Baradaran Baughman, S. "How Effective Are Police? The Problem of Clearance Rates and Criminal Accountability." *Alabama Law Review* 72, no. 1 (2020): 47–130.

Baradaran, M. *Color of Money: Black Banks and the Racial Wealth Gap*. Harvard University Press, 2017.

Bassichis, M., A. Lee, and D. Spade. "Building an Abolitionist Trans and Queer Movement with Everything We've Got." In *Captive Genders: Trans Embodiment and the Prison Industrial Complex*, edited by Eric A. Stanley and Nat Smith, 15–40. AK Press, 2011.

Bauer, G., and A. Scheim. *Transgender People in Ontario*. Statistics from the Trans PULSE Project to Inform Human Rights Policy, 2015.

Beck, B. "Op-ed: New York Should Make Milk, Not Prisons." *Thirteen.org*, February 24, 2012. https://www.thirteen.org/metrofocus/2012/02/op-ed-new-york-should-make-milk-not-prisons/.

Beck, R. R. *We Believe the Children: A Moral Panic in the 1980s*. PublicAffairs, 2015.

Beckett, K., and N. Murakawa. "Mapping the Shadow Carceral State: Toward an Institutionally Capacious Approach to Punishment." *Theoretical Criminology* 16, no. 2 (2012): 221–44.

Bell, M. "Abolition: A New Paradigm for Reform." *Law & Social Inquiry* 46, no. 1 (2021): 32–68. https://doi.org/10.1017/lsi.2020.21.

Bell, S.D. "The Long Shadow: Decreasing Barriers to Employment, Housing, and Civic Participation for People with Criminal Records Will Improve Public Safety and Strengthen the Economy." *Western State Law Review* 42, no. 1 (2014): 1–24.

Ben-Moshe, L. *The Tension between Abolition and Reform.* Brill, 2013.

Berger, D. "The Abolitionist Logic of 'Everyone for Everyone.'" *Jewish Currents*, December 1, 2023. https://jewishcurrents.org/the-abolitionist-logic-of-everyone-for-everyone.

Berger, D., and T. Losier. *Rethinking the American Prison Movement.* Routledge, 2017.

bergman, c, ed. *Trust Kids! Stories on Youth Autonomy and Confronting Adult Supremacy.* AK Press, 2022.

Berlant, L., and M. Warner. "Sex in Public." *Critical Inquiry* 24, no. 2 (1998): 547–66. http://www.jstor.org/stable/1344178.

Bernal, D.D. "Using a Chicana Feminist Epistemology in Educational Research." *Harvard Educational Review* 68, no. 4 (1998): 555–83.

Bernstein, E. "The Sexual Politics of the 'New Abolitionism.'" *Differences: A Journal of Feminist Cultural Studies* 18, no. 3 (2007): 128–51. https://doi.org/10.1215/10407391-2007-013.

Bey, M., and J.A. Goldberg. "Queer as in Abolition Now!" *GLQ* 28, no. 2 (2022): 159–63.

Blalock, H.M. *Toward a Theory of Minority-Group Relations.* John Wiley and Sons, 1967.

Blitz, C.L., N. Wolff, and J. Shi. "Physical Victimization in Prison: The Role of Mental Illness." *International Journal of Law and Psychiatry* 31, no. 5 (2008): 385–93.

Block, M. "Accusations of 'Grooming' Are the Latest Political Attack—with Homophobic Origins." *NPR*, May 11, 2022. https://www.npr.org/2022/05/11/1096623939/accusations-grooming-political-attack-homophobic-origins.

Blumer, H. "Race Prejudice as a Sense of Group Position." *Pacific Sociological Review* 1, no. 1 (1958): 3–7.

Bobo, L.D. "Prejudice as Group Position: Microfoundations of a Sociological Approach to Racism and Race Relations." *Journal of Social Issues* 55, no. 3 (1999): 445–72.

Bolden, C.L. *Out of the Red: My Life of Gangs, Prison, and Redemption.* Rutgers University Press, 2020.

Bonilla-Silva, E., C. Goar, and D.G. Embrick. "When Whites Flock Together: The Social Psychology of White Habitus." *Critical Sociology* 32, no. 2–3 (2006): 229–53. https://doi.org/10.1163/156916306777835268.

Boon-Kuo, L., E.R. Meiners, and P. Simpson. "Queer Interruptions: Policing Belonging in a Carceral State." In *Youth, Sexuality and Sexual Citizenship,* edited by Peter Aggleton, Rob Cover, Deana Leahy, Daniel Marshall, and Mary Lou Rasmussen, 34–49. Routledge, 2018.

Boucher, L., and R. Reynolds. "Decriminalisation, Apology and Expungement: Sexual Citizenship and the Problem of Public Sex in Victoria." *Australian Historical Studies* 49, no. 4 (October 2, 2018): 457–74. https://doi.org/10.1 080/1031461X.2018.1521853.

Brammer, J.P. "Behind the Weird Internet Scheme to Associate Pedophiles with the LGBTQ+ Community." *Them*, July 12, 2018. https://www.them.us /story/behind-the-weird-internet-scheme-to-associate-pedophiles-with-the -lgbtq-community.

Braunstein, M.D. "The Five Stages of LGBTQ Discrimination and Its Effects on Mass Incarceration." *Miami Race and Social Justice Law Review* 17 (2017): 217–46.

Britton, D.M. "The Epistemology of the Gendered Organization." *Gender & Society* 14, no. 3 (2000): 418–34.

Bronson, J., and M. Berzofsky. *Indicators of Mental Health Problems Reported by Prisoners and Jail Inmates, 2011–12*. U.S. Department of Justice, Bureau of Justice Statistics, Special Report NCJ 250612, June 2017.

Brown, G.R., and E. McDuffie. "Health Care Policies Addressing Transgender Inmates in Prison Systems in the United States." *Journal of Correctional Health Care* 15, no. 4 (2009): 280–91. https://doi.org/10.1177/1078345809340423.

Brown, M., and J. Schept. "New Abolition, Criminology and a Critical Carceral Studies." *Punishment & Society* 19, no. 4 (2017): 440–62.

Browne-Marshall, G.J. *She Took Justice: The Black Woman, Law, and Power— 1619 to 1969*. Routledge, 2021.

Brownmiller, S. *Against Our Will: Men, Women and Rape*. Simon & Schuster, 1975.

Bryant, A. *The Anita Bryant Story: The Survival of Our Nation's Families and the Threat of Militant Homosexuality*. Fleming H. Revell, 1977.

Buch, J. "ICE Criminal Investigators Ask to Be Distanced from Detentions, Deportations in Letter to Kirstjen Nielsen." *Texas Observer*, June 27, 2018. https://www.texasobserver.org/ice-hsi-letter-kirstjen-nielsen-criminal-civil -deportation-zero-tolerance/.

Buchanan, L., Q. Bui, and J.K. Patel. "Black Lives Matter May Be the Largest Movement in U.S. History." *New York Times*, July 3, 2020. https://www .nytimes.com/interactive/2020/07/03/us/george-floyd-protests-crowd-size .html.

Budd, K.M., and N. Monazzam. *Incarcerated Women and Girls*. Fact sheet. Sentencing Project, 2023. https://web.archive.org/web/20230705032605/https:// www.sentencingproject.org/fact-sheet/incarcerated-women-and-girls/.

Buist, C.L., and C. Stone. "Transgender Victims and Offenders: Failures of the United States Criminal Justice System and the Necessity of Queer Criminology." *Critical Criminology* 22, no. 1 (2014): 35–47.

Buist, C.L., and E. Lenning. *Queer Criminology*. 2nd ed. Routledge, 2022.

Buonanno, P., and J.F. Vargas. "Inequality, Crime, and the Long Run from Slavery." *Journal of Economic Behavior & Organization* 159 (2019): 539–52.

Burton, A. L., F. T. Cullen, V. S. Burton, A. Graham, L. C. Butler, and A. J. Thielo. "Belief in Redeemability and Punitive Public Opinion: 'Once a Criminal, Always a Criminal' Revisited." *Criminal Justice and Behavior* 47, no. 6 (June 2020): 712–32. https://doi.org/10.1177/0093854820913585.

Butts, J. A., and V. N. Schiraldi. *Recidivism Reconsidered: Preserving the Community Justice Mission of Community Corrections.* Harvard Kennedy School, 2018. https://www.hks.harvard.edu/sites/default/files/centers/wiener/programs/pcj/files/recidivism_reconsidered.pdf.

Camangian, P. R. "Teach Like Lives Depend on It: Agitate, Arouse, and Inspire." *Urban Education* 50, no. 4 (June 2015): 424–53. https://doi.org/10.1177/0042085913514591.

Cameron, J. J., and D. A. Stinson. "Gender (Mis)Measurement: Guidelines for Respecting Gender Diversity in Psychological Research." *Social and Personality Psychology Compass* 13, no. 11 (November 2019): e12506. https://doi.org/10.1111/spc3.12506.

Canada, K., S. Barrenger, C. Bohrman, A. Banks, and P. Peketi. "Multi-level Barriers to Prison Mental Health and Physical Health Care for Individuals with Mental Illnesses." *Frontiers in Psychiatry* 13 (2022): 777124. https://doi.org/10.3389/fpsyt.2022.777124.

Capers, I. B. "Cross Dressing and the Criminal." *Yale Journal of Law and the Humanities* 20, no. 1 (2008): 1–30.

Carlen, P., and L. A. França, eds. *Alternative Criminologies.* Routledge, 2018.

Carlton, B., and E. K. Russell. *Resisting Carceral Violence: Women's Imprisonment and the Politics of Abolition.* Palgrave, 2018.

Carpenter, L. F., and R. B. Marshall. "Walking While Trans: Profiling of Transgender Women by Law Enforcement, and the Problem of Proof." *William & Mary Journal of Women and the Law* 24, no. 1 (2017): 5–38.

Carpentier, C., L. Royuela, L. Montanari, and P. Davis. "The Global Epidemiology of Drug Use in Prison." In *Drug Use in Prisoners: Epidemiology, Implications, and Policy Responses*, edited by S. Kinner and J. Rich, 17–42. Oxford University Press, 2018.

Casey, L. S., S. L. Reisner, M. G. Findling, R. J. Blendon, J. M. Benson, J. M. Sayde, and C. Miller. "Discrimination in the United States: Experiences of Lesbian, Gay, Bisexual, Transgender, and Queer Americans." *Health Services Research* 54 (2019): 1454–66.

Center for American Progress. "Release: LGBT Immigrants in Detention Centers at Severe Risk of Sexual Abuse." May 30, 2018. https://www.americanprogress.org/press/release-lgbt-immigrants-detention-centers-severe-risk-sexual-abuse-cap-analysis-says/.

Center for Countering Digital Hate and Human Rights Campaign. *Digital Hate: Social Media's Role in Amplifying Dangerous Lies about LGBTQ+ People.* 2022. https://hrc-prod-requests.s3-us-west-2.amazonaws.com/CCDH-HRC-Digital-Hate-Report-2022-single-pages.pdf.

Centers for Disease Control and Prevention. *Preventing Youth Violence.* Fact sheet. 2022. https://www.cdc.gov/violenceprevention/pdf/yv/YV-factsheet_2022.pdf.

Césaire, A. *Discourse on Colonialism*. Translated by Robin D.G. Kelley. Monthly Review Press, 2000.

Chang, A., P. Jarenwattananon, and A. Sirianni. "Biden Hasn't Changed ICE's Budget, but He Has Changed the Agency's Approach." *NPR*, May 28, 2021. https://www.npr.org/2021/05/28/1001377999/biden-hasnt-changed-ices-budget-but-he-has-changed-the-agencys-approach.

Charmaz, K. *Constructing Grounded Theory: A Practical Guide through Qualitative Analysis*. Sage Publications, 2006.

Chenier, E. "The Natural Order of Disorder: Pedophilia, Stranger Danger and the Normalising Family." *Sexuality & Culture* 16, no. 2 (2012): 172–86.

"Children in Cages Are Not New." YouTube, June 29, 2019. Video, 2:41. https://youtu.be/fxoZtzZBGzA?feature=shared.

Child Welfare Information Gateway. *About CAPTA: A Legislative History*. U.S. Department of Health and Human Services, Children's Bureau, 2019.

Clarke, M. "Polls Show People Favor Rehabilitation over Incarceration." Prison Legal News, 2018. https://www.prisonlegalnews.org/news/2018/nov/6/polls-show-people-favor-rehabilitation-over-incarceration/.

Clarke, R., A. Killough, S. Moon, and P. Alvarez. "Texas Troopers Told to Push Back Migrants into Rio Grande and Ordered Not to Give Water amid Soaring Temperatures, Report Says." *CNN*, July 18, 2023. https://www.cnn.com/2023/07/18/us/texas-troopers-migrant-treatment-concerns.

Clear, T. *Imprisoning Communities: How Mass Incarceration Makes Disadvantaged Neighborhoods Worse*. Oxford University Press, 2007.

Cohen, C.J. "Punks, Bulldaggers, and Welfare Queens: The Radical Potential of Queer Politics." *GLQ* 3 (1997): 437–65.

Cohen, S. *Against Criminology*. Routledge, 2017.

Cohen, S.L. *The Gay Liberation Youth Movement in New York: An Army of Lovers Cannot Fail*. Routledge, 2008.

Collins, P.H. *Black Feminist Thought: Knowledge, Consciousness, and the Politics of Empowerment*. 2nd ed. Routledge, Taylor & Francis Group, 2009.

———. "Learning from the Outsider Within: The Sociological Significance of Black Feminist Thought." *Social Problems* 33, no. 6 (1986): 14–32. https://doi.org/10.2307/800672.

———. "The Social Construction of Black Feminist Thought." *Signs: Journal of Women in Culture and Society* 14 (1989): 745–73.

Collins, S.E., H.S. Lonczak, and S.L. Clifasefi. "Seattle's Law Enforcement Assisted Diversion (LEAD): Program Effects on Recidivism Outcomes." *Evaluation and Program Planning* 64, no. 1 (2017): 49–56. https://doi.org/10.1016/j.evalprogplan.2017.05.008.

Collin-Vézina, D., I. Daigneault, and M. Hébert. "Lessons Learned from Child Sexual Abuse Research: Prevalence, Outcomes, and Preventive Strategies." *Child and Adolescent Psychiatry and Mental Health* 7, no. 1 (2013): 1–9. https://doi.org/DOI:10.1186/1753-2000-7-22.

Conlin, M. "Off-Duty Black Cops in New York Feel Threat from Fellow Police." Reuters, December 23, 2014. https://www.reuters.com/article/us-usa-police-nypd-race-insight/off-duty-black-cops-in-new-york-feel-threat-from-fellow-police-idUSKBN0K11EV20141223/.

Connecticut Alliance to End Sexual Violence. "Fighting Anti-LGBTQ+ Grooming Rhetoric." 2023. https://endsexualviolencect.org/fighting-anti-lgbtq-grooming-rhetoric/.

Connell, R. W., and J. W. Messerschmidt. "Hegemonic Masculinity: Rethinking the Concept." *Gender & Society* 19, no. 6 (2005): 829–59.

Conover, T. *Newjack: Guarding Sing Sing.* Random House, 2000.

Conrad, R., ed. *Against Equality: Queer Revolution, Not Mere Inclusion.* AK Press, 2014.

Contreras, F., and M. Oropeza-Fujimoto. "College Readiness for English Language Learners (ELLs) in California: Assessing Equity for ELLs under the Local Control Funding Formula." *Peabody Journal of Education* 94, no. 2 (2019): 209–25. https://doi.org/10.1080/0161956X.2019.1598121.

Corradini, M., J. A. Kringen, L. Simich, K. Berberich, and M. Emigh. *Operation Streamline: No Evidence That Criminal Prosecution Deters Migration.* Vera Institute, 2018. https://www.vera.org/downloads/publications/operation_streamline-report.pdf.

Coulter, R. W., C. Mair, E. Miller, J. R. Blosnich, D. D. Matthews, and H. L. McCauley. "Prevalence of Past-Year Sexual Assault Victimization among Undergraduate Students: Exploring Differences by and Intersections of Gender Identity, Sexual Identity, and Race/Ethnicity." *Prevention Science* 18 (2017): 726–36.

Coulthard, G. S. *Red Skin, White Masks: Rejecting the Colonial Politics of Recognition.* University of Minnesota Press, 2014.

Council of State Governments Justice Center. "Confined and Costly: How Supervision Violations Are Filling Prisons and Burdening Budgets." 2019. https://csgjusticecenter.org/publications/confined-costly/.

Covington, S. S., and B. E. Bloom. "Gendered Justice: Women in the Criminal Justice System." In *Gendered Justice: Addressing Female Offenders*, edited by B. E. Bloom, 3–23. Carolina Academic Press, 2003.

Coyle, M. J., and J. Schept. "Penal Abolition and the State: Colonial, Racial and Gender Violences." *Contemporary Justice Review* 20, no. 4 (2017): 399–403.

Crenshaw, K. "Mapping the Margins: Intersectionality, Identity Politics, and Violence against Women of Color." *Stanford Law Review* 43, no. 6 (1991): 1241–99. https://doi.org/10.2307/1229039.

Crenshaw, K. W., and A. J. Ritchie. *Say Her Name: Resisting Police Brutality against Black Women.* African American Policy Forum, 2015.

Crissman, H. P., C. Czuhajewski, M. H. Moniz, M. Plegue, and T. Chang. "Youth Perspectives Regarding the Regulating of Bathroom Use by Transgender Individuals." *Journal of Homosexuality* 67, no. 14 (2020): 2034–49.

Critical Resistance. "Critical Resistance: Beyond the Prison Industrial Complex 1998 Conference." September 26, 2018. https://criticalresistance.org/updates/critical-resistance-beyond-the-prison-industrial-complex-1998-conference/.

———. "Reformist Reforms vs Abolitionist Steps in Policing." May 14, 2020. https://criticalresistance.org/resources/reformist-reforms-vs-abolitionist-steps-in-policing/.

———. *Reformist Reforms vs. Abolitionist Steps to End Imprisonment.* Poster. 2021. https://criticalresistance.org/wp-content/uploads/2021/08/CR _abolitioniststeps_antiexpansion_2021_eng.pdf.

Cunneen, C. *Defund the Police: An International Insurrection.* Policy Press, 2023.

Cunneen, C., and J.M. Tauri. "Indigenous Peoples, Criminology, and Criminal Justice." *Annual Review of Criminology* 2, no. 1 (2019): 359–81. https:// doi.org/10.1146/annurev-criminol-011518-024630.

Czopek, M. "Why It's Not 'Grooming': What Research Says about Gender and Sexuality in Schools." *PolitiFact,* May 11, 2022. https://www.politifact.com /article/2022/may/11/why-its-not-grooming-what-research-says-about-gend/.

Daly, K., and M. Chesney-Lind. "Feminism and Criminology." *Justice Quarterly* 5, no. 4 (1988): 497–538.

Daniels, E. *Building a Trauma-Responsive Educational Practice: Lessons from a Corrections Classroom.* Routledge, 2022.

Darder, A. *Reinventing Paulo Freire: A Pedagogy of Love.* Routledge, 2017.

Davis, A. "Masked Racism: Reflections on the Prison Industrial Complex." *Indigenous Law Bulletin* 4, no. 27 (2000): 4–7.

Davis, A. Y. *Abolition Democracy: Beyond Empire, Prisons, and Torture.* Seven Stories Press, 2005.

———. *Are Prisons Obsolete?* Seven Stories Press, 2003.

———. "Foreword: Transforming Anthropology." *Journal of Contemporary Ethnography* 48, no. 5 (2019): 487–97.

———. *Freedom Is a Constant Struggle: Ferguson, Palestine, and the Foundations of a Movement.* Haymarket Books, 2016.

Davis, A. Y., G. Dent, E. R. Meiners, and B. E. Richie. *Abolition. Feminism. Now.* Haymarket Books, 2022.

Davis, A .Y., and D. Rodriguez. "The Challenge of Prison Abolition: A Conversation." *Social Justice* 27, no. 3 (81) (2000): 212–18.

Decoster, A., and P. Cannoot. "The Abolition of Sex/Gender Registration in the Age of Gender Self-Determination: An Interdisciplinary, Queer, Feminist and Human Rights Analysis." *International Journal of Gender, Sexuality and Law* 1, no. 1 (2020). https://doi.org/10.19164/ijgsl.v1i1.1328.

DeMillo, A. "Arkansas Gov. Sanders Signs Bill Creating School Vouchers." AP News, March 8, 2023. https://apnews.com/article/huckabee-sanders-vouchers -schools-lgbtq-education-teachers-bd56e89399d401ea44018cc92a5116ee.

Democracy Now! "'Horrendous': Black Men Tortured by White Mississippi Police 'Goon Squad' React to Guilty Pleas." August 9, 2023. https://www .democracynow.org/2023/8/9/michael_jenkins_eddie_parker_police_torture.

Desmond, M. *Poverty, by America.* Crown, 2023.

DeVeaux, M. "The Trauma of the Incarceration Experience." *Harvard Civil Rights–Civil Liberties Law Review* 48, no. 1 (2013): 257–78.

DeVuono-Powell, S., C. Schweidler, A. Walters, and A. Zohrabi. "Who Pays? The True Cost of Incarceration on Families." Ella Baker Center, 2015. https://nicic.gov/resources/nic-library/all-library-items/who-pays-true-cost -incarceration-families.

Dickens, C. *American Note for General Circulation and Pictures from Italy.* Chapman & Hall, 1913.

Dillon, S. *Fugitive Life: The Queer Politics of the Prison State.* Duke University Press, 2018.

Dilts, A. "Crisis, Critique, and Abolition." In *A Time for Critique*, edited by B. E. Harcourt and D. Fassin, 230–51. Columbia University Press, 2019.

Disclosure. Netflix, 2020.

Dolan, F. X. *Eastern State Penitentiary.* Arcadia Books, 2007.

Dream Defenders. "Sunday School: Abolition in Our Lifetime." YouTube, June 23, 2020. Video, 1:51:02. https://youtu.be/RtpRiAoIoy4.

Dunbar-Ortiz, R. *An Indigenous Peoples' History of the United States.* Beacon Press, 2023.

———. *Not a Nation of Immigrants: Settler Colonialism, White Supremacy, and a History of Erasure and Exclusion.* Beacon Press, 2021.

Duncan, G. J., K. Magnuson, A. Kalil, and K. Ziol-Guest. "The Importance of Early Childhood Poverty." *Social Indicators Research* 108, no. 1 (2012): 87–98. https://doi.org/10.1007/s11205-011-9867-9.

Duncan-Andrade, J. M. R. "Note to Educators: Hope Required When Growing Roses in Concrete." *Harvard Educational Review* 79, no. 2 (2009): 181–94.

Dvorsky, G., and J. Hughes. "Postgenderism: Beyond the Gender Binary." *Institute for Ethics and Emerging Technologies* 20 (2008): 44–57.

Economic Times. "The Cost of Immigration to United States." May 26, 2021. https://economictimes.indiatimes.com/nri/migrate/the-costs-of-immigrating -to-the-united-states/articleshow/82966455.cms?from=mdr.

Editorial Staff. "New York Mayoral Primary Election: Live Vote Results." *New York Times*, June 22, 2021. https://www.nytimes.com/interactive/2021/06/22 /us/elections/results-nyc-mayor-primary.html.

Eggleston, E., and J. Laub. "The Onset of Adult Offending: A Neglected Dimension of the Criminal Career." *Journal of Criminal Justice* 30, no. 6 (2002): 603–22.

Elias, N., and R. Colvin. "A Third Option: Understanding and Assessing Non-Binary Gender Policies in the United States." *Administrative Theory & Praxis* 42, no. 2 (2020): 191–211. https://doi.org/10.1080/10841806.2019.1659046.

Eskridge, W. N., Jr. *Dishonorable Passions: Sodomy Laws in America, 1861–2003.* Viking, 2008.

———. *Gaylaw: Challenging the Apartheid of the Closet.* Harvard University Press, 1999.

Fadel, L., T. Haney, A. Rezvani, and K. Gallego-Mackie. "'Citizenship Won't Save You': Free Speech Advocates Say Student Arrests Should Worry All." NPR, April 8, 2025. https://www.npr.org/2025/04/08/nx-s1-5349472 /students-protest-trump-free-speech-arrests-deportation-gaza.

Fallot, R. D., and M. Harris. "A Trauma-Informed Approach to Screening and Assessment." *New Directions for Mental Health Services* 89 (2001): 23–31. https://doi.org/10.1002/yd.23320018904.

Farley, A. P. "The Black Body as Fetish Object." *Oregon Law Review* 76, no. 3 (1997): 457–535.

F.-Dufour, I., M.-P. Villeneuve, and J. Martel. "Portrait de la criminologie québécoise des dix dernières années selon le courant, la méthodologie et l'appartenance institutionnelle des auteurs." *Criminologie* 51, no. 1 (2018): 143–67. https://doi.org/10.7202/1045311ar.

Feagin, J.R., and K. Ducey. *Racist America: Roots, Current Realities, and Future Reparations*. 4th ed. Routledge, 2019.

Feinberg, L. "Street Transvestite Action Revolutionaries." Workers World Party, September 24, 2006. https://www.workers.org/2006/us/lavender-red-73/.

Ferrell, J., and C.R. Sanders. *Cultural Criminology*. Northeastern University Press, 1995.

Fiala, A. "Anarchism." Stanford Encyclopedia of Philosophy, 2021. https://plato.stanford.edu/archives/win2021/entries/anarchism/.

Forman, J., Jr. *Locking Up Our Own: Crime and Punishment in Black America*. Farrar, Straus and Giroux, 2017.

Foucault, M. *Discipline and Punish: The Birth of the Prison*. Knopf Doubleday, 2012.

———. *Society Must Be Defended: Lectures at the Collège de France, 1975–1976*. St. Martin's Press, 1997.

Freedom to Marry. "Using Online Video to Make the Case for the Freedom to Marry." n.d. http://www.freedomtomarry.org/pages/using-online-video-to-make-the-case-for-the-freedom-to-marry-in-the-court.

Freire, P. *Pedagogy of the Oppressed*. Herder and Herder, 1970.

Friedman, M.S., M.P. Marshal, T.E. Guadamuz, C. Wei, C.F. Wong, E.M. Saewyc, and R. Stall. "A Meta-Analysis of Disparities in Childhood Sexual Abuse, Parental Physical Abuse, and Peer Victimization among Sexual Minority and Sexual Nonminority Individuals." *American Journal of Public Health* 101, no. 8 (2011): 1481–94.

Fuller, D.A., E. Sinclair, H.R. Lamb, J.D. Cayce, and J. Snook. *Emptying the "New Asylums": A Beds Capacity Model to Reduce Mental Illness behind Bars*. Treatment Advocacy Center, January 2017. https://www.treatmentadvocacycenter.org/new-asylums.

Gabbay, Z.D. "Justifying Restorative Justice: Theoretical Justification for the Use of Restorative Justice Practices." *Journal of Dispute Resolution* 2005, no. 2 (2005): 349–98.

Gamio Cuervo, Á., A. Smith, E. Chang, and D. La Fazia. "'Solidarity and Community on Our Terms and through Our Lens': Community Care and Shared Trauma for Transgender and Nonbinary Peer Supporters during the COVID-19 Pandemic." *Psychology of Sexual Orientation and Gender Diversity* 11, no. 4 (2024): 690–702. https://doi.org/10.1037/sgd0000626.

Garnets, L., and D. Kimmel, eds. *Psychological Perspectives on Lesbian, Gay, and Bisexual Experiences*. Columbia University Press, 2003.

Garnette, L., A. Irvine, C. Reyes, and S. Wilber. "Lesbian, Gay, Bisexual, and Transgender (LGBT) Youth and the Juvenile Justice System." In *Juvenile Justice: Advancing Research, Policy, and Practice*, edited by F.T. Sherman and F.H. Jacobs, 156–73. Wiley, 2011.

Gates, G.J. *LGBT Adult Immigrants in the United States*. UCLA Williams Institute, 2013.

Gerena, C. E. "Clinical Implications for LGBT Asylum Seekers in US Detention Centers." *Journal of Gay & Lesbian Social Services* 34, no. 4 (2022): 489–501. https://doi.org/10.1080/10538720.2022.2041522.

Gewirtz-Meydan, A., and D. Finkelhor. "Sexual Abuse and Assault in a Large National Sample of Children and Adolescents." *Child Maltreatment* 25, no. 2 (2020): 203–14.

Giallombardo, R. *Society of Women: A Study of a Women's Prison*. John Wiley & Sons, 1966.

Gilbert, D. "New York Police Grabbed a Trans Protester and Threw Her into an Unmarked Van." *Vice News*, July 29, 2020. https://www.vice.com/en/article/dyzwxm/new-york-police-grabbed-a-trans-protester-and-threw-her-into-an-unmarked-van.

Gilbert, S. L. "Intimate Partner Violence in a Native American Community: An Exploratory Study." Master's thesis, Boise State University, 2020. https://doi.org/10.18122/td/1688/boisestate.

Gilbert, S. L., and K. Z. Armenta Rojas. "Indigenous Victimization and the Colonized Rainbow." In *Queer Victimology: Understanding the Victim Experience*, edited by S. Kelley, S. Clevenger, and K. Ratajczak, 106–14. Routledge, 2023.

Gillborn, D. "Education Policy as an Act of White Supremacy: Whiteness, Critical Race Theory and Education Reform." *Journal of Education Policy* 20, no. 4 (2005): 485–505.

———. "Heads I Win, Tails You Lose: Anti-Black Racism as Fluid, Relentless, Individual and Systemic." *Peabody Journal of Education* 93, no. 1 (2018): 66–77.

Gilmore, R. W. *Abolition Geography: Essays towards Liberation*. Verso, 2023.

———. *Change Everything: Racial Capitalism and the Case for Abolition*. Haymarket Books, 2023.

———. *Golden Gulag: Prisons, Surplus, Crisis, and Opposition in Globalizing California*. University of California Press, 2007.

Ginwright, S. *Hope and Healing in Urban Education: How Urban Activists and Teachers Are Reclaiming Matters of the Heart*. Routledge, 2015.

GLAAD. "PSA: Protect Our Families." YouTube, April 3, 2022. Video, 1:00. https://www.youtube.com/watch?v=xbad3efCic8.

Goffman, E. *Asylums: Essays on the Social Situation of Mental Patients and Other Inmates*. Anchor Books, 1961.

Golash-Boza, T. M. *Deported: Immigrant Policing, Disposable Labor, and Global Capitalism*. New York University Press, 2015.

Goldberg, S. K., and K. J. Conron. *LGBT Adult Immigrants in the United States*. UCLA School of Law Williams Institute, February 2021. https://williamsinstitute.law.ucla.edu/wp-content/uploads/Adult-LGBT-Immigrants-Feb-2021.pdf .

Goodmark, L. *Decriminalizing Domestic Violence: A Balanced Policy Approach to Intimate Partner Violence*. University of California Press, 2018.

———. *Imperfect Victims: Criminalized Survivors and the Promise of Abolition Feminism*. University of California Press, 2023.

Goomany, A., and T. Dickinson. "The Influence of Prison Climate on the Mental Health of Adult Prisoners: A Literature Review." *Journal of Psychiatry and Mental Health Nursing* 22, no. 6 (2015): 413–22.

Gottschalk, M. "Democracy and the Carceral State in America." *The Annals of the American Academy of Political and Social Science* 651, no. 1 (January 2014): 288–95. https://doi.org/10.1177/0002716213503787.

Gould, D. B. *Moving Politics: Emotion and ACT UP's Fight against AIDS.* University of Chicago Press, 2009.

Gramlich, J. "U.S. Public Divided over Whether People Convicted of Crimes Spend Too Much or Too Little Time in Prison." Pew Research Center, 2021. https://www.pewresearch.org/short-reads/2021/12/06/u-s-public-divided-over-whether-people-convicted-of-crimes-spend-too-much-or-too-little-time-in-prison/.

———. "What the Data Says (and Doesn't Say) about Crime in the United States." Pew Research Center, 2020. https://www.pewresearch.org/short-reads/2020/11/20/facts-about-crime-in-the-u-s/.

Grande, S. *Red Pedagogy: Native American Social and Political Thought.* Rowman & Littlefield, 2015.

Grant, J. M., L. A. Mottet, J. J. Tanis, and D. Min. *Transgender Discrimination Survey.* National Center for Transgender Equality and National Gay and Lesbian Task Force, 2011.

Grassini, M., S. Terp, B. Fischer, S. Ahmed, M. Ross, N. Frenzen, E. Burner, and P. Parmar. "Characteristics of Deaths among Individuals in US Immigration and Customs Enforcement Detention Facilities, 2011–2018." *JAMA Network Open* 4, no. 7 (2021): 1–11. https://doi.org/10.1001/jamanetworkopen.2021.16019.

Green, A. E., M. Price-Feeney, S. H. Dorison, and C. J. Pick. "Self-Reported Conversion Efforts and Suicidality among US LGBTQ Youths and Young Adults, 2018." *American Journal of Public Health* 110, no. 8 (2020): 1221–27. https://doi.org/10.2105/AJPH.2020.305701.

Greenbank, P. "The Role of Values in Educational Research: The Case for Reflexivity." *British Educational Research Journal* 29, no. 6 (2003): 791–801.

Greene, J. "Gender Bound: Making, Managing, and Navigating Prison Gender Boundaries, 1941–2018." *American Journal of Sociology* 128, no. 4 (2023): 993–1030.

Greene, M. *Releasing the Imagination: Essays on Education, the Arts, and Social Change.* Jossey-Bass, 1995.

Greey, A. "Queer Inclusion Precludes (Black) Queer Disruption: Media Analysis of the Black Lives Matter Toronto Sit-in during Toronto Pride 2016." *Leisure Studies* 37, no. 6 (2018): 662–76.

Gruenewald, D. A. "The Best of Both Worlds: A Critical Pedagogy of Place." *Educational Researcher* 32, no. 4 (2003): 3–12.

Guadalupe-Diaz, X. L., and J. Jasinski. "'I Wasn't a Priority, I Wasn't a Victim': Challenges in Help Seeking for Transgender Survivors of Intimate Partner Violence." *Violence against Women* 23, no. 6 (2017): 772–92.

Guishard, M. A., D. A. Heyward, J. T. Brown, and M. Stoddard-Pennant. "What We Not Finna Do: Respectfully Collaborating with Skinfolk and Kinfolk in

Black Feminist Participatory Action Research." *Global Journal of Community Psychology Practice* 12, no. 2 (2021): 1–36.

Hadden, S.E. *Slave Patrols: Law and Violence in Virginia and the Carolinas.* Harvard University Press, 2003.

Haggerty, K.D., and S. Bucerius. "The Proliferating Pains of Imprisonment." *Incarceration* 1, no. 1 (2020): 2632666320936432. https://doi.org/10.1177/2632666320936432.

Hall, S., C. Critcher, T. Jefferson, J. Clarke, and B. Roberts. *Policing the Crisis: Mugging, the State, and Law and Order.* Macmillan, 1978.

Haney, C. "Restricting the Use of Solitary Confinement." *Annual Review of Criminology* 1 (2018): 285–310.

Harney, S., and F. Moten. *The Undercommons: Fugitive Planning and Black Study.* Minor Compositions, 2013.

Hart, P.D. *Changing Public Attitudes toward the Criminal Justice System.* Open Society Institute, February 2002. https://www.prisonpolicy.org/scans/CJI-Poll.pdf .

Hartsock, N.C.M. "The Feminist Standpoint: Developing the Ground for a Specifically Feminist Historical Materialism." In *Discovering Reality*, edited by S. Harding and M.B. Hintikka, 238–310. D. Reidel, 1983.

Hayes, S., and S. Jeffries. "Romantic Terrorism: An Auto-ethnographic Analysis of Gendered Psychological and Emotional Tactics in Domestic Violence." *Journal of Research in Gender Studies* 6, no. 2 (2016): 38–61.

Haynes, S.H., A.C. Cares, and R.R. Barry. "Reducing the Harm of Criminal Victimization: The Role of Restitution." *Violence and Victims* 30, no. 3 (2015): 450–69.

Healey, J.F., and E. O'Brien. "Assimilation and Pluralism: From Immigrants to White Ethnics." In *Race, Ethnicity, Gender, and Class: The Sociology of Group Conflict and Change*, 6th ed. Sage, 2009, 43–94.

Hegarty, P., Y.G. Ansara, and M.J. Barker. "Nonbinary Gender Identities." In *Gender, Sex, and Sexualities: Psychological Perspectives*, edited by N.K. Dess, J. Marecek, and L.C. Bell, 53–76. Oxford University Press, 2018.

Heitzeg, N.A. "Education or Incarceration: Zero Tolerance Policies and the School to Prison Pipeline." Forum on Public Policy, 2009. https://files.eric.ed.gov/fulltext/EJ870076.pdf.

Hereth, J. "'Where Is the Safe Haven?': Transgender Women's Experiences of Victimization and Help-Seeking across the Life Course." *Feminist Criminology* 16, no. 4 (2021): 461–79.

Hernández, C.C.G. *Migrating to Prison: America's Obsession with Locking Up Immigrants.* New Press, 2023.

Herring, K. "Was a Prison Built Every 10 Days to House a Fast-Growing Inmate Population?" *PolitiFact*, July 31, 2015. https://www.politifact.com/factchecks/2015/jul/31/cory-booker/was-prison-built-every-10-days-house-fast-growing-/.

Herzing, R., and J. Piché. *How to Abolish Prisons: Lessons from the Movement.* Haymarket Books, 2024.

Himmelstein, D.U., R.M. Lawless, D. Thorne, P. Foohey, and S. Woolhandler. "Medical Bankruptcy: Still Common despite the Affordable Care Act."

American Journal of Public Health 109, no. 3 (2019): 431–33. https://doi
.org/10.2105/AJPH.2018.304901.

Himmelstein, K. E., and H. Bruckner. "Criminal-Justice and School Sanctions against Nonheterosexual Youth: A National Longitudinal Study." *Pediatrics* 127, no. 1 (2011): 49–57.

Hing, B. O. "Institutional Racism, ICE Raids, and Immigration Reform." *USFL Review* 44 (2009): 307. https://repository.usfca.edu/usflawreview/vol44 /iss2/5.

Hinton, E. *From the War on Poverty to the War on Crime: The Making of Mass Incarceration in America*. Harvard University Press, 2016.

Hirschel, D., and P. D. McCormack. "Same-Sex Couples and the Police: A 10-Year Study of Arrest and Dual Arrest Rates in Responding to Incidents of Intimate Partner Violence." *Violence against Women* 27, no. 9 (2021): 1119–49.

Hirschi, T. *Causes of Delinquency*. Routledge, 1969.

Hocquenghem, G. *Gay Liberation after May '68*. Duke University Press, 2022.

Hodge, D. *Colouring the Rainbow: Blak Queer and Trans Perspectives*. Wakefield Press, 2015.

Hoffman, S. D., and R. A. Maynard. *Kids Having Kids: Economic Costs and Social Consequences of Teen Pregnancy*. Urban Institute of Justice, 2008.

Holas, N. "Police Raid at Hares & Hyenas Building." *Saturday Paper*, May 24, 2019. https://www.thesaturdaypaper.com.au/news/law-crime/2019/05/18 /police-raid-hares-hyenas-building/15581016008157#hrd.

Holmes, A. "Marching with Pride? Debates on Uniformed Police Participating in Vancouver's LGBTQ Pride Parade." *Journal of Homosexuality* 68, no. 8 (2021): 1320–52. https://doi.org/10.1080/00918369.2019.1696107.

hooks, b. *Teaching to Transgress: Education as the Practice of Freedom*. Routledge, 1994.

Hudson, K. D., and M. Romanelli. "'We Are Powerful People': Health-Promoting Strengths of LGBTQ Communities of Color." *Qualitative Health Research* 30, no. 8 (2020): 1156–70.

Huling, T. "Building a Prison Economy in Rural America." In *Invisible Punishment: The Collateral Consequences of Mass Imprisonment*, edited by M. Mauer and M. Chesney-Lind, 197–213. New Press, 2002.

Human Rights Campaign. "Tools for Equality and Inclusion." 2023. https:// www.hrc.org/resources/.

Human Rights Watch. "Criminal Justice." n.d. https://www.hrw.org/united -states/criminal-justice.

———. "'Do You See How Much I'm Suffering Here?' Abuse against Transgender Women in US Immigration Detention." March 23, 2016. https://www .hrw.org/report/2016/03/24/do-you-see-how-much-im-suffering-here/abuse -against-transgender-women-us.

———. "US: New York Police Planned Assault on Bronx Protesters." September 30, 2020. https://www.hrw.org/news/2020/09/30/us-new-york-police -planned-assault-bronx-protesters.

Hunt, J., and A. Moodie-Mills. "The Unfair Criminalization of Gay and Transgender Youth: An Overview of the Experiences of LGBT Youth in the Juvenile Justice System." *Center for American Progress* 29 (2012): 1–12.

"'I Barely Did Anything': Video Shows Emory Professor Thrown to the Ground, Arrested during Protest." YouTube, April 26, 2024. Video, 2:55. https://www.youtube.com/watch?v=L5t5ldOXvwQ.

Ifeonu, C., K. D. Haggerty, and S. M. Bucerius. "Calories, Commerce, and Culture: The Multiple Valuations of Food in Prison." *Punishment & Society* 25, no. 3 (2023): 665–82. https://doi.org/10.1177/14624745221097367.

Indian Health Services. "Two Spirit: Health Resources." 2021. https://www.ihs.gov/lgbt/health/twospirit/.

International Lesbian, Bisexual, Gay, Trans, and Intersex Association. "Legal Frameworks." ILGA World Database, 2023. https://database.ilga.org/criminalisation-consensual-same-sex-sexual-acts.

Irvine, A., and A. Canfield. "The Overrepresentation of Lesbian, Gay, Bisexual, Questioning, Gender Nonconforming and Transgender Youth within the Child Welfare to Juvenile Justice Crossover Population." *Journal of Gender, Social Policy & the Law* 24, no. 2 (2015): 243–62.

Isom, D. A. *Gratuitous Angst in White America: A Theory of Whiteness and Crime.* Routledge, 2024.

Itskovich, E., and R. Factor. "Economic Inequality and Crime: The Role of Social Resistance." *Journal of Criminal Justice* 86 (2023): 1–9. https://doi.org/10.1016/j.jcrimjus.2023.102065.

Jackson, G. "Authoritarian Leftists: Kill the Cop in Your Head." libcom.org, 1996. https://libcom.org/article/authoritarian-leftists-kill-cop-your-head-greg-jackson.

Jacobs, A. "Prison Power Corrupts Absolutely: Exploring the Phenomenon of Prison Guard Brutality and the Need to Develop a System of Accountability." *California Western Law Review* 41, no. 1 (2004): 277–302.

James, S. E., J. L. Herman, S. Rankin, M. Keisling, L. Mottet, and M. Anafi. *The Report of the 2015 U.S. Transgender Survey.* National Center for Transgender Equality, 2016. https://transequality.org/sites/default/files/docs/usts/USTS-ExecutiveSummary-Dec17.pdf.

Johnson, J. R. "Cisgender Privilege, Intersectionality, and the Criminalization of CeCe McDonald: Why Intercultural Communication Needs Transgender Studies." *Journal of International and Intercultural Communication* 6, no. 2 (2013): 135–44.

Jones, A. "Visualizing the Unequal Treatment of LGBTQ People in the Criminal Justice System." Prison Policy Initiative, 2021. https://www.prisonpolicy.org/blog/2021/03/02/lgbtq/.

Jouet, M. *Exceptional America: What Divides Americans from the World and from Each Other.* University of California Press, 2017.

Just Beginnings Collaborative. "Wayfinding Project." December 15, 2023. https://justbeginnings.org/wayfinding/.

JusticeTrans. *2STNBGN Perspectives on Access to Justice: A Legal Needs Assessment.* 2022. https://justicetrans.org/wp-content/uploads/2023/09/2/2STNBGN_Perspectives_on_Access_to_Justice-Report.pdf.

Kaba, M. *We Do This 'til We Free Us: Abolitionist Organizing and Transforming Justice.* Haymarket Books, 2021.

———. "Yes, We Mean Literally Abolish the Police." *New York Times*, June 12, 2020.

Kaba, M., and K. Hayes. "A Jailbreak of the Imagination: Seeing Prisons for What They Are and Demanding Transformation." Truthout, May 3, 2018. https://truthout.org/articles/a-jailbreak-of-the-imagination-seeing-prisons-for-what-they-are-and-demanding-transformation/.

Kaba, M., and A. J. Ritchie. *No More Police: A Case for Abolition*. New Press, 2022.

Kappeler, V. E., and G. W. Potter. *The Mythology of Crime and Criminal Justice*. 5th ed. Waveland Press, 2018.

Karpman, B. "The Sexual Psychopath." *Journal of Criminal Law and Criminology* 42, no. 2 (1951): 184–98.

Kazemian, L. "Longest Sentences: An International Perspective." Council on Criminal Justice's Task Force on Long Sentences, 2022. https://counciloncj.foleon.com/tfls/long-sentences-by-the-numbers/an-international-perspective.

Keller, B. "Is 'Abolish Prisons' the Next Frontier in Criminal Justice?" Bloomberg, June 12, 2019.

Kelley, K. "The Playboy Interview with Anita Bryant." *Playboy*, May 1, 1978. https://www.playboy.com/read/the-playboy-interview-with-anita-bryant.

Kelley, R. D. G. *Freedom Dreams: The Black Radical Imagination*. 20th anniv. ed. Beacon Press, 2022.

Kempe, C. H. "The Battered-Child Syndrome." *JAMA* 181, no. 1 (1962): 17. https://doi.org/10.1001/jama.1962.03050270019004.

Kennedy, B. P., I. Kawachi, D. Prothrow-Stith, B. Gibbs, and K. Lochner. "Social Capital, Income Inequality and Firearm Violent Crime." *Social Science Medical Journal* 47 (1998): 7–17.

Keveney, B. "Weaponized Grooming Rhetoric Is Taking a Toll on LGBTQ Community and Child Sex Abuse Survivors." *Phys.Org*, May 2, 2022. https://phys.org/news/2022-05-weaponized-grooming-rhetoric-toll-lgbtq.html.

Kilgore, J. *Understanding Mass Incarceration: A People's Guide to the Key Civil Rights Struggle of Our Time*. New Press, 2015.

Kim, D. Y. "Prison-Based Economic Development: What the Evidence Tells Us." *International Journal of Rural Criminology* 7, no. 3 (2023): 357–85.

Kindy, K. "Historic Surge in Bills Targeting Transgender Rights Pass at Record Speed." *Washington Post*, April 17, 2023. https://www.washingtonpost.com/politics/2023/04/17/gop-state-legislatures-lgbtq-rights/.

Kirchick, J. "The Long, Sordid History of the Gay Conspiracy Theory." *New York Magazine*, May 31, 2022. https://nymag.com/intelligencer/2022/05/the-long-sordid-history-of-the-gay-conspiracy-theory.html.

Kirk, D. S., and S. Wakefield. "Collateral Consequences of Punishment: A Critical Review and Path Forward." *Annual Review of Criminology* 1, no. 1 (2018): 171–94.

Kitossa, T., and G. S. Tanyildiz. "Anti-Blackness, Criminology and the University as Violence Work: Diversity as Ritual and the Professionalization of Repression in Canada." In *Diversity in Criminology and Criminal Justice Studies*, edited by D. M. D. Silva and M. Deflem, vol. 27, 39–61. Emerald, 2022.

Knopp, F.H., B. Boward, M.J. Brach, S. Christianson, M.A. Largen, J. Lewin, J. Lugo, M. Morris, and W. Newton. *Instead of Prisons: A Handbook for Abolitionists*. Prison Research Education Action Project, 1976.

Koch-Rein, A., E. Haschemi Yekani, and J.J. Verlinden. "Representing Trans: Visibility and Its Discontents." *European Journal of English Studies* 24, no. 1 (2020): 1–12. https://doi.org/10.1080/13825577.2020.1730040.

Kopan, T., and N. Chavez. "There Are 2,300 Children Separated from Their Parents. What Will Happen to Them?" *CNN*, June 21, 2018. https://www.cnn.com/politics/live-news/immigration-border-children-separation/h_d553 540e1824a39c5520af408cf73f5e.

Kosciw, J.G., C.M. Clark, and L. Menard. *The 2021 National School Climate Survey: The Experiences of LGBTQ+ Youth in Our Nation's Schools*. GLSEN, 2022.

Krafft, E.K. "Marxist Criminology Abolishes Lombroso, Marxist Criminology Abolishes Itself." In *Abolish Criminology*, edited by M. Coyle, V. Saleh-Hanna, and J. Williams, 156–69. Routledge, 2023.

Kramer, R., and B. Remster. "Stop, Frisk, and Assault? Racial Disparities in Police Use of Force during Investigatory Stops." *Law & Society Review* 52, no. 4 (2018): 960–93. https://doi.org/10.1111/lasr.12366.

Kumashiro, K.K. "Toward a Theory of Anti-oppressive Education." *Review of Educational Research* 70, no. 1 (2000): 25–53.

Kunzel, R. *Criminal Intimacy: Prison and the Uneven History of Modern American Sexuality*. University of Chicago Press, 2008.

Kurti, Z., and M. Brown. "Carceral Reckoning and Twenty-First Century US Abolition Movements: Generational Struggles in the Fight against Prisons." *Punishment & Society* 25, no. 5 (2023): 14624745231171364. https://doi.org/10.1177/14624745231171364.

Kushner, R. "Is Prison Necessary? Ruth Wilson Gilmore Might Change Your Mind." *New York Times*, April 17, 2019. https://www.nytimes.com/2019/04/17/magazine/prison-abolition-ruth-wilson-gilmore.html.

Ladson-Billings, G. "Toward a Theory of Culturally Relevant Pedagogy." *American Educational Research Journal* 32, no. 3 (1995): 465–91.

Lambda Legal. "Protected and Served?: Executive Summary." 2015. https://lambdalegal.org/wp-content/uploads/2022/05/ps_executive-summary.pdf.

Lamble, S. "Practising Everyday Abolition." In *Abolishing the Police*, edited by K. Duff, 147–60. Dog Section Press, 2021.

———. "Queer Necropolitics and the Expanding Carceral State: Interrogating Sexual Investments in Punishment." *Law and Critique* 24, no. 3 (2013): 229–53.

———. "Unknowable Bodies, Unthinkable Sexualities: Lesbian and Transgender Legal Invisibility in the Toronto Women's Bathhouse Raid." *Social & Legal Studies* 18, no. 1 (2009): 111–30. https://doi.org/10.1177/0964663908100336.

Lamusse, T. "Politics at Pride?" *New Zealand Sociology* 31, no. 6 (2016): 49–70.

Lancaster, R.N. *Sex Panic and the Punitive State*. University of California Press, 2011.

Landivar, L.C., N.L. Graf, and G.A. Rayo. *Childcare Prices in Local Areas: Initial Findings from the National Database of Childcare Prices*. Issue brief.

Women's Bureau, U.S. Department of Labor, January 2023. https://www
.dol.gov/sites/dolgov/files/WB/NDCP/WB_IssueBrief-NDCP-final.pdf?_ga=
2.140175475.174781248.1692043680-1145242922.1692043680.

Latessa, E. J., and B. Lovins. *Corrections in the Community*. 7th ed. Routledge,
2019.

Law, V. "Against Carceral Feminism." *Jacobin*, October 17, 2014. https://
jacobin.com/2014/10/against-carceral-feminism/.

Leachman, M., N. Albares, K. Masterson, and M. Wallace. *Most States Have Cut
School Funding, and Some Continue Cutting*. Center on Budget and Policy
Priorities, December 10, 2015. https://media.azpm.org/master/document
/2015/12/9/pdf/most-states-have-cut-school-funding-and-some-continue
-cutting.pdf .

Lean, T. "Why I Am an Abolitionist." Overland, 2021. https://overland.org
.au/2021/06/why-i-am-an-abolitionist/.

Lee, Y., J. E. Eck, and N. Corsaro. "Conclusions from the History of Research
into the Effects of Police Force Size on Crime—1968 through 2013: A Historical Systematic Review." *Journal of Experimental Criminology* 12 (2016):
431–51. https://doi.org/10.1007/s11292-016-9269-8.

Lennard, N. "New York City's Cops Are Waging War on Subway Performers."
Vice, 2014. https://www.vice.com/en/article/nem9vm/new-york-citys-cops
-are-waging-war-on-subway-performers.

Lenning, E., and S. Brightman. "Taking Stock of Queer Victimology." In *Queer
Victimology: Understanding the Victim Experience*, edited by S. Kelley, S.
Clevenger, and K. Ratajczak, 3–22. Routledge, 2023.

Leslie, C. R. "Creating Criminals: The Injuries Inflicted by 'Unenforced' Sodomy
Laws." *Harvard Civil Rights–Civil Liberties Law Review* 35 (2000):
103–81.

Letourneau, E., and L. Malone. "America Has Been Going about Stopping
Child Sex Abuse the Wrong Way." *Time*, February 15, 2023. https://time
.com/6253908/america-child-sex-abuse-prevention/.

Levenson, J. S., and G. M. Willis. "Implementing Trauma-Informed Care in
Correctional Treatment and Supervision." *Journal of Aggression, Maltreatment & Trauma* 28, no. 4 (2019): 481–501. https://doi.org/10.1080/10926
771.2018.1531959.

Levin, B. "After the Criminal Justice System." *SSRN Electronic Journal*, 2023.
https://doi.org/10.2139/ssrn.4372330.

Lewis, C. "Guards Join Striking Prisoners in Alabama." *BuzzFeed News*, September 26, 2016. https://www.buzzfeednews.com/article/coralewis/guards
-join-striking-prisoners-in-alabama.

Linnemann, T. *The Horror of Police*. University of Minnesota Press, 2022.

Lipsey, M. W., and F. T. Cullen. "The Effectiveness of Correctional Rehabilitation: A Review of Systematic Reviews." *Annual Review of Law and Social
Science* 3, no. 1 (2007): 297–320.

Looney, A., and N. Turner. *Work and Opportunity before and after Incarceration*. Economic Studies at the Brookings Institution, March 2018. https://
mykairos.org/docs/conference/Work%20and%20opportunity%20
before%20and%20After%20Incarceration.pdf.

Love, B.L. *We Want to Do More than Survive: Abolitionist Teaching and the Pursuit of Educational Freedom.* Beacon Press, 2019.

Luibhéid, E., and K.R. Chávez, eds. *Queer and Trans Migrations: Dynamics of Illegalization, Detention, and Deportation.* University of Illinois Press, 2020.

Lvovsky, A. *Vice Patrol: Cops, Courts, and the Struggle over Urban Gay Life before Stonewall.* University of Chicago Press, 2021.

MacDonald, M. "Overcrowding and Its Impact on Prison Conditions and Health." *International Journal of Prisoner Health* 14, no. 2 (2018): 65–68.

Malatino, H. *Trans Care.* University of Minnesota Press, 2020.

Malkin, M.L., and C. DeJong. "Protections for Transgender Inmates under PREA: A Comparative Study of Correctional Policies in the United States." *Sexuality Research and Social Policy* 16 (2019): 393–407.

Mallory, C., A. Hasenbush, and B. Sears. *Discrimination and Harassment by Law Enforcement Officers in the LGBT Community.* Williams Institute, March 2015. https://williamsinstitute.law.ucla.edu/wp-content/uploads/LGBT-Discrimination-by-Law-Enforcement-Mar-2015.pdf.

Manion, J. *Female Husbands: A Trans History.* Cambridge University Press, 2020.

Marcoux Rouleau, A. "Lessons from Insiders: Embracing Subjectivity as Objectivity in Victimology." *International Review of Victimology* 30, no. 2 (2023): 1–23. https://doi.org/10.1177/02697580231179489.

Marcoux Rouleau, A., I. Melouka, and M. Pérusse-Roy. "Whose Criminology? Marginalised Perspectives and Populations within Student Production at the Montreal School of Criminology." In *Marginalised Voices in Criminology,* edited by Kelly J. Stockdale and Michelle Addison, 182–200. Routledge, 2024.

Martensen, K.M. "Teaching Abolition to Future Police Officers: A Reflective Essay on Pedagogies of Response and Care." *Contemporary Justice Review* 23, no. 2 (2020): 139–47.

Martensen, K.M., and B.E. Richie. "Prison Abolition." In *Oxford Research Encyclopedia of Criminology and Criminal Justice.* Oxford University Press, 2021.

Mathiesen, T. *The Politics of Abolition.* Wiley, 1974.

———. "The Prison Movement in Scandinavia." *Crime and Social Justice* 1, no. 1 (1974): 45–50.

Maynard, R. *Policing Black Lives: State Violence in Canada from Slavery to the Present.* Fernwood, 2017.

Mbembe, A. "Necropolitics." In *Foucault in an Age of Terror: Essays on Biopolitics and the Defence of Society,* edited by Stephen Morton and Stephen Bygrave, 152–82. Palgrave Macmillan, 2008.

McCallum, M.J.L. *Indigenous Women, Work, and History: 1940–1980.* University of Manitoba Press, 2014.

McDowell, M.G., and L.A. Fernandez. "'Disband, Disempower, and Disarm': Amplifying the Theory and Practice of Police Abolition." *Critical Criminology* 26, no. 3 (2018): 373–91. https://doi.org/10.1007/s10612-018-9400-4.

McQuire, A. "National Accounts: Black and White Witness." *Meanjin* 78, no. 2 (2019): 1–6.

Meiners, E.R. "Ending the School-to-Prison Pipeline/Building Abolition Futures." *Urban Review* 43, no. 4 (2011): 547–65.

Mendoza, B. "Coloniality of Gender and Power: From Postcoloniality to Decoloniality." In *The Oxford Handbook of Feminist Theory*, edited by L. Disch and M. Hawkesworth, 100–121. Oxford Handbooks, 2015.

Menkel-Meadows, C. "Restorative Justice: What Is It and Does It Work?" *Annual Review of Law and Social Science* 3, no. 1 (2007): 161–87.

Messerschmidt, J. *Crime as Structured Action: Gender, Race, Class, and Crime in the Making*. Sage, 1997.

Messerschmidt, J.W. "The Salience of Hegemonic Masculinity." *Men and Masculinities* 22, no. 1 (2019): 85–91.

Messinger, A.M., and S. Koon-Magnin. "Sexual Violence in LGBTQ Communities." In *Handbook of Sexual Assault and Sexual Assault Prevention*, edited by William T. O'Donohue and Paul A. Schewe, 661–74. Springer, 2019.

Messner, S. "Poverty, Inequality, and the Urban Homicide Rate: Some Unexpected Findings." *Criminology* 20 (1982): 103–14.

Meyer, D. "Resisting Hate Crime Discourse: Queer and Intersectional Challenges to Neoliberal Hate Crime Laws." *Critical Criminology* 22 (2014): 113–25.

Mikell, T. "Trans Black Women Deserve Better: Expanding Queer Criminology to Unpack Trans Misogynoir in the Field of Criminology." In *Abolish Criminology*, edited by V. Saleh-Hanna, J. Williams, and M. Coyle, 93–104. Routledge, 2023.

Minero, L.P., S. Domínguez, S.L. Budge, and B. Salcedo. "Latinx Trans Immigrants' Survival of Torture in U.S. Detention: A Qualitative Investigation of the Psychological Impact of Abuse and Mistreatment." *International Journal of Transgender Health* 23 (2022): 1–2, 36–59. https://doi.org/10.1080/26895269.2021.1938779.

Mitchum, P., and A.C. Moodie-Mills. *Beyond Bullying: How Hostile School Climate Perpetuates to School-to-Prison Pipeline for LGBT Youth*. Center for American Progress, February 27, 2014. https://www.americanprogress.org/issues/lgbtq-rights/reports/2014/02/27/84179/beyond-bullying/.

Mittelstadt, M., B. Speaker, D. Meissner, and M. Chishti. "Through the Prism of National Security: Major Immigration Policy and Program Changes in the Decade since 9/11." *Migration Policy Institute* 2 (2011): 1–17.

Mogul, J.L., A.J. Ritchie, and K. Whitlock. *Queer (In)Justice: The Criminalization of LGBT People in the United States*. Beacon Press, 2011.

Mongibello, A. "From 'Berdache' to 'Two-Spirit': Naming Indigenous Women-Men in Canada." In *Miss Man? Languaging Gendered Bodies*, edited by G. Balirano and O. Palusci, 156–67. Cambridge Scholars, 2018.

Montalvo, T., and J. Ortiz. "Perpetual Punishment: One Man's Journey Post-incarceration." In *Prisoner Reentry in the 21st Century: Critical Perspectives of Returning Home*, edited by K.M. Middlemass and C.J. Smiley, 275–87. Routledge, 2020.

Moreton-Robinson, A. *The White Possessive: Property, Power, and Indigenous Sovereignty*. University of Minnesota Press, 2015.

Morgan, I., and A. Amerikaner. "Funding Gaps 2018: An Analysis of School Funding Equity across the U.S. and within Each State." EdTrust, February 27, 2018. https://eric.ed.gov/?id=ED587198.

Morris, M. *Pushout: The Criminalization of Black Girls in Schools*. New Press, 2016.

Moten, F., and S. Harney. "The University and the Undercommons: Seven Theses." *Social Text* 22, no. 2 (2004): 101–15.

Mottet, L. "Modernizing State Vital Statistics Statutes and Policies to Ensure Accurate Gender Markers on Birth Certificates: A Good Government Approach to Recognizing the Lives of Transgender People." *Michigan Journal of Gender & Law* 19, no. 2 (2013): 373. https://repository.law.umich.edu/mjgl/vol19/iss2/4.

Movement Advancement Project. "HIV Criminalization Laws." 2023. https://www.lgbtmap.org/equality-maps/hiv_criminalization_laws.

———. "Messaging Guides." 2023. https://www.mapresearch.org/talking-about-lgbt-issues-series.

———. *Talking about Anti-LGBTQ School Bills & False "Groomer" Attacks*. 2022. https://www.lgbtmap.org/file/talking-about-anti-lgbtq-school-bills-false-groomer-attacks.pdf.

———. *Talking about Transgender People & Restrooms*. 2021. https://www.lgbtmap.org/file/talking-about-transgender-people-and-restrooms.pdf.

———. *Talking about Transgender Students & School Facilities Access*. 2017. https://www.mapresearch.org/file/talking-about-transgender-students-school-facilities-access.pdf.

———. *Talking about Transgender Youth Participation in Sports*. 2021. https://www.lgbtmap.org/file/talking-about-transgender-youth-sports-participation.pdf.

Muñoz, J. E. *Cruising Utopia: The Then and There of Queer Futurity*. New York University Press, 2009.

Murakawa, N. *The First Civil Right: How Liberals Built Prison America*. Oxford University Press, 2014.

Myers, J. E. B. "A Short History of Child Protection in America." *Family Law Quarterly* 42, no. 3 (2008): 449–63.

Mystal, E. "Bill de Blasio Has Failed the Test of This Moment." *The Nation*, June 5, 2020. https://www.thenation.com/article/society/de-blasio-policing-failure/.

Mzezewa, T. "USC Has Canceled Its Main Graduation." *The Cut*, April 26, 2024. https://www.thecut.com/article/usc-graduation-canceled-protests-israel-gaza.html.

National Association of Mandated Reporters. "A History of CAPTA Legislation." 2021. https://namr.org/news/a-history-of-capta-legislation.

National Cancer Institute. "Homeostasis." n.d. https://www.cancer.gov/publications/dictionaries/cancer-terms/def/homeostasis.

National Child Traumatic Stress Network. *Why Don't They Tell? Teens and Sexual Assault Disclosure*. 2018. https://www.nctsn.org/resources/why-they-dont-tell-teens-and-sexual-assault-disclosure.

National Institute on Drug Abuse. "Drug Fact: Criminal Justice." 2020. https://nida.nih.gov/sites/default/files/drugfacts-criminal-justice.

Nef, H. "The Aesthetics of Survival." TEDx, Connecticut College, April 2016. Video, 12:28. https://www.ted.com/talks/hari_nef_the_aesthetics_of _survival.

Nettelbeck, A., and L. Ryan. "Salutary Lessons: Native Police and the 'Civilising' Role of Legalised Violence in Colonial Australia." *Journal of Imperial and Commonwealth History* 46, no. 1 (2018): 47–68. https://doi.org/10 .1080/03086534.2017.1390894.

New York City Independent Budget Office. "Fiscal History: NYPD." n.d. https://ibo.nyc.ny.us/RevenueSpending/nypd.html.

"Noelle McAfee, Emory University's Philosophy Department Chair, Detained in Pro-Palestine Protest." YouTube, April 25, 2024. Video, 0:20. https://www .youtube.com/watch?v=INZo7x3_XPk.

O'Connor, M. "Prosecutors Have Levied Serious Charges against Pro-Palestine College Protesters." The Appeal, November 4, 2024. https://theappeal.org /pro-palestine-college-protesters-face-serious-charges/.

Ohi, K. "Molestation 101: Child Abuse, Homophobia, and the Boys of St. Vincent." *GLQ* 6, no. 2 (2000): 195–248.

O'Neal, S. "Gaza's Queer Palestinians Fight to Be Remembered." *The Nation*, November 17, 2023. https://www.thenation.com/article/world/gaza-queering -the-map/.

Ore, A. "No Proof a 2,700 Boost in Victorian Police Numbers Has Improved Safety, Audit Finds." *The Guardian Australia*, September 1, 2022. https:// www.theguardian.com/australia-news/2022/sep/01/no-proof-a-2700-boost -in-victorian-police-numbers-has-improved-safety-audit-finds.

Orth, U. "Secondary Victimization of Crime Victims by Criminal Proceedings." *Social Justice Research* 15, no. 4 (2002): 313–25. https://doi.org/10.1023 /A:1021210323461.

Ortiz, J. "From East New York to the Ivy Tower: How Structural Violence and Gang Membership Made Me a Critical Scholar." In *Survivor Criminology*, edited by K. Cook, 69–92. Rowman & Littlefield, 2022.

Ortiz, J., and Hayley Jackey. "The System Is Not Broken, It Is Intentional: The Prisoner Reentry Industry as Deliberate Structural Violence." *Prison Journal* 99, no. 4 (2019): 484–503.

Ortiz, J., and K. Wrigley. "The Invisible Enclosure: How Community Supervision Inhibits Successful Reentry." *Corrections: Policy, Practice, and Research* 7, no. 3 (2022): 230–45.

Ortiz, P. *An African American and Latinx History of the United States.* Beacon Press, 2018.

Pager, D. "The Mark of a Criminal Record." *American Journal of Sociology* 108 (2003): 937–75.

Panfil, V.R. "Young and Unafraid: Queer Criminology's Unbounded Potential." *Palgrave Communications* 4, no. 110 (2018). https://doi.org/10.1057 /s41599-018-0165-x.

Panfil, V.R., and D. Peterson. *Handbook of LGBT Communities, Crime, and Justice.* Springer, 2014.

Papalia, N., B. Spivak, M. Daffern, and J.R.P. Ogloff. "A Meta-Analytic Review of the Efficacy of Psychological Treatments for Violent Offenders in Correctional and Forensic Mental Health Settings." *Clinical Psychology Science and Practice* 26, no. 2 (2019): 12282. https://doi.org/10.1111/cpsp.12282.

Paris, D., and H.S. Alim. *Culturally Sustaining Pedagogies: Teaching and Learning for Justice in a Changing World.* Teachers College Press, 2017.

———. "What Are We Seeking to Sustain through Culturally Sustaining Pedagogy? A Loving Critique Forward." *Harvard Educational Review* 84, no. 1 (2014): 85–100.

Parsons, A.E. *From Asylum to Prison: Deinstitutionalization and the Rise of Mass Incarceration after 1945.* University of North Carolina Press, 2018.

Parsons, J., and T. Bergin. "The Impact of Criminal Justice Involvement on Victims' Mental Health." *Journal of Traumatic Stress* 23, no. 2 (2010): 182–88. https://doi.org/10.1002/jts.20505.

Peitzmeier, S.M., M. Malik, S.K. Kattari, E. Marrow, R. Stephenson, M. Agenor, and S.L. Reisner. "Intimate Partner Violence in Transgender Populations: Systematic Review and Meta-Analysis of Prevalence and Correlates." *American Journal of Public Health* 100, no. 9 (2020): 1–14.

Perry, C., M. Thurston, and K. Green. "Involvement and Detachment in Researching Sexuality: Reflections on the Process of Semistructured Interviewing." *Qualitative Health Research* 14, no. 1 (2004): 135–48.

Pettit, B., and C. Gutierrez. "Mass Incarceration and Racial Inequality." *American Journal of Economic Sociology* 77, no. 3 (2018): 1153–82. https://doi.org/10.1111/ajes.12241.

Pew Charitable Trusts. *More Imprisonment Does Not Reduce State Drug Problems: Data Show No Relationship between Prison Terms and Drug Misuse.* Issue brief. March 8, 2018. https://www.pewtrusts.org/en/research-and-analysis/issue-briefs/2018/03/more-imprisonment-does-not-reduce-state-drug-problems.

Pew Research Center. "Most Americans Favor the Death Penalty despite Concerns about Its Administration." June 2, 2021. https://www.pewresearch.org/politics/2021/06/02/most-americans-favor-the-death-penalty-despite-concerns-about-its-administration/.

Phifer, H. "For Angela Davis and Gina Dent, Abolition Is the Only Way." *Harper's Bazaar*, January 14, 2022. https://www.harpersbazaar.com/culture/art-books-music/a38746835/angela-davis-gina-dent-abolition-feminism-now-interview/.

Pierson, E., C. Simoiu, and J. Overgoor. "A Large-Scale Analysis of Racial Disparities in Police Stops across the United States." *Nature Human Behavior* 4 (2020): 736–45. https://doi.org/10.1038/s41562-020-0858-1.

Plotka, R., and N.A. Busch-Rossnagel. "The Role of Length of Maternity Leave in Supporting Mother–Child Interactions and Attachment Security among American Mothers and Their Infants." *International Journal of Child Care and Education Policy* 12, no. 2 (2018): 1–18. https://doi.org/10.1186/s40723-018-0041-6.

Plummer, C.A. "The History of Child Sexual Abuse Prevention: A Practitioner's Perspective." *Journal of Child Sexual Abuse* 7, no. 4 (1999): 77–95. https://doi.org/10.1300/J070v07n04_06.

Pluralism Project. *The Right to Be Different*. Harvard University, 2020. https://pluralism.org/files/pluralism/files/the_right_to_be_different.pdf.

Ponton, D. "Clothed in Blue Flesh: Police Brutality and the Disciplining of Race, Gender, and the 'Human.'" *Theory & Event* 19, no. 3 (2016). https://muse.jhu.edu/pub/1/article/623994.

Porter, A. "The Criminal Foundations of Australian Policing." In *When Cops Are Criminals*, edited by Veronica Gorrie, 1–16. Scribe, 2024.

Porter, A., N. Ironfield, and T. Hopkins. "Racial Profiling, Australian Criminology and the Creation of Statistical 'Facts': A Response to Shepherd and Spivak." *Decolonization of Criminology and Justice* 4, no. 2 (2023): 77–102. https://doi.org/10.24135/dcj.v4i2.41.

Potier, C., V. Laprevote, F. Dubois-Arber, O. Cottencin, and B. Rolland. "Supervised Injection Services: What Has Been Demonstrated? A Systematic Literature Review." *Drug and Alcohol Dependence* 145, no. 1 (2014): 48–68.

Prager, S. "Queer People Organizing in Solidarity with Palestine Continues to Grow." Prism, February 5, 2024. https://prismreports.org/2024/02/05/queer-people-organizing-solidarity-palestine/.

Pratt, J. "The Rise and Fall of Homophobia and Sexual Psychopath Legislation in Postwar Society." *Psychology, Public Policy, and Law* 4, no. 1–2 (1998): 25–49.

Prison Discipline Society. *Thirteenth Annual Report of the Board of Managers of the Prison Discipline Society*. 1838. https://books.google.je/books?id=4Pc7AQAAMAAJ&printsec=frontcover.

Prison Policy Initiative. "United States Profile." 2023. https://www.prisonpolicy.org/profiles/US.html.

Purnell, D. *Becoming Abolitionists: Police, Protests, and the Pursuit of Freedom*. Astra, 2022.

Queer Nation. "Queers Read This." 1990. https://archive.qzap.org/index.php/Detail/Object/Show/object_id/184.

Queirolo, R., L. Repetto, B. Sotto, and E. Alvarez. "Explaining the Impact of Legal Access to Cannabis on Attitudes toward Users." *International Journal of Public Opinion Research* 35, no. 2 (2023): edado10. https://doi.org/10.1093/ijpor/edado10.

Rabuy, B., and D. Kopf. "Prisons of Poverty: Uncovering the Pre-incarceration Incomes of the Imprisoned." Press release. Prison Policy Initiative, July 9, 2015. https://www.prisonpolicy.org/reports/income.html.

Race, K. "Public Orders: The Sex Crimes of Policing." *Alternative Law Journal* 48, no. 3 (2023). https://doi.org/10.1177/1037969x231196983.

RAINN. "The Criminal Justice System: Statistics." n.d. https://www.rainn.org/statistics/criminal-justice-system.

Rayman, G., J. Jorgensen, and L. McShane. "Hundreds of NYPD Cops Turn Backs to de Blasio in Protest as He Speaks at Funeral for Slain Officer Miosotis Familia." *New York Daily News*, July 11, 2017. https://www.nydailynews.com/2017/07/11/hundreds-of-nypd-cops-turn-backs-to-de-blasio-in-protest-as-he-speaks-at-funeral-for-slain-officer-miosotis-familia/.

Razack, S.H. "Settler Colonialism, Policing and Racial Terror: The Police Shooting of Loreal Tsingine." *Feminist Legal Studies* 28, no. 1 (2020): 1–20. https://doi.org/10.1007/s10691-020-09426-2.

Redburn, K. "Before Equal Protection: The Fall of Cross-Dressing Bans and the Transgender Legal Movement, 1963–86." *Law and History Review* 40, no. 4 (2022): 679–723.

Redd, C., and E.K. Russell. "'It All Started Here, and It All Ends Here Too': Homosexual Criminalisation and the Queer Politics of Apology." *Criminology & Criminal Justice* 20, no. 5 (2020): 590–603. https://doi.org/10.1177/1748895820939244.

Reiter, K. *23/7: Pelican Bay Prison and the Rise of Long-Term Solitary Confinement.* Yale University Press, 2016.

Reiter, K., J. Ventura, D. Lovell, D. Augustine, M. Barragan, T. Blair, K. Chesnut et al. "Psychological Distress in Solitary Confinement: Symptoms, Severity, and Prevalence in the United States, 2017–2018." *American Journal of Public Health* 110, no. 1 (2020): 56–62. https://doi.org/10.2105/AJPH.2019.305365.

Rengifo, A.F., L.A. Slocum, and V. Chillar. "From Impressions to Intentions: Direct and Indirect Effects of Police Contact on Willingness to Report Crimes to Law Enforcement." *Journal of Research in Crime and Delinquency* 56, no. 3 (2019): 412–50.

Reuter, T.R., M.E. Newcomb, S.W. Whitton, and B. Mustanski. "Intimate Partner Violence Victimization in LGBT Young Adults: Demographic Differences and Associations with Health Behaviors." *Psychology of Violence* 7, no. 1 (January 2017): 101–9. https://doi.org/10.1037/vio0000031.

Richie, B. *Arrested Justice: Black Women, Male Violence, and the Build Up of a Prison Nation.* New York University Press, 2012.

Richie, B.E., and K.M. Martensen. "Resisting Carcerality, Embracing Abolition: Implications for Feminist Social Work Practice." *Affilia* 35, no. 1 (2020): 12–16.

Riggs, D.W. *Priscilla, (White) Queen of the Desert: Queer Rights/Race Privilege.* Peter Lang, 2006.

Ritchie, A.J. *Invisible No More: Police Violence against Black Women and Women of Color.* Beacon Press, 2017.

Rizer, A. "The Race Effect on Wrongful Convictions." *William Mitchell Law Review* 29, no. 3 (2003): 845–68.

Roberts, D. *Killing the Black Body: Race, Reproduction, and the Meaning of Liberty.* Vintage, 2014.

———. *Torn Apart: How the Child Welfare System Destroys Black Families—and How Abolition Can Build a Safer World.* Basic Books, 2022.

Roberts, D.E. "Abolition Constitutionalism." *Harvard Law Review* 133, no. 1 (2019). https://harvardlawreview.org/print/vol-133/abolition-constitutionalism/.

Robertson, D.L., A.M. Pow, D. Hunt, B. Hudson, and R. Mickelsen. "We Are Just People: Transgender Individuals' Experiences of a Local Equal Rights Debate." *Journal of LGBT Issues in Counseling* 13, no. 3 (2019): 178–97.

Robinson, M. *Media Coverage of Crime and Criminal Justice.* 3rd ed. Carolina Academic Press, 2018.

Robles, B., B. Leondar-Wright, and R. Brewer. *The Color of Wealth: The Story behind the US Racial Wealth Divide*. New Press, 2006.

Rodriguez, D. "Abolition as Praxis of Human Being: A Foreword." *Harvard Law Review* 132, no. 6 (2019). https://harvardlawreview.org/print/vol-132/abolition-as-praxis-of-human-being-a-foreword/.

Roman, C.G., and J. Travis. "Where Will I Sleep Tomorrow? Housing, Homelessness, and the Returning Prisoner." *Housing Policy Debate* 17 (2006): 389–418.

Romano, A. "The Right's Moral Panic over 'Grooming' Invokes Age-Old Homophobia." *Vox*, April 21, 2022. https://www.vox.com/culture/23025505/leftist-groomers-homophobia-satanic-panic-explained.

Ross, C.T., B. Winterhalder, and R. McElreath. "Racial Disparities in Police Use of Deadly Force against Unarmed Individuals Persist after Appropriately Benchmarking Shooting Data on Violent Crime Rates." *Social Psychological and Personality Science* 12, no. 3 (2021): 323–32. https://doi.org/10.1177/1948550620916071.

Ross, J.I. "Deconstructing Correctional Officer Deviance: Toward Typologies of Actions and Controls." *Criminal Justice Review* 38, no. 1 (2013): 110–26. https://doi.org/10.1177/0734016812473824.

Rothman, D.J. *Conscience and Convenience: The Asylum and Its Alternatives in Progressive America*. Longman, 1980.

Rozsa, M. "Why the Moral Panic over 'Grooming' Is So Effective at Manipulating the Right-Wing Mind." *Salon*, January 30, 2023. https://www.salon.com/2023/01/30/why-the-moral-panic-over-grooming-is-so-effective-at-manipulating-the-right-wing-mind/.

Rubinstein, D., and J.C. Mays. "Police Union Discloses Arrest of de Blasio's Daughter in Privacy Breach." *New York Times*, June 1, 2020. https://www.nytimes.com/2020/06/01/nyregion/chiara-de-blasio-arrest.html.

Ruggiero, V. "How Public Is Public Criminology?" *Crime, Media, Culture: An International Journal* 8, no. 2 (2012). https://doi.org/10.1177/1741659012444432.

Russell, E., and J. Ison. "Why the Violence of Policing Is a Queer Issue." *Overland*, June 2019. https://overland.org.au/2019/06/why-the-violence-of-policing-is-a-queer-issue/.

Russell, E.K. "Carceral Pride: The Fusion of Police Imagery with LGBTI Rights." *Feminist Legal Studies* 26, no. 3 (2018): 331–50. https://doi.org/10.1007/s10691-018-9383-2.

———. *Queer Histories and the Politics of Policing*. Routledge, 2020.

———. "Queer Penalities: The Criminal Justice Paradigm in Lesbian and Gay Anti-violence Politics." *Critical Criminology* 25, no. 1 (2017): 21–35. https://doi.org/10.1007/s10612-016-9337-4.

———. "'Seeing Like a Cop': Police Perception in Spaces of Gender and Racial Criminalization." *British Journal of Criminology*, 2024. https://doi.org/10.1093/bjc/azae042.

Ryan, H. *The Women's House of Detention: A Queer History of a Forgotten Prison*. Bold Type Books, 2022.

Sabati, S., F. Pour-Khorshid, E. Meiners, and C. A. Z. Hernandez. "Dismantle, Change, Build: Lessons for Growing Abolition in Teacher Education." *Teachers College Record* 124, no. 3 (2022): 177–206.

Saldana, J. *The Coding Manual for Qualitative Researchers*. 2nd ed. Sage, 2013.

Saleh-Hanna, V. "An Abolitionist Theory on Crime: Ending the Abusive Relationship with Racist-Imperialist-Patriarchy [R.I.P.]." *Contemporary Justice Review* 20, no. 4 (2017): 419–44.

———. "A Call for Wild Seed Justice." In *Abolish Criminology*, edited by M. Coyle, V. Saleh-Hanna, and J. Williams, 13–26. Routledge, 2023.

———. "Feminist Hauntology: Rememory the Ghosts of Abolition?" *Champ Pénal/Penal Field* 12 (2015). https://doi.org/10.4000/champpenal.9168.

Sampath, N., M. Obradovic, H. Burns, and C. L. Keller. "For College Students Arrested Protesting the War in Gaza, the Fallout Was Only Beginning." AP News, August 2, 2024. https://apnews.com/article/college-protest-israel -hamas-war-arrest-charges-7cb75debddc2e8bd795d16515d07de09.

Santos, A., and S. Iaboni. "What's in a Prison Meal?" Marshall Project, July 7, 2015. https://www.themarshallproject.org/2015/07/07/what-s-in-a-prison -meal.

Santos, F. "It's Children against Federal Lawyers in Immigration Court." *New York Times*, August 20, 2016. https://www.nytimes.com/2016/08/21/us /in-immigration-court-children-must-serve-as-their-own-lawyers.html.

Sawyer, W., and P. Wagner. "Mass Incarceration: The Whole Pie 2023." Prison Policy Initiative, 2023. https://www.prisonpolicy.org/reports/pie2023 .html.

Scarlett, A. V. "Doctors Speak to Claims about Gender-Confirming Care." *Medium*, January 22, 2023. https://medium.com/keep-fighting/doctors -speak-to-claims-about-gender-confirming-care-7533fc80360c.

Schenwar, M., and V. Law. *Prison by Any Other Name: The Harmful Consequences of Popular Reforms*. New Press, 2020.

Schmid, M. "'The Eye of God': Religious Beliefs and Punishment in Early Nineteenth-Century Prison Reform." *Theology Today* 59, no. 4 (2003): 546–58.

Schrader, B. E. "Palestinians: LGBTQ+ Not Welcome Here—Opinion." *Jerusalem Post*, June 20, 2022. https://www.jpost.com/opinion/article-709930.

Sedgwick, E. K. "Queer and Now." In *The Routledge Queer Studies Reader*, edited by Donald Hall and Annamarie Jagose, 3–17. Routledge, 2013.

Seigel, M. "Violence Work: Policing and Power." *Race & Class* 59, no. 4 (2018): 15–33. https://doi.org/10.1177/0306396817752617.

Sentas, V. *Traces of Terror: Counter-Terrorism Law, Policing, and Race*. Oxford University Press, 2014.

Shapiro, D. M., and C. Hogle. "The Horror Chamber: Unqualified Impunity in Prison." *Notre Dame Law Review* 93, no. 5 (2018): 2021–64.

Shatz, S. F., G. L. Pierce, and M. L. Radelet. "Race, Ethnicity, and the Death Penalty in San Diego County: The Predictable Consequences of Excessive Discretion." *Columbia Human Rights Law Review* 51, no. 3 (2020): 1070–98.

Shelby, R. *The Idea of Prison Abolition.* Princeton University Press, 2022.

Sherman, A. D. F., K. D. Clark, K. Robinson, T. Noorani, and T. Poteat. "Trans* Community Connection, Health, and Wellbeing: A Systematic Review." *LGBT Health* 7, no. 1 (2020): 1–14.

Siegel, D. P. "We Are Not 'Groomers': How Anti-LGBTQ Stereotypes Inhibit Reproductive Justice." *Rewire News Group*, March 14, 2023. https://rewirenewsgroup.com/2023/03/14/we-are-not-groomers-how-anti-lgbtq-stereotypes-inhibit-reproductive-justice/.

Siennick, S. E., M. Picon, J. M. Brown, and D. P. Mears. "Revisiting and Unpacking the Mental Illness and Solitary Confinement Relationship." *Justice Quarterly* 39, no. 4 (2022): 772–801. https://doi.org/10.1080/07418825.2020.1871501.

Simon, J. *Mass Incarceration on Trial: A Remarkable Court Decision and the Future of Prisons in America.* New Press, 2016.

Simpson, D., G. Joe, B. Fletcher, R. Hubbard, and M. D. Anglin. "A National Evaluation of Treatment Outcomes for Cocaine Dependence." *Archive of General Psychiatry* 56, no. 6 (1999): 507–14. https://doi.org/10.1001/pubs.ArchGenPsychiatry-ISSN-0003-990x-56-6-yoa8260.

Skolnick, J. "Corruption and the Blue Code of Silence." *Police Practice and Research* 3, no. 1 (2002): 7–19.

Smith, L. T. *Decolonizing Methodologies: Research and Indigenous Peoples.* 2nd ed. Zed Books, 2012.

Snapp, S. D., J. M. Hoenig, A. Fields, and S. T. Russell. "Messy, Butch, and Queer: LGBTQ Youth and the School-to-Prison Pipeline." *Journal of Adolescent Research* 30, no. 1 (2015): 57–82.

Soss, J., and V. Weaver. "Police Are Our Government: Politics, Political Science, and the Policing of Race–Class Subjugated Communities." *Annual Review of Political Science* 20, no. 1 (2017): 565–91. https://doi.org/10.1146/annurev-polisci-060415-093825.

Spade, D. *Love in a F*cked-up World: How to Build Relationships, Hook Up, and Raise Hell Together.* 1st ed. Algonquin Books of Chapel Hill, 2025.

———. *Normal Life: Administrative Violence, Critical Trans Politics, and the Limits of Law.* 2nd ed. Duke University Press, 2015.

———. "Under the Cover of Gay Rights." *NYU Review of Law & Social Change* 37 (2013): 79–100.

Speri, A. "Bill de Blasio Promised to Change the NYPD. His Courage Failed Him, and Us." *The Intercept*, July 14, 2020. https://doi.org/10/bill.

Squillacote, R. "To the Editors." *New Labor Forum* 30, no. 1 (2021): 127. https://doi.org/10.1177/1095796020983016.

Squirrell, T., and J. Davey. "A Year of Hate: Understanding Threats and Harassment Targeting Drag Shows and the LGBTQ+ Community." Institute for Strategic Dialogue, 2023. https://www.isdglobal.org/isd-publications/a-year-of-hate-understanding-threats-and-harassment-targeting-drag-shows-and-the-lgbtq-community/.

Stand, K. "What Kind of Job: A Series on Unions and Prisons." Personal blog, 2003.

Stand, L. F. "Every Family Has One." Personal blog, 2005.

Stanley, E. A. *Atmospheres of Violence: Structuring Antagonism and the Trans/Queer Ungovernable.* Duke University Press, 2021.

Stanley, E. A., and N. Smith. *Captive Genders: Trans Embodiment and the Prison Industrial Complex.* AK Press, 2011.

Stardust, Z., C. Treloar, E. Cama, and J. Kim. "'I Wouldn't Call the Cops If I Was Being Bashed to Death': Sex Work, Whore Stigma and the Criminal Legal System." *International Journal for Crime, Justice and Social Democracy* 10, no. 3 (2021): 142–57. https://doi.org/10.5204/ijcjsd.1894.

Stevenson, M., and S. Mayson. "The Scale of Misdemeanor Justice." *Boston University Law Review* 98, no. 3 (2018): 731–78.

Strout, J. "The Massachusetts Transgender Equal Rights Bill: Formal Legal Equality in a Transphobic System." *Harvard Journal of Law & Gender* 35 (2012): 515–21.

Sudbury, J. "Maroon Abolitionists." *Meridians* 9, no. 1 (2009): 1–29. https://doi.org/10.2979/MER.2008.9.1.1.

Surette, R. *Media, Crime, and Criminal Justice: Images, Realities, and Policies.* 5th ed. Cengage, 2015.

Sutherland, E. H. "The Sexual Psychopath Laws." *Journal of Criminal Law and Criminology* 40, no. 5 (1950): 543–54.

Sutherland, R., N. Sindicich, E. Barrett, E. Whittaker, A. Peacock, S. Hickey, and L. Burns. "Motivations, Substance Use, and Other Correlates among Property and Violent Offenders Who Regularly Inject Drugs." *Addictive Behaviors* 45, no. 2 (2015): 207–13.

Swanson, J. W., and C. M. Belden. "The Link between Mental Illness and Being Subjected to Crime in Denmark vs the United States: How Much Do Poverty and the Safety Net Matter?" *JAMA Psychiatry* 75, no. 7 (2018): 669–70. https://doi.org/10.1001/jamapsychiatry.2018.0528.

Sykes, G. M. *The Society of Captives: A Study of a Maximum Security Prison.* Princeton University Press, 1958.

Tamarkin, S. "Why Queer Solidarity with Palestine Is Not 'Chickens for KFC.'" *Them*, November 22, 2022. https://www.them.us/story/lgbtq-solidarity-palestine-saed-atshan.

Taylor, M. "Adult Earnings of Juvenile Delinquents: The Interaction of Race/Ethnicity, Gender, and Juvenile Justice Status on Future Earnings." *Justice Policy Journal* 13, no. 2 (2016): 1–24.

Terp, S., S. Ahmed, E. Burner, M. Ross, M. Grassini, B. Fischer, and P. Parmar. "Deaths in Immigration and Customs Enforcement (ICE) Detention: FY2018–2020." *AIMS Public Health* 8, no. 1 (2021): 81–89. https://doi.org/10.3934/publichealth.2021006.

Thoma, B. C., T. L. Rezeppa, S. Choukas-Bradley, R. H. Salk, and M. P. Marshal. "Disparities in Childhood Abuse between Transgender and Cisgender Adolescents." *Pediatrics* 148, no. 2 (2021): 2020016907. https://doi.org/10.1542/peds.2020-016907.

Thompson, H. *Blood in the Water: The Attica Prison Uprising of 1971 and Its Legacy.* Pantheon Books, 2016.

Thompson, L. "Feminist Methodology for Family Studies." *Journal of Marriage and Family* 54, no. 1 (1992): 3–18.

Thompson, V. E. "Policing in Europe: Disability Justice and Abolitionist Intersectional Care." *Race & Class* 62, no. 3 (2021): 61–76. https://doi .org/10.1177/0306396820966463.

Thorneycroft, R., and N. L. Asquith. "Cripping Criminology." *Theoretical Criminology* 25, no. 2 (2021): 187–208.

Torrey, E. F., A. D. Kennard, D. Eslinger, R. Lamb, and J. Pavie. *More Mentally Ill Persons Are in Jails and Prisons than Hospitals: A Survey of the States*. Treatment Advocacy Center and National Sheriffs' Association Report. The Treatment Advocacy Center and the National Sheriffs' Association, 2010. https:// www.ojp.gov/ncjrs/virtual-library/abstracts/more-mentally-ill-persons-are -jails-and-prisons-hospitals-survey.

Transportation Security Administration. "Transgender/Non Binary/Gender Nonconforming Passengers." n.d. https://web.archive.org/web/20230307133536 /https://www.tsa.gov/transgender-passengers.

Treitler, V. B. *The Ethnic Project: Transforming Racial Fiction into Ethnic Factions*. Stanford University Press, 2013.

Tuck, E., and K. W. Yang. "Decolonization Is Not a Metaphor." *Decolonization: Indigeneity, Education & Society* 1, no. 1 (2012): 1–40.

Tylka, B. "Getting to Tarasoff: A Gender-Based History of Tort Law Doctrine." *California Legal History* 16 (2021): 237.

Uggen, C. "Work as a Turning Point in the Life Course of Criminals: A Duration Model of Age, Employment, and Recidivism." *American Sociological Review* 65, no. 4 (2000): 529–46. https://doi.org/10.2307/2657381.

United Nations High Commissioner for Refugees. "LGBTIQ+ Persons." 2023. https://www.unhcr.org/lgbtiq-persons.

U.S. Department of Justice. "2022 FBI Hate Crimes Statistics." U.S. Department of Justice Archives, October 2023. https://www.justice.gov/crs/ highlights /2022-hate-crime-statistics.

U.S. Immigration and Customs Enforcement. "History of ICE." February 23, 2023. https://www.ice.gov/history.

———. "Mission." May 9, 2023. https://www.ice.gov/mission.

Vaughn, M. S., and L. Smith. "Practicing Penal Harm Medicine in the United States: Prisoners' Voices from Jail." *Justice Quarterly* 16, no. 1 (1999): 175–231. https://doi.org/10.1080/07418829900094101.

Vincent, B. W. "Studying Trans: Recommendations for Ethical Recruitment and Collaboration with Transgender Participants in Academic Research." *Psychology & Sexuality* 9, no. 2 (2018): 102–16.

Violence Policy Center. "When Men Murder Women: An Analysis of 2020 Homicide Data." 2023. https://vpc.org/when-men-murder-women/.

Vitale, A. S. *The End of Policing*. Verso, 2017.

Vitale, A. S., and B. J. Jefferson. "The Emergence of Command and Control Policing in Neoliberal New York." In *Policing the Planet: Why the Policing Crisis Led to Black Lives Matter*, edited by Jordan T. Camp and Christina Heatherton, 157–72. Verso Books, 2016.

Vitulli, E. W. "Queering the Carceral." *GLQ: A Journal of Lesbian and Gay Studies* 19, no. 1 (January 1, 2013): 111–23. https://doi.org/10.1215 /10642684-1729563.

Wacquant, L. "The New Peculiar Institution: On the Prison as Surrogate Ghetto." *Theoretical Criminology* 4 (2000): 377–89.

Wahl, T., and N. Pittman. "Injustice: How the Sex Offender Registry Destroys LGBTQ Rights." *The Advocate*, August 5, 2016. https://www.advocate .com/commentary/2016/8/05/injustice-how-sex-offender-registry-destroys.

Wald, J., and D. J. Losen. "Defining and Redirecting a School-to-Prison Pipeline." *New Directions for Youth Development* 2003, no. 99 (2003): 9–15.

Walker, A. "Police Do Not Protect Us, and Other Lessons I Learned as a Queer Victim." In *Queer Victimology: Understanding the Victim Experience*, edited by Shelly Clevenger, Shamika Kelley, and Kathleen Ratajczak, 143–46. Routledge, 2023.

———. "Preventing Child Abuse Should Not Be Controversial. My Own Hate Mail Reveals That It Is." *Scientific American*, 2024. https://www .scientificamerican.com/article/preventing-child-abuse-should-not-be -controversial-my-own-hate-mail-reveals-that-it-is/.

———. "Transphobic Discourse and Moral Panic Convergence: A Content Analysis of My Hate Mail." *Criminology* 61, no. 4 (2023): 994–1021. https://doi.org/10.1111/1745-9125.12355.

Walker, A., A. M. Petersen, A. Wodda, and A. Stephens. "Why Don't We Center Abolition in Queer Criminology?" *Crime & Delinquency* 70, no. 5 (2024): 1443–61. https://doi.org/10.1177/00111287221134595.

Walker, A., J. Valcore, B. Evans, and A. Stephens. "Experiences of Trans Scholars in Criminology and Criminal Justice." *Critical Criminology* 29 (2021): 37–56. https://doi.org/10.1007/s10612-021-09561-5.

Walker, S. *A Critical History of Police Reform: The Emergence of Professionalism*. Lexington Books, 1977.

Wang, L., and W. Sawyer. "New Data: State Prisons Are Increasingly Deadly Places." Prison Policy Initiative, June 8, 2021. https://www.prisonpolicy.org /blog/2021/06/08/prison_mortality/.

Warner, T. *Never Going Back: A History of Queer Activism in Canada*. University of Toronto Press, 2002.

Washington, John. "What Is Prison Abolition?" *The Nation*, July 31, 2018. https://www.thenation.com/article/archive/what-is-prison-abolition/.

Weissert, W., and A. Gomez Licon. "Immigration Reform Stalled Decade after Gang of 8's Big Push." AP News, April 3, 2023. https://apnews.com/article /immigration-asylum-trump-biden-gang-of-eight-3d8007e72928665b 66d8648be0e3e31f.

Weissinger, S. E., D. A. Mack, and E. Watson, eds. *Violence against Black Bodies: An Intersectional Analysis of How Black Lives Continue to Matter*. Routledge, 2017.

Whitaker, Tracy R., and Cudore L. Snell. "Parenting While Powerless: Consequences of 'the Talk.'" *Journal of Human Behavior in the Social Environment* 26, no. 3–4 (2016): 303–9. https://doi.org/10.1080/10911359.2015 .1127736.

Whyte, K. "Settler Colonialism, Ecology, and Environmental Injustice." *Environment and Society* 9, no. 1 (2018): 125–44.

Williams, J. E. "Secondary Victimization—Confronting Public Attitudes about Rape." *Victimization* 9, no. 1 (1984): 66–81.

Winn, M. T. *Justice on Both Sides: Transforming Education through Restorative Justice*. Harvard Education Press, 2018.

Wodda, Aimee, and Vanessa R. Panfil. *Sex-Positive Criminology*. Routledge, 2020.

Wolf Harlow, C. *Education and Correctional Populations*. U.S. Department of Justice, Bureau of Justice Statistics Special Report NCJ 195670, January 2003. https://bjs.ojp.gov/content/pub/pdf/ecp.pdf.

Wolfe, P. "Settler Colonialism and the Elimination of the Native." *Journal of Genocide Research* 8, no. 4 (2006): 387–409.

Wolff, K. B., and C. L. Cokely. "'To Protect and to Serve?': An Exploration of Police Conduct in Relation to the Gay, Lesbian, Bisexual, and Transgender Community." *Sexuality and Culture* 11 (2007): 1–23.

Wolff, N., J. Shi, and J. A. Siegel. "Patterns of Victimization among Male and Female Inmates: Evidence of an Enduring Legacy." *Violence and Victims* 24, no. 4 (2009): 469–84. https://doi.org/10.1891/0886-6708.24.4.469.

Woodall, D. "We Are All Criminals." *Social Justice* 45, no. 4 (2019): 117–40.

Woods, J. B. "Queer Contestations and the Future of a Critical 'Queer' Criminology." *Critical Criminology* 22 (2014): 5–19.

Zehr, H. *The Little Book of Restorative Justice*. Good Books, 2002.

Zeidman, S. "Eradicating Assembly-Line Justice: An Opportunity Lost by the Revised American Bar Association Criminal Justice Standards." *Hofstra Law Review* 46, no. 1 (2018): 14. https://scholarlycommons.law.hofstra.edu/cgi/viewcontent.cgi?article=2997&context=hlr.

Zempi, I. "Researching Victimisation Using Auto-ethnography: Wearing the Muslim Veil in Public." *Methodological Innovations* 10, no. 1 (2017): 2059799117720617. https://doi.org/10.1177/2059799117720617.

Ziadah, Rafeef. "We Teach Life, Sir." *Wasafiri* 27, no. 4 (2012): 50–51. https://doi.org/10.1080/02690055.2012.718879.

Zinn, H. *A People's History of the United States*. Harper Collins, 1980.

Contributors

IHSAN AL-ZOUABI is a PhD candidate at Rutgers-Newark School of Criminal Justice, studying family regulation across historical and contemporary contexts. She holds a BS and MS in criminal justice from UNC Charlotte. Ihsan enjoys painting, K-pop, and liberation for all.

Native to Baja California, Mexico, KAREN ARMENTA ROJAS navigated complex immigration processes as a transborder and international student and now as an immigrant, experiencing both the privilege and vulnerability associated with documentation. Her journey highlights the discriminatory US asylum and migration processes. Her research focuses on juvenile delinquency, vulnerable population experience, neighborhoods and crime, and gender studies.

SUSANA AVALOS is an assistant professor at the University of Missouri Kansas City in the Department of Criminal Justice and Criminology. Susana's research explores how trans people navigate and resist victimization in public, private, and online spaces, as well as the role of community support in overcoming transphobic violence.

KARL BEAULIEU holds a master's degree in criminology and is currently pursuing a PhD in social work at Université du Québec à Montréal. His PhD thesis focuses on mobile unit intervention teams composed of police officers and social workers. His research interests include social control, the penalization of injustices, and the carceralization of care services. Finally, Karl also works as a practitioner in the field of addiction rehabilitation in Montreal.

CANDICE CRUTCHFIELD is a PhD candidate in sociology at The Ohio State University. She studies prisons, punishment, and their impact on families and other social ties. Grounded in Black feminist theory and praxis, her work often critiques carceral systems and envisions abolitionist futures rooted in justice and collective care.

JENANI DEVI (they/them) is a 2023–2025 Soros Justice Fellow, the project director at the Georgia Survivor Defense Project, and the National Movement Incubator at Just Beginnings Collaborative. Devi centers system-impacted survivors, young survivors, and the queer and trans community. After spending a decade in Atlanta, Georgia, they now reside in Brooklyn, New York. Outside of work, they are a novice rock climber, a frequent traveler, and an enjoyer of creative things.

DR. JANE HERETH'S (she/they) research examines the impacts of interpersonal and state violence among LGBTQIA+ communities. Dr. Hereth's research and teaching are informed by her social work practice and community organizing work with LGBTQIA+ youth and survivors of victimization.

ALEXIS MARCOUX ROULEAU is a PhD candidate in criminology at the University of Montreal, Canada. Their dissertation is rooted in standpoint and abolitionist epistemologies and explores experiences of leisure in women's prisons. More broadly, Alexis's research focuses on social and penal control of marginalized populations.

DR. TONIQUA MIKELL is an assistant professor of crime and justice studies at the University of Massachusetts Dartmouth. She is a BlaQueer feminist and intersectional criminologist whose work centers Black feminism, queer criminology, and critical race theory to understand the social control of Black women and femme-identifying individuals within carceral states.

ALESSANDRA MILAGROS EARLY is an assistant professor of criminal justice at John Jay College of Criminal Justice. Her research focuses on spatial dynamics, identity formation, and behavior. Specifically, her work has explored the complex interplay between queer social spaces, heterosexual social spaces, and queer identity formation through substance use.

JENNIFER M. ORTIZ, PhD, is an associate professor of criminology at the College of New Jersey. Her research interests center on structural violence within the criminal legal system. Ortiz serves as division chair for the American Society of Criminology's Division of Convict Criminology and as book review editor for the *Critical Criminology Journal*.

MAX OSBORN is an assistant professor of sociology and criminology at Villanova University. His research, published in outlets including *Critical Criminology*, *Feminist Criminology*, and *Trauma, Violence & Abuse*, addresses queer and transgender people's experiences within the carceral system, depictions of trans people in crime news, and consequences of victimization.

AMANDA M. PETERSEN is an independent scholar. Their research primarily focuses on leftist approaches to addressing anti-Blackness and its intersection with the US carceral state.

MONICA RAMSY (she/they) is the Wayfinding Project's project coordinator at Just Beginnings Collaborative. A disabled queer person of color, Monica is an educator, bridge builder, and storyteller deeply invested in building toward radically relational futures. As a sociology PhD student, Monica examines how the ongoing institutionalization of restorative/transformative justice practices intersects with race, gender, and disability.

ALISON REBA (they/them/theirs) is a Black trans and mixed-race shape shifter, sibling, community organizer, and flower essence therapist who centers relationship building as a means to transform ourselves and our communities. Previously, they served as Project NIA's youth training coordinator, where they coordinated the Abolitionist Youth Organizing Institute (AYO, NYC!). Currently, they act as the youth organizing consultant for the Wayfinding Project at Just Beginnings Collaborative.

EMMA K. RUSSELL is an associate professor of crime, justice, and legal studies at La Trobe University, sited on the unceded lands of the Wurundjeri peoples of the Kulin Nation in so-called "Australia." Her research and public advocacy focuses on prisons, policing, and social in/justice.

ROSA SQUILLACOTE is a lecturer at John Jay College, City University of New York, with over twenty years in the criminal justice movement. Her academic interests focus on the history and practices of carceral administrative agencies. She lives in the South Bronx with two children and enjoys good books, good beer, and old movies.

DR. ASH STEPHENS (he/they) is an assistant professor in the Department of Criminology, Law and Justice at UIC. Their research explores trans and gender-nonconforming people's experiences with and strategies to resist state-sanctioned violence. Abolitionist feminism guides their teaching with the Prison Neighborhood Arts & Education Project (PNAP) in Chicago.

CATHERINE THERRIEN is a former academic. After pursuing graduate studies in criminology, she decided to work in the nonprofit sector in Montreal, Canada. She counsels and supports individuals with unmet needs, helps solidify positive relationships, and aims to prevent violence.

ALLYN WALKER (they/them) is an assistant professor of criminology at Saint Mary's University in Kjipuktuk/Halifax. Their ongoing research focuses on noncriminalizing strategies to address the root causes of harm while supporting people who have lived through violence and marginalization. They are the author of *A Long, Dark Shadow: Minor-Attracted People and Their Pursuit of Dignity*.

AIMEE WODDA is an associate professor of criminal justice, law, and society at Pacific University and coauthor of *Sex-Positive Criminology*.

Index

Founded in 1893,
UNIVERSITY OF CALIFORNIA PRESS
publishes bold, progressive books and journals
on topics in the arts, humanities, social sciences,
and natural sciences—with a focus on social
justice issues—that inspire thought and action
among readers worldwide.

The UC PRESS FOUNDATION
raises funds to uphold the press's vital role
as an independent, nonprofit publisher, and
receives philanthropic support from a wide
range of individuals and institutions—and from
committed readers like you. To learn more, visit
ucpress.edu/supportus.

www.ingramcontent.com/pod-product-compliance
Lightning Source LLC
Chambersburg PA
CBHW020840270326
41928CB00006B/497